CENTRO STUDI GIACOMO PUCCINI
PREMIO ROTARY GIACOMO PUCCINI RICERCA

2

ARMAN SCHWARTZ

PUCCINI'S SOUNDSCAPES: REALISM AND MODERNITY IN ITALIAN OPERA

FIRENZE
LEO S. OLSCHKI EDITORE
MMXVI

Casa Editrice Leo S. Olschki
Viuzzo del Pozzetto, 8
50126 Firenze
www.olschki.it

Il volume è stato pubblicato grazie al contributo del Rotary Club Lucca
e della Fondazione Cassa di Risparmio di Lucca

ISBN 978 88 222 6447 3

PRESENTAZIONE

Siamo lieti di offrire con *Puccini's Soundscapes: Realism and Modernity in Italian Opera* i risultati della ricerca del vincitore della seconda edizione del Premio Rotary Giacomo Puccini Ricerca, istituito nel 2005 a Lucca – la città natale di Giacomo Puccini – grazie al fruttuoso accordo tra il Rotary Club Lucca, la Fondazione Cassa di Risparmio di Lucca e il Centro studi Giacomo Puccini.

Alla seconda edizione del Premio, la commissione giudicatrice, composta da Vittorio Armani, Virgilio Bernardoni, Gabriella Biagi Ravenni, Giovanni Cattani, Massimo Fino, Gaetano Giani Luporini, Michele Girardi e Arthur Groos, scelse di sostenere il progetto di ricerca presentato da Arman Schwartz per l'originalità della proposta, intuendone la ricchezza di implicazioni per il futuro della ricerca pucciniana.

Il saggio prodotto da Schwartz, e ora edito nella collana del Centro studi Giacomo Puccini presso l'editore Olschki di Firenze, mantiene le premesse del progetto dal quale è scaturito. Illustrando il percorso creativo di Puccini dal punto di osservazione inconsueto delle idee di suono realizzate in opere esemplari quali *Tosca*, *Suor Angelica*, *Gianni Schicchi* e *Turandot*, mette in rilievo la continua tensione modernista del teatro pucciniano nel suo complesso, la natura peculiare del suo impianto realistico e la sua capacità di registrare i mutamenti culturali e sociali del suo tempo.

La pubblicazione in lingua inglese dello studio di Schwartz testimonia l'internazionalità del Premio Rotary Giacomo Puccini Ricerca, nato per incentivare la nuova ricerca pucciniana nel mondo. Con esso il Centro studi Giacomo Puccini accoglie nel proprio raggio d'azione un giovane studioso di valore, chiamato dopo questa prova – come già Riccardo Pecci, vincitore della prima edizione – a far parte del suo Comitato scientifico e d'ora in avanti a contribuire attivamente alla continuità delle sue attività di ricerca.

Giorgio Serafini	Arturo Lattanzi	Gabriella Biagi Ravenni
Presidente	Presidente	Presidente
Rotary Club Lucca	Fondazione Cassa di Risparmio di Lucca	Centro studi Giacomo Puccini

Lucca, maggio 2016

PREMIO ROTARY GIACOMO PUCCINI RICERCA

2006	Riccardo Pecci	*Puccini, il 'principe reale', e Catalani, il 'perti-chino'.Consonanze e dissonanze di due lucche-sialla corte di Verdi*
2008	Arman Schwartz	*Puccini's Soundscapes: Geography and Moderni-ty in Italian Opera*
2010	Suzanne Scherr Steger	*Tempo in the Operatic Works of Giacomo Puccini*
	Progetti segnalati:	
	Matteo Giuggioli	*Ricezione e traduzione audiovisiva del melodramma pucciniano:* Madama Butterfly *in film*
	Vincenzina Ottomano	*Il monologo come strategia narrativa: Giacomo Puccini e l'estetica del dramma moderno*
2014	Federico Fornoni	*Scene di seduzione nell'opera italiana del secondo Ottocento: da* Rigoletto *a* Madama Butterfly

ACKNOWLEDGEMENTS

Thanks, above all, to the Rotary Club of Lucca, the Fondazione Cassa di Risparmio di Lucca, and the Centro Studi Giacomo Puccini. Without the extraordinary generosity of these institutions, this project would never have come to fruition. At the Centro itself, Art Groos and Gabriella Biagi Ravenni graciously guided me through the publication process. Their detailed comments on my final text – as well as those of Virgilio Bernardoni and Michele Girardi – led to significant improvements. I began thinking about *Tosca* at the American Academy in Rome thanks to a Marian and Andrew Heiskell Pre-Doctoral Rome Prize in Modern Italian Studies, and hope my chapter on the opera still bears the imprint of an enchanted year. An invitation from the incomparable Dana Prescott to visit Civitella Ranieri as a Director's Guest provided me with time, space, and an ideal setting to formulate my ideas about *Suor Angelica*. Further institutional support was provided by an Andrew Mellon Post-Doctoral Teaching Fellowship at the University of Pennsylvania, an American Council of Learned Societies New Faculty Fellowship at Columbia University, and by the University of Birmingham.

Although it would be impossible to thank the many, many friends and colleagues who contributed to, and sustained me during the course of, this project, I am especially grateful to the members of my original dissertation committee – Mary Ann Smart, Kate van Orden, and Celeste Langan – in dialogue with whom I developed many of the ideas that would inform this volume. Alessandra Campana invited me to present my research on *Gianni Schicchi* at the Mahindra Humanities Center at Harvard University, and provided a much needed jolt to the whole project. Emanuele Senici and David Levin have offered invaluable support and guidance over the years. A special note of gratitude is due to Roger Parker for first tempting me to forsake Darmstadt for the nineteenth century and, even more impressively, for reading everything I have written since. Thanks, finally, to my parents Reid and Mary Schwartz for their unbounded support, and to Heather Wiebe, for everything.

A significantly earlier version of Chapter Two appeared as *Rough Music: «Tosca» and «Verismo» Reconsidered*, «19th-Century Music», XXXI, 2008, pp. 228-

244. Earlier versions of Chapters Three and Five were published as *Puccini, in the Distance*, «Cambridge Opera Journal», XXIII, 2012, pp. 167-189; and *Mechanism and Tradition in Puccini's «Turandot»*, «Opera Quarterly», XXV, 2009, pp. 28-50. I am grateful to the University of California Press, Cambridge University Press, and Oxford University Press for the permission to republish all this material. This volume's publication costs were supported in part by a generous subvention from the AMS 75 PAYS Endowment of the American Musicological Society, funded in part by the National Endowment for the Humanities and the Andrew W. Mellon Foundation.

REHEARING PUCCINI

Attending the American premiere of Giacomo Puccini's *Tosca* (1900) at the Metropolitan Opera on 4 February 1901, a troubled critic for «Life» magazine encountered a composition in which the normal priorities of Italian opera seemed to have been turned progressively upside down:

The composer's work is practically limited to a cantilena – but an excellent one – sung by Cavaradossi, the painter – besides a graceful, languishing duo between him and Tosca. These melodic delights are confined to the first act. Throughout the remainder of the opera, the part allotted to the singers is mostly of the declamatory order, supported by the orchestra in ultra modern style, with bells and cannons thrown in left and right.[1]

Several aspects of this assessment might surprise us. Most immediately, it is strange to see *Tosca*, an opera now routinely dismissed as pandering to its audiences' basest instincts, stand accused instead for its lack of «melodic delights». «Vissi d'arte», «E lucevan le stelle»: how could these, and many other, tuneful set pieces have escaped a critic's ear? Even stranger is the reviewer's emphasis on the «ultra modern» sounds of «bells and cannons». On the one hand, the raw, environmental music he felt he had encountered – music so arbitrary, or so inhuman, that it betrayed scant evidence of a «composer's work» – would seem to place *Tosca* in the company of a much later, and more obviously experimental repertoire. On the other hand, there does not seem to be anything especially modern, let alone 'ultra' modern, about the specific sounds he heard. There are bells in Hector Berlioz's *Symphonie fantastique* (1830) and cannons in Pyotr Ilyich Tchaikovsky's *1812 Overture* (1880), after all, and given the variety of modernist innovations one might have encountered in a concert hall in 1901, it seems perverse to worry about *Tosca* as a manifestation of the dangerously new.

---

[1] MONSECRET, «*La Tosca*», «Life», XXXVII, 1901, p. 173.

As we shall see in Chapter Two, despair over the sheer noisiness of Puccini's operas was widespread in the years around 1900. Listeners in Europe and North America found the composer's unconventional use of unconventional instruments to be perhaps the most disturbing aspect of his style. Like the critic for «Life», they too felt that standard definitions of the «composer's work» had been betrayed. And yet, despite its early intensity, this way of thinking about Puccini had begun to fade by the First World War. In the ensuing century, all sense of menace has been lost. In part, of course, this is a product of Puccini's ever more established, ever more familiar place in the performing canon. (Indeed, if Puccini seems menacing nowadays, it is largely in his role as a stalwart of conservative values, clogging the repertories of major opera houses, and ruining audiences' appetites for more experimental fare). But it is also a sign that our priorities as listeners have changed. When we look for evidence of «ultra modern style», we are apt to speak of harmony, or perhaps of rhythm. To treat orchestration as an equally central feature of musical modernism is still uncommon, yet our reluctance to do so separates us from a vital aspect of the past.[2]

In recent years, scholars have started to rethink Puccini's place in the early twentieth century, questioning perceptions of the composer as a Romantic epigone born in the wrong age. Michele Girardi has shown how closely Puccini listened to (and was listened to by) his most advanced contemporaries: Claude Debussy and Richard Strauss, surely, but also Arnold Schoenberg and Igor Stravinsky.[3] No less a modernist than Anton Webern praised *La fanciulla del West* (1910) for containing «very special sounds», and «not a shade of kitsch».[4] The most international composer of his generation, Puccini was often denounced for forsaking the great traditions of

---

[2] For an important attempt to place orchestration at the forefront of discussions of musical modernity – and, indeed, at the forefront of musicological discourse more generally – see Emily I. Dolan, *The Orchestral Revolution: Haydn and the Technologies of Timbre*, Cambridge, Cambridge University Press, 2013. Discussions of fin-de-siècle music that argue for a critical sensitivity to issues of timbre and orchestration include David Code, *Hearing Debussy Reading Mallarmé: Music après Wagner in the «Prélude à l'après-midi d'une Faune»*, «Journal of the American Musicological Society», LII, 2001, pp. 93-154; and John J. Sheinbaum, *Adorno's Mahler and the Timbral Outsider*, «Journal of the Royal Musical Association», CXXXI, 2006, pp. 38-82. For an earlier study of the *giovane scuola's* own techniques of orchestration, see Jürgen Maehder, «*La giusta prospettiva dell'orchestra*»: *Grundlagen der Orchesterbehandlung bei Komponisten der «giovane scuola»*, «Studi pucciniani», 3, 2004, pp. 105-149. For an earlier study of Puccini's approach to sound and timbre, see Jürgen Leukel, *Sulla rappresentazione dell'extramusicale nelle opere di Puccini*, in *Esotismo e colore locale nell'opera di Puccini. Atti del primo Convegno internazionale sull'opera di Giacomo Puccini (Torre del Lago, 1983)*, ed. by Jürgen Maehder, Pisa, Giardini, 1985, pp. 241-245.

[3] See Michele Girardi, *Puccini: His International Art*, trans. by Laura Basini, Chicago, University of Chicago Press, 2000.

[4] Unpublished letter of 27 March 1918, quoted in Girardi, *Puccini*, pp. 284-285.

Italian music, indeed the idea of national style *tout court*. Alexandra Wilson has explored how Puccini's operas came to occupy a fraught place in the imaginary of post-Unification Italy, helping audiences and critics articulate their worst fears about modernity.[5] But this was not merely a discursive construct. Many of the same anxieties that haunted Puccini's critics – fears about urbanization, migration, changing gender roles, the decline of the Italian nation – also animated the composition of his works.[6]

If it is becoming somewhat more common to assert Puccini's place in the history of twentieth-century music – and if a burgeoning analytic discourse is enriching our sense of the formal complexity of Puccini's music – few have asked how renewed attention to the composer might prompt us to revise our understanding of modernism itself.[7] It is one thing to think about the fragmentary, austere, almost anti-narrative final act of *Manon Lescaut* (1893) alongside *Salome* (1905) and *Erwartung* (1909), but unless we are also prepared to ask how Puccini's operas might tell us something different from those of Strauss and Schoenberg, the composer will always seem a wallflower at the party, and our old narratives will remain intact. My contention is that listening closely to Puccini's 'soundscapes' may fuel just such a project, leading to new interpretations of his operas, and to new ways of 'hearing' the century in which he lived.

I

As anxious listeners to the first performances of *Tosca* may have feared, Puccini's orchestra would only grow stranger in the coming years. His next opera, *Madama Butterfly* (1904), called for an amazing array of on- and offstage instruments: a handbell, tubular chimes, Japanese bells, a viola d'amore, bird whistles, tam-tams, a cannon, chains. For *La fanciulla del West*, Puccini tried to invent a 'fonica', a set of bells that could be played electrically, without the mediation of human hands.[8] For *Il tabarro* (1918), he crafted a more explicitly urban soundscape; in the first few minutes of

---

[5] See ALEXANDRA WILSON, *The Puccini Problem: Opera, Nationalism, Modernity*, Cambridge, Cambridge University Press, 2007.

[6] For readings of one of Puccini's operas in terms of these larger issues, see the special issue *Puccini: «Manon Lescaut»*, ed. by Roger Parker, «Opera Quarterly», XXIV, 2008.

[7] See DEBORAH BURTON, *Recondite Harmony: Essays on Puccini's Operas*, Hillsdale, NY, Pendragon Press, 2012; NICHOLAS BARAGWANATH, *The Italian Traditions and Puccini: Compositional Theory and Practice in Nineteenth-Century Opera*, Bloomington, Indiana University Press, 2011; and ANDREW DAVIS, *«Il trittico», «Turandot», and Puccini's Late Style*, Bloomington, Indiana University Press, 2010.

[8] For a suggestive discussion of the fonica, see ELLEN LOCKHART, *Photo Opera: «La fanciulla del West» and the Staging Souvenir*, «Cambridge Opera Journal», XXIII, 2011, pp. 145-166: 160-161.

the opera, we encounter the long, melancholy whistle of a tugboat, punctuated by the staccato horn of an automobile. In addition to these literal noises, Puccini also drew on a variety of acoustic found objects. *Madama Butterfly* and *Turandot* (incomplete, premiered 1926) both contain tunes transcribed from exotic music boxes; there are Zuni melodies in *La fanciulla del West* and fox-trots in *La rondine* (1917); colloquial American speech resounds throughout *La fanciulla del West*, despite its nominally Italian-language text. And then there is Puccini's interest not just in sound itself, but in its physical placement: the opening scene of *Suor Angelica* (1918), to take just one example, contains nothing but a variety of noises (bells, chanting, an organ, birdsong) resonating from assorted locations offstage.

Numerous, seemingly fanciful analogies suggest themselves: to Charles Ives, with his frenzied recreations of American vernacular music making; to Edgard Varèse, with his combinations of conventional and unconventional, 'human' and 'electronic' instruments; to the *musique concrète* of Pierre Schaeffer. Perhaps a closer point of comparison, and one I will return to in the coming pages, is Italian Futurism, and its violent «art of noises». But how can we account for Puccini's interest in acoustic innovation? And what might it mean to include his name in a lineage of 'experimental' music?

A rapidly expanding body of literature suggests that the basic fabric of Western auditory culture was transformed during the last few decades of the nineteenth century, producing new ideas about the relationship between music, noise, and language; about ephemerality and preservation; about the nature of listening itself.[9] Thomas Edison's phonograph and Hermann von Helmholtz's new science of listening are usually taken, no doubt over-easily, as key agents in (and metonyms for) this process; the unprecedented noisiness of urbanization and industry played a role as well.[10] The narrative is usually framed as an international one, but it is striking how many of the iconic cultural manifestations of this shift emerged in Italy: Futurism, Guglielmo Marconi's wireless, Ferruccio Busoni's philosophy of microtonal music, even Ottorino Respighi's *Pini di Roma* (1924), the first orchestral composition to include a phonograph record in its score. In the sphere of performance, meanwhile, it was Enrico Caruso who would

---

[9] Especially influential studies include FRIEDRICH KITTLER, *Gramophone, Film, Typewriter* [1986], trans. by Geoffrey Winthrop-Young and Michael Wutz, Palo Alto, Stanford University Press, 1999; JONATHAN STERNE, *The Audible Past: Cultural Origins of Sound Reproduction*, Durham, University of North Carolina Press, 2003; JOHN M. PICKER, *Victorian Soundscapes*, Oxford, Oxford University Press, 2003; and MARK KATZ, *Capturing Sound: How Technology Has Changed Music*, Berkeley, University of California Press, 2010.

[10] For a study of Helmholtz in this context, see BENJAMIN STEEGE, *Helmholtz and the Modern Listener*, Cambridge, Cambridge University Press, 2012.

become the first star to master the new medium of sound recording, and Arturo Toscanini who would emerge as the first truly 'modern' orchestral conductor, «the great simplifier and depersonalizer of music», in Richard Taruskin's phrase, the man who «did more than anyone else toward modernizing musical performance and musical perception alike».[11] These examples add weight to a question once posed by Antonio Gramsci: «Why did Italian artistic "democracy" have a musical and not a "literary" expression?».[12] They suggest that for a rapidly and incompletely industrialized new nation – one whose public culture was marred by widespread illiteracy and the lack of a unified language, on the one hand, but uniquely dependent on opera and public oratory, on the other – modernity was imagined and explored in powerfully acoustic terms.[13]

Puccini's operas were a central – if not 'the' central – «musical expression» of this unsettled world. They deserve a place in a broader history of auditory culture, and can tell us things that studies of technologies and scientific practices can not. But if, as I am suggesting, musicology might play a more active role in the discourse of sound studies than it has done so far, the obverse should be true as well. For although our histories of acoustic modernity may start in the late nineteenth century, the stories we tell about the relationship between sound technology and musical composition still tend only to begin in earnest after the Second World War. Varèse, Schaeffer, John Cage: these are the composers that are described as exploring new technologies and modes of listening, new relationships between music and noise. True, there have been attempts to explore the impact of the phonograph on the aesthetics of neo-classicism and *Neue Sachlichkeit*, but these movements developed some fifty years after Edison's first patent.[14] By looking to Puccini, then, I want to ask how a late nineteenth-century operatic composer may have addressed fundamental shifts in auditory culture without the aid of tape and microphones, and during the generation in which they first emerged. And if listening to *Tosca* as if it were, say, *Poème électronique* (1958) – to cite an-

---

[11] RICHARD TARUSKIN, *The New Antiquity*, in *Text and Act: Essays on Musical Performance*, Oxford, Oxford University Press, 1995, pp. 202-234: 222. For an insightful discussion of Caruso and early sound recording, see DAVID SUISMAN, *Selling Sounds: The Commercial Revolution in American Music*, Cambridge, MA, Harvard University Press, 2009, pp. 125-149.

[12] ANTONIO GRAMSCI, *Selections from the Cultural Writings*, ed. by David Forgacs and Geoffrey Nowell-Smith, Cambridge, MA, Harvard University Press, 1991, p. 378.

[13] For an exploration of how Italian cultural history might be rethought from the perspective of sound studies, see *Italian Sound*, ed. by Deanna Shemek and Arielle Saiber, «California Italian Studies», IV, 2013.

[14] See CAROLYN ABBATE, *Outside the Tomb*, in *In Search of Opera*, Princeton, Princeton University Press, 2001, pp. 185-248; and ALEXANDER REHDING, *On the Record*, «Cambridge Opera Journal», XVIII, 2006, pp. 59-82.

other work that mixes primal human song with the rumble of the ultra-modern – may help shed new light on an overly-familiar work, it may also prompt us to think anew about the tradition that it helped inaugurate. I do not want to deny that Puccini was a populist and in many ways reactionary figure – indeed, Puccini's place in the emerging culture of Italian fascism will be one of my central themes – but I do want to suggest that the aesthetic and political anxieties his works address, and the specific compromises they propose, might encourage us to think more carefully about the newness, autonomy, and revolutionary power of the later avant-garde.

Puccini's century, as one might call it, began in an important sense with Richard Wagner. The German composer was a central figure for thinking about modernity in fin-de-siècle Italy and, predictably, the metonymy meant many (contradictory) things: foreignness, internationalism, anti-Semitism, scientism, progressivism, decadent sexuality, the ascendency of orchestral logic and the decline of naïve song.[15] All this is well known. I suspect, though, that Puccini and some of his Italian contemporaries also heard something else in the soundscape of the future: music that was astonishingly repetitive; music that made unprecedented use of strange, percussive instruments (the anvils in *Das Rheingold* [1869], the bells in *Parsifal* [1882]); music that originated from multiple locations on and off the stage. These are the very features of Wagner's music that Theodor Adorno found most pernicious: the «distant sounds» he called «phantasmagoria», where «music pauses and is made special, the near and the far are deceptively merged like the comforting Fata Morgana that brings the mirage of cities and caravans within reach and makes social models appear magically rooted in nature».[16] Listening to the first act finale of *Tosca* – whose bells, choruses, processions, and obsessive ostinati all seem drawn from the first act finale of *Parsifal* (a scene with which it also shares an interest in church interiors, esoteric ritual, and female temptresses) – one suspects these effects were also those that Puccini found most exciting.[17] That Puccini and Adorno, an unlikely pair, seem to have heard similar things in Wagner's operas goes some way toward validating the latter's theories.[18]

---

[15] On Wagner's reception in Italy, see WILSON, *The Puccini Problem*; AXEL KÖRNER, *Politics of Culture in Liberal Italy: From Unification to Fascism*, New York, Routledge, 2009, pp. 221-262; and JULIAN BUDDEN, *Wagnerian Tendencies in Italian Opera*, in *Music and Theatre: Essays in Honour of Winton Dean*, ed. by Nigel Fortune, Cambridge, Cambridge University Press, 1987, pp. 299-332.

[16] THEODOR ADORNO, *In Search of Wagner*, trans. by Rodney Livingstone, London, Verso, 2005[2], p. 75.

[17] For an alternative discussion of the origins of the *Tosca* finale, see PETER ROSS, *Die multidimensionale Szenenstruktur in der italienischen Oper am Ende des 19. Jahrhunderts*, «Studi pucciniani», 3, 2004, pp. 151-175.

[18] For a more extended discussion of the relationship between Puccini and Wagner's

The coincidence of their reactions suggests a new way of framing the very question of Wagner's 'influence'.[19]

A more detailed example may be instructive here. Immediately after the famous prelude to *Tristan und Isolde* (1865), Wagner composes a 'phantasmagorical' unaccompanied song for an offstage sailor. There are various ways to interpret this peculiar gesture: as an attack on the earlier nineteenth-century tradition of beginning operas with 'characteristic' choruses, or as an appeal to audiences to forsake easy spectacle and to train their ears on the beyond. As such, the sailor's song seems a clear precedent for the aesthetics of French symbolism; a line from the opening of *Tristan* to Mélisande's unaccompanied, offstage aria in the third act of Debussy's 1902 opera has been drawn convincingly.[20] But might it not also be possible to hear a connection between the opening of *Tristan* and that of *Cavalleria rusticana* (1890), where, once again, an orchestral prelude is interrupted by an invisible tenor singing a folk-like tune? Of course there are major differences here, but more significant than the contrast between Wagner's sublime prelude and Pietro Mascagni's clunkily orchestrated medley is the challenge posed to Wagnerian metaphysics by a new aesthetic that might well be called realist. For, although the precise location of Mascagni's singer is mysterious – indeed, more mysterious than Wagner's sailor on the mast – his words and music are both recognizably Sicilian, grounded far more thoroughly than earlier characteristic music in a specific time and place. Whether this gesture toward situatedness, an early instance of the acoustic materialism and the incorporation of 'found objects' that would soon come to occupy Puccini, is best understood as a self-conscious critique of Wagner's idealism or as the actualization of a previously unacknowledged dimension to music drama is difficult to say. Nonetheless, symbolism may begin to seem less an immediate or inevitable outgrowth of Wagner's aesthetics, and more a defensive attempt to reassert Romantic mystery in the face of what Giuseppe Verdi famously derided as «progress, science, realism», all bywords for the disenchantment of modernity, and all values that Puccini would soon embrace.[21]

'phantasmagoria', see my *Manon in the Desert, Wagner on the Beach*, in «Opera Quarterly», XXIV, 2008, pp. 51-61.

[19] Relevant studies of Wagner's legacy in this context include FRIEDRICH KITTLER, *World-Breath: On Wagner's Media Technology*, in *Opera through Other Eyes*, ed. by David J. Levin, Stanford, Stanford University Press, 1993, pp. 215-235; and MATTHEW WILSON SMITH, *The Total Work of Art: From Bayreuth to Cyberspace*, New York, Routledge, 2007.

[20] See CAROLYN ABBATE, *In Search of Opera*, pp. 153-154 and 169-171.

[21] «Ah il progresso, la scienza, il verismo... Ahi Ahi... Verista finché volete, ma... Shakespeare era un verista ma non lo sapeva». Letter to Giulio Ricordi, 20 November 1880, in *Car-*

II

Puccini's response to Wagner has an important precedent in the *œuvre* of the poet and composer Arrigo Boito (1842-1918), the man who is usually credited with importing German Idealist aesthetics into Italian opera. In my first chapter, I attempt to reinterpret Boito's poems, libretti, and compositions using the insights of sound studies; resisting conventional distinctions between media, I describe Boito's fascination with a type of rough, embodied sound that emerges in the space between music and verbal language. Many of his texts celebrate the negative, destructive force of this new acoustics, doing so in terms that anticipate some central preoccupations of High Modernism. His libretto for Verdi's *Falstaff* (1893), in contrast, attempts to contain the unruliness of pure sonority by martialing it into a nationalist fantasy of the Tuscan landscape. If Boito's acoustic materialism represents the key Italian model for Puccini's realism, so too do his reactionary anxieties.

Tosca, the subject of my second chapter, is a case in point. In the 1890s, the composers of the so-called *giovane scuola* (Puccini, Mascagni, Ruggero Leoncavallo, Umberto Giordano, Francesco Cilea) developed a new aesthetic of realist opera. Influenced by the militantly empiricist naturalism of the novelist Giovanni Verga, they experimented with a variety of acoustic effects designed to help them escape from the basic fiction of their medium. *Verismo* operas refuse musical transcendence, insisting on the objectivity of unmediated sound, and they do so in terms that seem inseparable from the new technology of phonographic transcription. *Tosca* might be described as the movement's most radical text, the climax of a decade of realist innovation. But Puccini's work also exhibits a pronounced ambivalence about *verismo*, a self-consciousness that sets it apart from its cohort.

It is telling, then, that in the years following *Tosca* Puccini seems to have become disillusioned with operatic positivism. Indeed, once we understand *verismo* in acoustic terms, we can begin to perceive a set of features – the lineaments of an ambivalent post-realist project – that lie behind the otherwise baffling heterogeneity of the composer's later works. As I suggest in Chapter Three, Puccini's operas after *Tosca* unleash a variety of mysterious sound effects that unsettle the strictures of *verismo*. The central document of this new manner is *Suor Angelica*, the second 'panel' of *Il trittico* (1918). The opera, somewhat notoriously, culminates with an apparition of the Virgin Mary. Some critics, perhaps beholden to realist biases of their own, have attempted to psychologize this miracle; in contrast, I attempt to take

---

teggio Verdi-Ricordi 1880-1881, ed. by Pierluigi Petrobelli, Marisa Di Gregorio Casati, and Carlo Matteo Mossa, Parma, Istituto di Studi Verdiani, 1988, p. 70.

it at face value, grounding it within the discourse of fin-de-siècle spiritualism, and exploring how Puccini's move away from phonographic realism may have been influenced by the new technology of wireless communication. If the phonograph has provoked significant musicological attention in recent years, the wireless has not, and I suggest a set of terms that may enable us to hear a radiophonic dimension of musical modernism.

Chapters Two and Three are designed as a pair; together they trace Puccini's move from a 'phonographic' to a 'radiophonic' understanding of operatic sound. In my two concluding chapters, I take a step back from this technological narrative, and ask how a new sensitivity to questions of sound and realism might help us rethink the 'politics' of Puccini's last two dramatic works. *Gianni Schicchi* (the subject of Chapter Four) and *Turandot* (the subject of Chapter Five) were written during some of the darkest years in twentieth-century Italy, a period that saw the nadir of the nation's already disastrous engagement in the First World War and then Mussolini's rise to power. Although some critics – both Puccini's contemporaries and more recent scholars – have interpreted these operas as uncharacteristically blunt (and distinctly right-wing) depictions of contemporary reality, they have also seemed like turns away from the immediate world, retreats into the stylization of *commedia dell'arte* and the anti-realist dramaturgy of Carlo Gozzi. Realism, that is to say, should be central to any discussion of Puccini's politics.

The relationship between *Gianni Schicchi* and *Falstaff* – routinely cited as the most obvious model for Puccini's only comedy – is especially interesting in this context. One the one hand, Puccini's opera seems grossly to amplify the Tuscan nationalism of Verdi and Boito's work, drawing on the full resources of *verismo* theater to restore a noble past. It did so, moreover, during a moment when Italian patriots were calling loudly for a politicized revival of Tuscan culture. On the other hand, *Gianni Schicchi* seems more ambivalent than *Falstaff* – and, indeed, Puccini's own earlier works – about the power of sound to recapture distant worlds. Acoustic realism is largely avoided, and when the noises of Dante's hell do intrude into the opera's charmed circle they undermine and call attention to the pretenses of the work as a whole. As in *Suor Angelica*, Puccini uses a climactic scene of resurrection to ponder dark questions about the realist project.

If *Gianni Schicchi* is reticent and anxious about sound, *Turandot* has long been praised – and, more recently, criticized – for its thoroughgoing attempts at acoustic authenticity. As noted above, Puccini derived several of its melodies from a Chinese music box, whose timbres chime throughout the score. I contend, however, that the composer was drawn to this music box not just as a source of information about a distant culture, but more importantly as a vehicle for reflecting on the logic of sound recording and transmission. What is more, Puccini's treatment of the music box material in *Turandot* suggests an increasingly pessimistic attitude toward technology itself. Frequently cast in the role of the Last Italian Opera, *Turandot* seems melancholically aware of its own historical position. Its struggle to reconcile competing imperatives of positivism and enchantment – to mourn the destructive effects of mechanical reproduction while also harnessing their mystic power – speaks to some of the central dilemmas of fascist modernism.

III

Throughout this volume, I suggest that by thinking about acoustic materiality, realism, and their larger material and political contexts, we may gain a better understanding of the questions that motivated and gave shape to Puccini's career, and of the distinctive anxieties and compromises that informed the Italian experience of modernity during the fin-de-siècle. I aim to provide a new set of terms for thinking about sound in opera, and a new approach to a repertoire that is too often described (and set aside) as 'late Romantic'. To preview some aspects of my overarching argument, it may be instructive to compare three moments across Puccini's *œuvre*. All three might be described as 'soundscapes', to adopt R. Murray Schafer's term, in that unlike so much previous operatic music, they are less concerned with plot, character, or song than with the delineation of specifically acoustic ecosystems. Schafer declared, triumphantly, that «Today all sounds belong to a continuous field of possibilities lying *within the comprehensive domain of music*. Behold the new orchestra: the sonic universe!».[22] Puccini's operas share something of this enthusiasm, but they also consider a darker obverse to Schafer's proposal: subjective human expression turned back into the raw materials of nature.

My first example comes from the third act of *La bohème*. The act opens with a sharp dominant-tonic tattoo: the sound of a curtain rising or a mechanism being turned on, perhaps, but also an exaggeratedly tonal gesture that seems designed to place all that follows in especially stark relief. For the next 112 bars, the bass will play nothing but a constant tremolo on the notes D and A; the extremely sparse upper voices alternate between cascades of parallel fifths in D Minor and a modest theme constructed entirely from first-inversion triads in D Major, as if a child were moving her right hand across a piano keyboard (see III, 1-3). The pedal point, the lack of proper voice leading, and the modal mixture all seem designed not just to avoid harmonic motion, but to banish it. Atop this meager canvas, Puccini adds a series of barely musical sounds. They are, in order: the unpitched screams of a group of street cleaners, accompanied by the stamping of their feet (on-

---

[22] R. Murray Schafer, *The Soundscape: Our Sonic Environment and the Tuning of the World*, Rochester, VT, Destiny Books, 1993, p. 5.

stage); a drinking chorus, accompanied by the sound of glasses pounding on a table (offstage); Musetta, wordlessly vocalizing on the melody of her Act Two waltz (offstage); the unpitched screams of a group of milk sellers and carters (onstage); the voices of peasant women, pitched but confined to a single note (onstage). Four minutes have now passed, and we have yet to hear much that might be conventionally described as 'music'.

Camille Bellaigue must have had this passage in mind when he described the music of *La bohème* as «not fearing to sacrifice itself to word or action, or to theatrical display and purely scenic effects». Although he greeted this «music from which music is almost absent» with guarded enthusiasm, others were horrified.[23] For Eduard Hanslick,

In the most diverse scenes there arise columns of ascending and descending parallel fifths of such obtrusive ugliness [...] that one asks oneself in vain, what the composer wanted to accomplish with these rude monstrosities? The text does not offer the remotest motivation for them, for with these ghastly fifth-rods Puccini beats the conversation of the friends in the garret as well as the crowd scene in front of the café, and even the customs officers at the barrière.[24]

Hanslick's complaint is, at root, a defense of traditional harmony, but he also seems to have intuited that there was something radically anti-subjective about Puccini's music. That is why he imagines the orchestra 'beating' the characters into submission, and why he despairs that Puccini's harmonic experiments are indiscriminate, uninterested in revealing any inner truth. (It is this peculiar relationship between sound and subject, incidentally, that distinguishes Puccini's use of noise from that of a more conventionally Romantic composer like Berlioz).

This privileging of 'objective' presentation over psychological interpretation is a hallmark of *verismo* opera, and versions of *La bohème*'s soundscape scene appear in countless works from the 1890s and early 1900s. When the curtain rises of the first act of Leoncavallo's *Pagliacci* (1892), the score instructs that «*si sentono squilli di tromba stonata alternantisi con dei colpi di cassa, ed insieme risate, grida allegre, fischi di monelli e un vociare che vanno appressandosi*» (*the sound of an out-of-tune trumpet is heard, alternating with the banging of a drum, together with laughter, gay shouts, urchins whistling, and approaching voices*). Franco Leoni's *L'Oracolo* (1905) provides perhaps the most extreme example of the trend: it begins with three strokes on a drum, followed by a rooster crowing, a chorus of gamblers chanting un-

---

[23] Quoted in ARTHUR GROOS and ROGER PARKER, *Giacomo Puccini: «La bohème»*, Cambridge, Cambridge University Press, 1986, p. 136.

[24] Quoted in GROOS and PARKER, *La bohème*, p. 135.

pitched 'Chinese' syllables (we are in an opium den in San Francisco), wild laughter, and then an unaccompanied song for one of the main characters. Several aspects of these scenes (the conflation of music, speech, and noise; the denial of artistic mediation; the static, repetitive interruption of the normal flow of time) suggest that Italian composers approached realism in terms that were distinctly 'phonographic'. And although similar passages will appear in many of Puccini's later operas, they are often marked by signs of increasing self-awareness and skepticism about the realist project.

Consider the extended 'sunrise' scene that opens the third act of *Madama Butterfly*. Like the parallel scene in *La bohème*, this is a passage in which conventional narrative cedes to «purely scenic effects». Here too are a variety of non- and barely musical offstage sounds: sailors' cries, clanging chains, bird calls, bells. On the one hand, this is a significantly more 'dynamic' – and, indeed, more conventionally 'psychological' – scene: essentially, an extended crescendo over a sustained dominant function, which paints both the rising sun and Butterfly's own, anxious state. On the other hand, the extraordinarily elaborate lighting effects called for here – effects which, famously, first stimulated Puccini's interest in Belasco's source play – suggest that the composer may still be more interested in technologically fueled spectacle than in the nuances of character development.

But perhaps the greatest difference between this scene and its precedent in *La bohème* comes from its attempt to thematize its own effects. The image we see onstage, after all, is of a woman, utterly immobile, peering through two holes in a paper screen. This is an allegory of objective observation, of eyes cut off from bodies and from the surrounding world. It is not an especially comforting image, and given Butterfly's inability to understand the awful truth of her situation, her militantly scientific gaze might be construed as calling the desirability of unmediated spectatorship into question. (Similarly, the strange, inscrutable humming chorus that initiated her vigil at the end of the previous act seems there to suggest that there are forces in this world that realism alone will never fully grasp).

The music makes a similar point. In the middle of this scene, the orchestra plays an accelerated version of a pentatonic melody that had sounded at several points during Act One (see III, 6-9). W. Anthony Sheppard has recently suggested that Puccini transcribed this melody from a Chinese music box; he also notes that, especially at this moment in Act Three, Puccini seems to be appropriating not just the melody, but the actual sound of the device.[25] The tempo is close to that of the original music box, and the

---

[25] W. Anthony Sheppard, *Puccini and the Music Boxes*, «Journal of the Royal Musical Association», CXL, 2015, pp. 41-92: 53.

shrill piccolo and oboe that double the melody, accompanied by scratchy strings *sul ponticello*, approach its reedy whine. It would be possible to interpret this appropriation as a newly triumphant (and newly imperialist) form of Puccini's realism, an attempt to bring the actual sounds of exotic lands into his orchestra. But it would also be possible to say that, by foregrounding the sound of the mechanism as mechanism, the composer is calling attention to the crude facts of mediation, in a way that separates this scene from its unself-conscious counterpart in *La bohème*. This latter interpretation also helps account for the fact that the re-orchestrated, fast version of the melody seems intentionally drained of the delicate magic it claimed in the first act. A beautiful image has been replaced by the thing itself, and the results are disappointing.

Similar tensions between realism and enchantment, concealment and revelation, are even more attenuated in my last example, taken from the start of *La fanciulla del West*. After the self-contained prelude (an oddly stodgy gesture, as Emanuele Senici has noted, interpreting it as an attempt to self-consciously thematize the role of the orchestra from the very beginning of the score), Puccini writes what may now seem like a predictable soundscape scene: from various locations offstage, we hear the unpitched cries of men, making heavy use of American dialect; there are snippets of quoted folk-song and carefully notated bangs of fists; everything is supported by a static and thinly orchestrated orchestral fabric.[26] All this will change, though, when Jake Wallace, the camp's minstrel, enters the scene and begins to sing (see I, $20^{+1\text{-}11}$). Many aspects of his song are 'realistic' in the manner of the preceding music: his voice originates offstage, and his melody is based on a 'correct' Native American tune. Puccini could have easily accompanied this diegetic performance with any manner of 'authentic' instruments; instead he uses an offstage harp with paper between its strings. This weird offstage sound (described ambivalently in the score as «imitando un banjo») is made significantly more mysterious by the use of a second harp in the orchestra, suggesting an impossible instrument that sounds from two places at once. And, crucially, both of these harps continue to play – now amplified by strings and clarinets – when Wallace arrives on stage strumming his guitar, an instrument that is neither the banjo we have briefly been led to expect nor in any way adequate to the wonders that we hear (see I, 21-22).

In the time between the opening soundscape music and the start of Wallace's performance, we have left blunt realism behind in favor of some-

---

[26] See EMANUELE SENICI, *Landscape and Gender in Italian Opera: The Alpine Virgin from Bellini to Puccini*, Cambridge, Cambridge University Press, 2005, pp. 251-252. For a close reading of this opening scene, see LOCKHART, *Photo Opera*.

thing more sensual and, indeed, more conventionally operatic. If the successive statements of the music-box theme in *Madama Butterfly* suggest a move from enchantment to demystification, here Puccini traces an opposite path, as if in an effort to occlude or elide the differences between the two. When the miners begin to sing, taking up Wallace's tune as a richly polyphonic chorus, we no longer feel the need to ask why they are singing, or where they learned counterpoint. This is especially ironic, given that 'phenomenal' songs had, in previous generations, been a *locus classicus* of operatic self-consciousness and intrusions of the real. It would be possible to accuse Puccini of bad faith here, but it might be more accurate to hear the composer as himself responding to Wallace's «canto nostalgico». As the miners give themselves over to the delights of melody, they may well be mourning their lost dogs and homes in Cornwall, but they also sound like they are longing for a more innocent moment in the history of opera itself.

CHAPTER ONE

BOITO'S MATERIALS

In 1898, the architect, critic, and occasional fabulist Camillo Boito published a short story entitled *Il maestro di setticlavio*. Set in Venice during the early 1850s – a time, the narrator reminds us, when Verdi's *Rigoletto* was still «fresco fresco» – the story focuses on Luigi Zen, an elderly singing master and the victim of a singular affliction.[1] It is an era when fixed Do is on the rise, and he remains wedded to an outmoded method of teaching sight singing. So fanatical is Zen's commitment to moveable Do that neither the advice of his fellow musicians nor the steady flight of his students will cause him to relent: it remains, he insists, «The gospel of music: the only true faith».[2] As the story opens, the evangelist is engaged in one of many attempted conversions:

> – Tell me, what is the tonic in the key of C?
> – Do.
> – Good. And what is Mi?
> – The third scale degree.
> – And Si?
> – The seventh.
> – Now listen, what is the interval between Do and Mi?
> – A major third.
> – Thus when you say Do Mi you speak and sing a major third.
> – Of course.
> – When you sing Si Do what interval do you produce?
> – A semitone.
> – Thus when you say Si Do, just like Mi Fa, you speak and sing a semitone.
> – Certainly.
> – Now answer me. If in your cursed system of sight-singing, which they call 'common', you sing, for example, in the key of D, what does Do Mi become?

---

[1] CAMILLO BOITO, *Il maestro di setticlavio*, in *Storielle vane*, ed. by Chiara Cretella, Bologna, Edizioni Pendragon, 2007, pp. 237-284: 238.

[2] «Il setticlavio è il vangelo della musica: la sola vera credenza». BOITO, *Il maestro*, p. 239.

– A minor third.

– And Mi Fa or Si Do?

– A whole tone.

– Oh, see, see what misery, what infamous confusion! You read one thing and you sing another. There are no longer rules, one no longer understands anything.[3]

Zen's passion for moveable Do is only one symptom of his «angry conservatism» (he also detests Verdi), but his argument has an undeniable logic.[4] As he describes it, fixed Do unsettles any unitary relationship between verbal name and scalar function, transforming the seven solfège syllables into arbitrary and polyvalent signs.

In the course of the story, Zen's views make him increasingly desolate. A vocal recital designed to advertise the glories of his method is mocked by the Venetian press; various other projects – «a journal in dialect to place moveable Do in ever greater light», «a *History of Song from Antiquity to the Present Day*» – come to naught.[5] Even his closest friends abandon him. The mounting sense of gloom is magnified by a second narrative, which traces the seduction of Nene, an orphaned virgin left under Zen's protection, by the lusty gondolier Mirate, whose gorgeous but intuitive tenor voice Zen has been working to perfect. (Given that Raffaele Mirate was the tenor who created the role of the Duke in *Rigoletto*, this narrative seems designed to replay ironically the plot of Zen's least favorite opera). Both stories climax during the premiere of a much anticipated mass in the church of San Clemente. Written by a «celebrated Bolognese composer», it had been the talk of the town for weeks: not only would it feature Mirate but, in an unprecedented move, it was rumored not to contain «the customary fugue»:

---

[3] «Dimmi, qual è la tonica nella chiave di *Do?* –. – Il *Do* –. – Bene. E il *Mi* che cosa è? –. – La terza –. – E il *Si?* –. – La settima –. – Ora senti, dal *Do* al *Mi* che salto si fa? –. – di terza maggiore –. – Dunque quando dici *Do Mi* dici e canti una terza maggiore –. – Sicuro –. – Quando canti *Si Do* che intervallo fai? –. – Di mezzo tono –. – Dunque quando dici *Si Do* come *Mi Fa* dici e canti un mezzo tono –. – Certamente –. – Adesso rispondi. Se nel tuo maledetto sistema di lettura, che chiamano comune, canti, per esempio, in chiave di *Re*, il *Do Mi* che cosa diventa? –. – Una terza minore –. – E il *Mi Fa* o il *Si Do?* –. – Un tono intiero d'intervallo –. – Oh, vedi, vedi che miserabile, che infame confusione. Si legge una cosa e si canta l'altra. Non c'è più regola, non si capisce più nulla –». Boito, *Il maestro*, pp. 239-240.

[4] «Il basso Zen era conservatore arrabbiato. Per esempio, non poteva soffrire le opere del Verdi: ne diceva un mondo di male, specialmente il *Rigoletto*, allora fresco fresco». Boito, *Il maestro*, p. 238.

[5] «Un giorno gli viene in mente di pubblicare un giornale in dialetto per mettere in sempre maggior luce il setticlavio e dire al prossimo la verità: fortuna che in meno di un mese il foglio era bello e sotterrato. Un altro giorno annunzia su tutte le cantonate della città la *Storia del canto dall'antichità fino ad oggi*, raccoglie firme e quote di associati: l'opera rimane alla prima faccia della prefazione». Boito, *Il maestro*, p. 256.

There was an anxiety in the city, as much as if one had spoken of a new opera by Verdi at La Fenice: in the cafes, in the clubs, walking up and down Saint Mark's Square or along the Molo one spoke of nothing else. It was like waiting for a musical revolution.[6]

The performance, however, does not take place. At the last minute it is discovered that Mirate has escaped from the city during the previous night, and no one else can perform his part. Abandoned by her lover, Nene soon falls ill and dies; Zen is committed to an insane asylum. The story ends much as it began: «He had chosen for his companions the least melancholic patients, and he got busy teaching them to solfège and to sing. The rooms, the corridors, and the garden often echoed with voices, which repeated for hours on end: *Do Re, Do Mi, Do Fa, Do Sol, Do La, Do Si*».[7]

Camillo Boito is most remembered for another of his Venetian stories, *Senso*, which served as the basis for Luchino Visconti's film of 1954. Visconti's *Senso*, in turn, is best known for a rousing sequence in which the crowd at La Fenice is seen interrupting a performance of *Il trovatore*. That famous depiction of Risorgimento patriotism does not, however, appear in the original story, and the director might be described as co-opting Boito into a familiar, even triumphalist, history of Italian opera. *Il maestro di setticlavio* suggests that Boito's true concerns were rather different. Instead of Austrian oppression, it worries about the arbitrary nature of the linguistic sign. But that is generally thought to be a much later problem; it is modernism's great subject, and seemingly not at stake in anything as solid as *Rigoletto*.

Camillo Boito left few other writings on music, yet *Il maestro di setticlavio* might serve as an invitation to revisit the more distinguished brother with whom he shared an apartment in Milan. Arrigo Boito, after all, was closely associated with Zen's despised Verdi; and, if he was hardly a «celebrated Bolognese composer», his notoriously unconventional opera *Mefistofele* did find favor first with that city's audiences. This chapter suggests that an intensive investigation into the relationship between music, language, and pure sonority – a theme broached summarily in *Il maestro di setticlavio* – constitutes a fundamental, if largely overlooked dimension of Arrigo Boito's thought. His poems, compositions, and libretti thus represent perhaps

---

[6] «Ma, appunto per questo, era un'ansia per la città, quanto se si fosse trattato di un'opera nuova del Verdi al teatro della Fenice: nelle botteghe da caffè, nei ritrovi, passeggiando su e giù in piazza di San Marco o sul Molo non si parlava d'altro. C'era come l'attesa di una rivoluzione musicale». Boito, *Il maestro*, p. 269.

[7] «Aveva scelto fra i suoi compagni, tutti tranquilli, i meno malinconici, e s'affaccendava nell'insegnar loro a solfeggiare e a cantare. Le sale, i corridoi e il giardino echeggiavano spesso di voci, che ripetevano per ore ed ore: *Do Re, Do Mi, Do Fa, Do Sol, Do La, Do Si*». Boito, *Il maestro*, p. 281.

the key Italian precedent for the more aggressive (and more explicitly 're-alistic') experiments with acoustic materiality to be discussed in Chapter Two. Like *verismo* operas, Boito's works often seem to be struggling against the limited resources and generic conventions of their respective media, using a variety of humble devices – solfège syllables, whistles, chanting, onomatopoeia – to raise quite sophisticated questions about sound. What is more, and again like Puccini and his contemporaries, Boito seems wary of the more unsettling implications of his own discoveries. In his libretto for Verdi's *Falstaff*, to be discussed in the conclusion of this chapter, we can observe the poet both unleashing and trying to master a proto-modernist linguistic riot, incorporating the unruly nature of vocalized sound into a romanticized poetics of the Italian language. Although *Falstaff* is often described as a twilight work, I aim instead to locate it at the start of a new and troubled moment in the history of Italian opera.

I

Arrigo Boito in fact makes a fleeting appearance in *Il maestro di setticlavio*, by way of an allusion obscure enough to suggest it may have been intended as a family joke. During his final descent into madness, Zen makes a last attempt to convince his companions of the viability of his system. «Moveable Do is still respected», he insists. «It is known, for example, that the city of Arezzo has decided to raise, with the aid of European donations, a monument to Guido Monaco. And what was Guido d'Arezzo's great invention? Solfège, or, to put it in other words, moveable Do».[8] Although Zen's logic is dubious, he does have his facts straight; and when the Tuscan city unveiled its Guido monument on 2 September 1882, Camillo's brother was extensively involved. A preview of the event published in «Il teatro illustrato» would have made Zen proud:

As soon as the curtain that now hides the likeness of Guido from the view of spectators is raised, thirty bands will play two instrumental works composed for the occasion: one by maestro Cosimo Burali, and one by maestro Gandolfi, after which will follow the overture to Verdi's *Nabucco*. Then a hymn by Luigi Mancinelli on verses by Boito will be sung. That evening the theater will open with a grand operatic spectacle, the aforementioned Boito's *Mefistofele*. Celebrations of every type will follow in the succeeding days: academic presentations in honor of Guido, races, processions by torchlight, electric illuminations, and much else.[9]

---

8 «Il setticlavio anzi è in onore. Ella sa, per esempio, che la città di Arezzo deliberò di alzare, col mezzo di una colletta europea, un monumento a Guido Monaco. Quale fu la gloriosa invenzione dell'aretino? Il solfeggio o, per dirlo con un'altra parola, il setticlavio. È vero o non è vero?». BOITO, *Il maestro*, p. 279.

9 «Allorché verrà calata la tela, che toglie ora il simulacro di Guido alla vista dei riguardan-

This strange admixture of scholastic ambition and popular entertainment follows the general outline of many other commemorative festivals in post-Unification Italy, from those accompanying the five-hundredth anniversary of Dante's birth in 1865 to those marking the centenary of Verdi's in 1913.[10] (As we shall see in Chapter Four, the model would persist, with little modification, throughout the Fascist period). Acts of collective memorialization aided the cause of Italian unity, building a shared mythology of great men through ritual contact with the past.

Yet why lavish such attention on a medieval pedagogue? It is worth noting, first of all, that commemorative festivals were especially common in Tuscany. This is partially explained by the province's disproportionately high quotient of artistic genius, but a more important factor was the central role that medieval Tuscany played in the ideology of the new nation.[11] During a period distinguished by a corrupt and barely functional parliamentary system, an antagonistic relationship between church and state, the explosion of regional and class factionalism, and the appalling legacy of medieval sharecropping systems, Tuscan history offered a model of enlightened leadership, robust secularism, civic unity, and productive agriculture. And for a small city like Arezzo (a village of «peaches and cabbages», according to Henry James, where «the historic, the romantic decoction seemed to reach one's lips in less stiff doses» than elsewhere in the province) a bid for a place in the cultural pantheon was also a bid for a position in the new economy of high-minded tourism.[12]

---

ti, saranno suonati, da trenta bande, due brani strumentali appositamente composti, l'uno dal maestro Cosimo Burali e l'altro dal maestro Gandolfi, ai quali pezzi farà seguito la sinfonia del *Nabucco* di Verdi. Indi verrà cantato un inno musicato da Luigi Mancinelli sopra versi di Boito. Alla sera, il teatro s'aprirà con grande spettacolo d'opera, e cioè col *Mefistofele*, dello stesso Boito. Seguiranno, nei giorni successivi, feste d'ogni genere, tornate accademiche in onore di Guido, corse, ritirate con fiaccole, illuminazione elettrica, e che altro mai». *Le feste di Arezzo*, «Il teatro illustrato», September 1882, pp. 135-136: 135.

[10] On the Verdi festival, see LAURA BASINI, *Cults of Sacred Memory: Parma and the Verdi Centennial Celebration of 1913*, «Cambridge Opera Journal», XIII, 2001, pp. 141-161. On Italian memorial culture more generally, see UMBERTO LEVRA, *Fare gli Italiani: memoria e celebrazione del Risorgimento*, Turin, Comitato di Torino dell'Istituto per la storia del Risorgimento, 1992.

[11] See *Donatello among the Blackshirts: History and Modernity in the Visual Culture of Fascist Italy*, ed. by Claudia Lazzaro and Roger J. Crum, Ithaca, Cornell University Press, 2005; D. MEDINA LASANSKY, *The Renaissance Perfected: Architecture, Spectacle, and Tourism in Fascist Italy*, University Park, Pennsylvania, Pennsylvania State University Press, 2004; and WALTER L. ADAMSON, *Avant-Garde Florence: From Modernism to Fascism*, Cambridge, MA, Harvard University Press, 1993.

[12] HENRY JAMES, *A Chain of Cities* [1873], in *Italian Hours*, ed. by John Auchard, New York, Penguin Books, 1995, pp. 205-219: 218. For more on Arezzo in this context, see LASANSKY, *The Renaissance Perfected*, pp. 107-182; and BENJAMIN GEORGE MARTIN, *Celebrating the Nation's Poets: Petrarch, Leopardi, and the Appropriation of Cultural Symbols in Fascist Italy*, in *Donatello among the Blackshirts*, pp. 187-202. It should be noted that the cult of Piero della Francesca – whose fresco

Although hardly as distinguished as Dante or Verdi, then, Guido d'Arezzo could nonetheless be imagined as a more practical sort of hero: as the father of modern musical notation, and of a deeply embodied method of teaching sight-singing, he exemplified the newly vital arts of memory and transmission. «Il teatro illustrato» insisted on the monk's contemporary relevance, celebrating his skill at bringing the mysteries of music to the populace:

Guido's principal merit is to have renounced, in an art where practice plays so great a role, the philosophical and mathematic disquisitions of his predecessors, to adopt a relatively easy language, popular as one would say today. He understood the poverty of the art of his time, and demonstrated the necessity of putting it on the path of progress and great innovations.[13]

The journal's vision of a music both inclusive and innovative, participatory and progressive, was furthermore reflected in the musical program itself: the popular marches (for thirty bands!); Verdi's rousing overture, with its paraphrase of the Risorgimento icon «Va', pensiero»; Boito's experimental opera. The city of Arezzo demonstrated the «path of progress» in a different way: Guido's statue was placed just outside the new train station, on the boulevard that leads uphill through the historic center.

No work was more elaborately tailored to the aims of the occasion than Boito's text for the central ode.[14] As *Il maestro di setticlavio* makes clear, Guido's most famous innovation was the invention of solmization syllables to identify the six notes of the hexachord. Guido had pulled these syllables (ut, re, mi, fa, sol, la) from the text of a popular Latin hymn; Boito reversed the process, placing Guido's phonemes in a new linguistic reliquary:

> *Util* di Guido *re*gola superna,
> *Mi*suratrice *fa*cile de' suoni,

---

cycle *La legenda della vera Croce* has firmly placed Arezzo at the heart of culturally ambitious Tuscan tourism today – is an exclusively twentieth-century phenomenon. See Auchard's footnote in *Italian Hours*, p. 218.

[13] «Il merito principale di Guido è d'aver rinunciato, in un'arte in cui la pratica ha tanta parte, alle disquisizioni filosofiche e matematiche dei suoi predecessori, per adottare un linguaggio relativamente facile come si direbbe oggi *popolare*. Egli comprese la povertà dell'arte del suo tempo, e dimostrò la necessità di mettersi sulla via del progresso e delle grandi innovazioni». AMINTORE GALLI, *Guido d'Arezzo*, «Il teatro illustrato», September 1882, pp. 136-138.

[14] Boito describes his plans for the ode in a letter to Luigi Mancinelli dated 1 August 1882, in LUIGI MANCINELLI, *Epistolario*, ed. by Antonio Mariani, Lucca, Akademos, 2000, pp. 70-72. In addition to his compositional activities, Mancinelli (1848-1921) was the one of the most important Italian conductors of his generation.

> *Solenne* or tu *laude* a te stessa intuoni;
> *Sillaba* eterna![15]

[Guido's useful supreme rule, | easy measurer of sounds, | now you sing to yourself a solemn song of praise; | eternal syllable!]

Allowing Guido's ancient syllables literally to echo through his own modern verses, Boito provided a model of historical continuity. And, by forcing his secular voice into conformity with the style of his monastic ancestor, he performed a gloss of sorts on Guido's original hymn: «That thy servants may freely proclaim the wonders of thy deeds, absolve the sins of their unclean lips, O Saint John».[16]

II

On closer inspection, though, Boito's message begins to seem rather less straightforward. «Useful» and «easy» are terms of faint praise, especially from the pen of a militantly esoteric poet; meanwhile, the convoluted diction makes it unclear who, or what, is the subject of the third line's «tu»: is it Guido himself, or only his method, that is being lauded? This subjective ambiguity is intensified in the strange conceit of sounds praising themselves, which deprives both Boito and the celebrants in Arezzo of any authorial agency. Instead, the poem presents itself as a mysteriously self-generating and self-performing text, as if Guido's syllables had given rise to the lyric without any human intervention. The uncanny effect continues through the final line. Does the «sillaba eterna» connote one specific (if unnamed) phoneme, the whole set of solfège syllables, or some other sound echoing outside the confines of the text?

Similar ambiguities are exploited in several other Boito poems that make use of solfège syllables, texts that dwell on the peculiar ontological identity of Guido's syllables, and on their strangely mystic charm. Perhaps the richest of these is a poem entitled *Do mi sol... la do mi...* originally published in 1865.[17] It begins in an almost Baudelarian world of synesthesia:

> L'armonia del vostro viso
> mi ripete una canzon,

---

[15] Arrigo Boïto, *Per la celebrazione di Frate Guido*, in *Tutti gli scritti* (hereafter *TGS*), ed. by Piero Nardi, Verona, Mondadori, 1942, p. 1368. This poem (as well as the passage from *Iràm* I analyze below) is also discussed in Laura Basini, *Reviving the Past: Italian Music History and Verdi*, Ph.D. diss., University of California Berkeley, 2003. Basini's emphasis on linguistic experimentation in these texts is a key precedent for my own work.

[16] The original Latin reads: «*Ut* queant laxis | *re*sonare fibris, | *mi*ra gestorum | *fa*muli tuorum, | *sol*ve polluti | *la*bii reatum, | Sancte Ioannes».

[17] A. Boïto, *Do mi sol... la do mi...*, in *TGS*, p. 1365.

> che non so trascriver fiso
> né col verso né col suon;
> ora è bianca ed ora è bruna,
> ora è sole ed ora è luna,
> ora è carme ed ora è runa,
> la melodica vision.

[The harmony of your face | repeats a song to me, | that I don't know how to fix in written words, | neither with verse nor with sounds; | now it is white and now it is brown, | now it is sun and now it is moon, | now it is song and now it is rune, | the melodic vision.]

Unfolding a chain of opposing concepts that are neither mutually exclusive nor indeed precisely opposite, Boito suggests that even the seemingly stable polarity of verse and sound is inadequate to represent his experience, the «melodic vision» of a face that sings.

The undermining of discrete sign-systems continues through the second stanza:

> Quando sboccia il vostro labro,
> come un fiore di cinabro,
> e discioglie al riso il vol,
> entro l'anima mi scuote,
> come il tocco di tre note,
> do mi sol, do mi sol.

[When your lip opens, | like a flower of cinnabar, | and the flight dissolves into laughter, | it shakes my soul, | like the sounding of three notes, | do mi sol, do mi sol.]

If this passage begins with a conventional simile that likens a woman's lips to a flower in bloom, it ends by taking leave of poetic language completely, yet the flight from meaning culminates in sounds that are curiously didactic and banal.[18] One might interpret the final solfège syllables within the framework developed by Carolyn Abbate to make sense of similarly disappointing noises in Verlaine and Debussy, treating them as merely the place-holders for impossible songs outside the proper limits of the text.[19] Another way to avoid the obviousness of the syllables would be to train our ears to their purely verbal music. That is to say, perhaps we should hear the chord's pat-

---

[18] The second half of Boito's poem, not discussed here, traces an almost identical movement: in the third stanza the poet again praises the woman's beauty and, in the fourth, his description culminates in the line «la do mi, la do mi».

[19] See CAROLYN ABBATE, *Debussy's Phantom Sounds*, in *In Search of Opera*, Princeton, Princeton University Press, 2001, pp. 145-184.

tern of vowel sounds (O I O) as echoing the poet's own name, as if the woman's face was addressing 'Boito' directly. Yet both approaches may overemphasize the writing on the page. Something more magical happens when you allow yourself to sing along. Spoken syllables become notes of a musical scale, verse cues sound, and the poem dissolves into pure sonority, enacting the collapse of independent media that it had previously described.

This last interpretation is corroborated by a musical setting Boito made of the poem (it is the only art song listed in his catalogue). Most of the song is a tarantella-like ditty, whose tuneful melody is followed closely by the piano. At the words «entro l'anima mi scuote», however, the texture breaks, as the piano sounds the notes C, E, and G over the space of five octaves (see Ex. 1.1). For the next two measures the dance rhythm disappears; the piano outlines a C-major triad in close formation and the voice echoes it at pitch, intoning the syllables «do mi sol». It is as if the song has suddenly

Ex. 1.1. Boito, *Do mi sol... La do mi...* The 'mystic triad' emerges.

(continues)

Ex. 1.1. *(conclusion)*

turned into a warm-up exercise, or as if the soprano has briefly stopped to adjust her pitch. The passage sits strangely with the song as a whole: its literal joining of text and music is out of place in a piece that avoids all word-painting, let alone any clear correspondence between poetic and musical affects. Much as the syllables that appear in Boito's poem are not quite language, the arpeggios that interrupt his song are not quite music.

There is one final observation to be made about this setting: Boito is thinking in terms of fixed Do. The syllable «do», that is to say, connotes not just any tonic note, but rather the precise pitch C. This conceit intensifies the song's blurring of boundaries, for only in a fixed system can the letters «do» imply both a specific phonetic sound and a specific musical pitch, thus truly merging song with language. This point is necessary to make sense of another early poem that employs solfège syllables, the *Ballata dei tre tuo-ni* of 1867.[20] Boito's ballad tells the story of a troubadour seduced by the

---

[20] BOITO, *La ballata dei tre tuoni*, in *TGS*, pp. 1377-1380.

voice of a woman singing to him from the sea. The conventional narrative is given a twist, however: instead of luring the minstrel to his death, this Siren poses him a challenge:

> «Son la ninfa dell'Oceano
> più leggiadra sotto il ciel;
> odi, o vago giovincel:
> se con voce alta e serena
> canti questa cantilena
> entrerai nel mio vascel».

[«I am the nymph of the Ocean, | the lightest under the sky; | Listen, O beautiful youth: | If with a voice high and serene | you sing this cantilena | you will enter in my vessel».]

If Homer's Sirens lured their sailors with promises of fortune, Boito's creature seems more interested in a good time. Her accessibility – captured in the double sense of «vascel» – is further emphasized in the cantilena itself, which is almost comically straightforward:

> «Mi, re; do, re, mi.
> Ballata
> di fata
> è lunga a cantar,
> è affanno ed inganno,
> ci vuol più d'un anno,
> ci vuol più d'un dì.
> mi, re; do, re, mi».

[«Mi, re; do, re, mi. | Ballad | of fairies, | it is difficult to sing, | it is sorrow and trickery, | it takes longer than a year, | it takes longer than a day. | Mi, re; do, re, mi.»]

As the protagonist will soon learn, however, even if the voice sounds like Maria von Trapp, the song is not without its mystery.

The poem skips ahead to the following year: the troubadour returns to the shore, sounds a C-major chord, and sings the song. Yet, although he seems to reproduce it perfectly, the nymph vanishes into thin air. A year later he returns once more, sounds a D-major chord, repeats the cantilena, and she vanishes again. Finally on his third try, when he begins his song on E, he wins the girl, providing perhaps the first happy ending to the Siren myth in history:

> E all'ultimo suon
> di quella canzon,
> s'è visto vagar,
> s'è visto danzar

      sui flutti del mar
      la fata e il garzon.

    [And on the last note | of that song, | one saw wandering, | one saw dancing | on the ocean's waves, | the fairy and the boy.]

The key to the mystery, it seems, was quite literally its key: for the minstrel has discovered that the Siren's song is not transposable. Only when his starting pitch (E) matches the first syllable of the tune (Mi) does he gain access to the enchanted creature. This tuning of music and language, or so I read the lesson of the poem, may seem an ordinary sort of magic, but it is magic nonetheless.

III

In *Per la celebrazione di Frate Guido*, *Do mi sol*, and *La ballata dei tre toni*, Boito seems to use solfège syllables to explore, and even celebrate, the blurring of discrete sign systems. Boito scholars, however, have more commonly described the poet as obsessed with a rigidly binaristic logic. The perception originates in Boito's own self-presentation: he placed his poem *Dualismo* at the head of his collected verses, and its famous opening couplet – «Son luce ed ombra; | angelica farfalla o verme immondo» (I am light and shade; | angelic butterfly or filthy worm) – has seemed the key to his whole aesthetic program. Benedetto Croce argued that an opposition between good and evil dominates all Boito's major texts, and more recent critics have explored further polarities, between poetry and composition, northern and southern art.[21] While dualism is clearly an essential component of his thinking, it is also important to stress the extent to which Boito is fascinated by the unity of music and language, a unity that not only lacks a specific moral valence, but robs Manichean distinctions of their meaning.

For although the solfège poems discussed so far present the marriage of sound with language as a happy prospect, there are other texts that dwell

---

[21] See Benedetto Croce, *Arrigo Boito*, in *La letteratura della nuova Italia. Saggi critici*, I, Bari, Laterza, 1967, pp. 255-273. For the suggestion that Boito's dualistic philosophy essentially reinscribes his lifelong struggle between poetry and composition, see William Ashbrook, *Boito, Arrigo*, in *Grove Music Online*, ed. by L. Macy (accessed 16 January 2008), <http: | |grovemusic. com>. For an interpretation of Boito's aeshetics in light of debates on the relative merits of German and Italian culture, see Adriana Guarnieri Corazzol, *Indizi letterari del primo Mefistofele*, in *Musica e letteratura in Italia*, Milan, Sansoni, 2001, pp. 51-70. An important doctoral dissertation by Rosa Solinas explores further connections between the world of *Dualismo* and Boito's later work: see Rosa Solinas, *Arrigo Boito: The Legacy of Scapigliatura*, PhD diss., Oxford University, 1999. Essential recent discussions of Boito include Alessandra Campana, *Opera and Modern Spectatorship in Late Nineteenth-Century Italy*, Cambridge, Cambridge University Press, 2015; and Emanuele d'Angelo, *Arrigo Boito drammaturgo per musica. Idee, visioni, forma e battaglie*, Venice, Marsilio, 2010.

on the dystopian dimensions of the union. These are explored to (seemingly) comic effect in a scene from Boito's libretto for Cesare Dominiceti's obscure opera *Iràm*.[22] Like *Do mi sol*, this scene begins with an invocation of synaesthetic experience, although here the protagonist is inspired not by a beautiful woman but rather by too much beer:

> Il mondo è un trillo
> per l'uomo brillo,
> un trillo enorme
> di suoni e forme,
> di flauti e cetere,
> che scorre a vol
> dall'onda all'etere,
> dai prati al sol.[23]

[The world is a trill | for the man with a buzz, | an enormous trill | of sounds and forms, | of flutes and lyres, | that breaks into flight | from the waves to the ether, | from the fields to the sun.]

As some readers will have noted, this *brindisi* contains a few striking anticipations of Boito's most hallowed texts, resonances to be discussed in more detail below. Here I wish only to note that, as in *Do mi sol*, the transcending of conventional sense-perception provokes a song based on solfège syllables, as Iràm improvises what he calls a «cantus firmus»:

> *Do*mine va in cantina,
> *re*cipe un'ampia tina,
> *mi*sura cinque gotti,
> *fa* gorgogliar le botti,
> *sol*feggerò così,
> *la*udando la tua spina,
> *si*no al novello dì.
> *do*mine va in cantina.

[The Lord goes to the cellar, | prescribes a big vat, | measures five glasses, | makes the barrels gurgle, | I will solfège like this, | praising your tap, | until the new day. | The Lord goes to the cellar.]

Boito matches these blasphemous verses with an equally irreverent treatment of Guido's system, its holy syllables (originally used to describe the purification of lips) now serving as the basis for a bawdy drinking song.

---

[22] It is unclear if this text was ever performed or, indeed, set to music. The dating of Boito's libretto is similarly murky. See Nardi's commentary in *TGS*, p. 1536.

[23] Boito, *Iràm: commedia lirica in tre atti*, in *TGS*, pp. 819-876: 824-826.

This reversal of sacred and secular is not Boito's most subversive move. For the very fact that Guido's syllables can appear in both contexts reminds us that they are mere phonemes with no identity of their own, no inherent difference from the gurgles produced by an open spigot, itself a perverse image of the human mouth. The sounds of language may resemble less exalted music and more the rude, meaningless noises of the natural world. And, if this is true, perhaps language itself is nothing more than a random succession of empty sounds. Falstaff, in his famous deconstruction of the hallowed word «honor», puts it best: «Ch'è dunque? Una parola. | Che c'è in questa parola? C'è dell'aria che vola» (What is it then? A word. What is in this word? Only air that flies).

IV

In the wake of Saussurean linguistic theory, this realization will come as no surprise, yet Boito approached it with grim and dogged fascination. Indeed, he made an ability to turn coherent language into empty sound one of the defining features of his Mefistofele, the protagonist of his only completed opera (1868, revised 1875). This power is explored most extensively in Mefistofele's Act I aria «Son lo spirito che nega», through which he reveals his true identity to an astonished Faust:

> Son lo Spirito che nega
> sempre, tutto: l'astro, il fior.
> Il mio ghigno e la mia bega
> turban gli ozi al Creator.
> Voglio il Nulla e del Creato
> la ruina universal.
> È atmosfera mia vital
> ciò che chiamasi peccato,
> morte e Mal.
> Rido e avvento – questa sillaba:
> «No».
> Struggo, tento,
> ruggo, sibilo.
> «No».
> Mordo, invischio,
> fischio! fischio! fischio! (*fischia violentemente colle dita fra le labbra*).

[I am the sprit that denies | everything always; the star, the flower. | My sneer and my bicker | disturb the Creator's leisure. | I desire the Nothing and, as for Creation, | universal ruin. | My vital element is | that which they call sin, | Death and Evil. | I laugh and I howl this syllable: | «No». | I destroy, I tempt, | I roar, I hiss: | «No». | I taunt, I ensnare, | I whistle! I whistle! I whistle! (*he whistles violently with his fingers between his lips*).]

The first half of the text is little more than a litany of demonic sentiments, the sort of menacing but stock pronouncements that have given Boito's philosophizing such a bad name. Both the style and the sentiment soon change, however: steady *ottonari* break apart into lines of unequal length; the conventional opening rhyme scheme stutters; metaphysical doctrines are replaced with a series of blunt verbs.[24] Readers will also note that Mefistofele identifies his «no» not as a word to be spoken, but rather as a «syllable» that is laughed, howled, roared and hissed. These shifts from elevated language to raw phonation culminate in the final line: projecting nothing but empty air through his lips, Mefistofele begins to whistle.[25]

Each stage in this process of linguistic decomposition has a parallel in Boito's music for the aria. Mefistofele begins the piece by rehearsing many of the signifiers of evil available to a nineteenth-century composer: excessive chromaticism, prominent tritones, lines descending into the lowest depths of the male voice. Then, with the words «Rido e avvento», these standard tropes cede to a procession of deliberately ugly vocal gestures: first a flurry of sixteenth-notes on a single pitch, then a pattern of rising, arpeggiated diminished chords that ascend the chromatic scale to an E above the staff. The whistle, of course, is the final touch: it is an inherently unmusical sound, and one Boito makes no attempt to notate. The high-pitched noise sounds especially strange coming from an otherwise hyper-masculine bass voice. The effect would be doubly weird, if, following a wonderful instruction in the *disposizione scenica*, the whistle actually sounded from another body, concealed off-stage:

As soon as Mefistofele has placed his fingers in his lips in order to whistle, a man (an extra, a stage hand, a member of the chorus, in short someone who knows how to whistle extremely violently) hidden behind the first flat will whistle as loudly as he can, until the beginning of the orchestral ritornello.[26]

Lest the effect remain unclear, Faust's reaction is also specified. Having «approached [Mefistofele] with curiosity» during the passage beginning «Rido

---

[24] For a more detailed analysis of the poetic structure of this aria, see the commentary in ARRIGO BOITO, *Il primo Mefistofele*, ed. by Emanuele d'Angelo, Venice, Marsilio, 2012, p. 174.

[25] Solinas interprets this whistling scene rather differently, as staging Boito's own antagonistic relationship with his audience (who, after all, whistled at the premiere). See *The Legacy of Scapigliatura*, pp. 165-170. See also, D'ANGELO, *Arrigo Boito*, p. 78.

[26] «Appena Mefistofele avrà messe le dita nelle labbra per fischiare, un uomo (comparsa, servo di scena, corista, infine uno che sappia fischiare *violentissimamente*) nascosto dietro il primo piano fischierà più forte che potrà finché attacca il ritornello d'orchestra». The *disposizione* is reprinted in *Mefistofele di Arrigo Boito*, ed. by William Ashbrook and Gerardo Guccini, Milan, Ricordi, 1998, pp. 35-145: 62.

e avvento», now, «at the whistle's violence he plugs his ears with his hands, and rapidly passes in front of Mefistofele and goes to the right».[27]

As is often the case with operatic staging manuals, this excess of information might seem to compensate for some other lack.[28] No human whistle, not even one supported by a full orchestra shrieking a diminished-seventh chord, could possibly produce the horrifying sound that is called for so emphatically. As was the case with the C-major triad that interrupts the tarantella in *Do mi sol*, there is a seemingly ineradicable distance between the power that Boito invests in sonic materiality and his actual ability to call this power into being. Yet in the final moments of his revised, 1875 version of *Mefistofele*, Boito makes another, more aggressive, attempt to represent the devil's whistle. After Faust has renounced evil and ecstatically embraced his death, the opera concludes with a screaming match of sorts between Mefistofele and the angels. (Both parties sing in a style that imitates religious chanting, rapidly intoning their words over a single pitch. This effect, which makes the poetry almost inaudible, suggests that, for Boito, there is no absolute sonic difference between good and evil. Or, perhaps more accurately, that incantation – another way of blending language and music – renders the moral distinction irrelevant):

MEFISTOFELE

Diluvian le rose
sull'arsa mia testa,
le membra ho corrose
dai raggi e dai fior.
M'assale la mischia
di mille angioletti,
trionfan gli eletti,
ma il reprobo fischia!

I CHERUBINI

Spargiamo un profluvio di rose,
sul mostro, e le gelide e irose
sue membra contorca, furente,
in mezzo alla pioggia rovente
che spargano i cherubi d'oro.[29]

---

[27] «Alla violenza del fischio tura le sue orecchie colle mani, passa rapidamente innanzi a Mefistofele e va a destra». See *Mefistofele*, p. 62.

[28] For a consideration of the issues involved in interpreting these documents, see ROGER PARKER, *Reading the Livrets, or the Chimera of 'Authentic Staging'*, in *Leonora's Last Act: Essays in Verdian Discourse*, Princeton, Princeton University Press, 1997, pp. 126-147.

[29] Here I reproduce the text as it appears in Ricordi's 1876 piano-vocal score. Boito's published libretto contains several additional lines of text and other small variants not set to music.

[Mefistofele The roses shower down | on my burning head, | my limbs are corroded | by light and flowers. | A gaggle of thousands of angels | assails me, | the elected ones have prevailed, | but the reprobate whistles! Cherubim We scatter a profusion of roses | upon the monster, | his cold wrathful limbs contort, furiously, | amidst the red-hot rain | that the golden cherubs shower.]

First between Mefistofele's phrases, and then again after their conclusion, an unusual sound rises from the orchestra: a flute, doubled by two piccolos an octave higher, plays a rapid scale which functions as an appoggiatura to a sustained high E, a sound piercing enough to be heard clearly above the full orchestra and chorus. This whistle effect is truly uncanny, produced by no single human body, emanating from outside the confines of the stage world. It was perhaps Boito's most extreme musical invention.

V

Most of the texts discussed thus far form part of the 'avant-garde' side of Boito's corpus: lyric poems intended for a limited circulation, an opera remarkable for its lack of concern with audience. Yet the issues I have been exploring are also at play, in a more mediated form, in many of Boito's more popular works, and it may be instructive to consider his libretto for Amilcare Ponchielli's 1876 operatic warhorse *La Gioconda* in this context. Boito worked on this text concurrently with his revised version of *Mefistofele*, and although *La Gioconda* does not contain the extravagant sonic effects of that opera and of earlier works, I want to suggest that it also compensates for that lack, replacing the rude mechanics of pure sonority with a more abstract thematics of vocal production.

It is certainly hard to think of a nineteenth-century libretto that represents the act of singing more obsessively. The *dramatis personae* is dominated by professional singers: La Cieca and La Gioconda make their livings singing prayers and songs for hire; the spy Barnaba is also a *cantastorie* (minstrel) who prowls the stage with a guitar; a group of *cantori* (street singers) come to Gioconda's aid in the last act. The opera is also full of diegetic performances: La Cieca's prayers, which pepper the first act; the organ prelude, echoing from San Marco, which brings that act to its conclusion; the two *marinaresche* (the first sung by the sailors, the second initiated by Barnaba) in Act II; the serenade sung by the *cantori* in Act III and repeated in Act IV. In addition to these standard vehicles of operatic self-reflection, Boito also, and much more strangely, repeatedly calls visual attention to his singers' mouths. A stage direction at the beginning of the second act instructs each member of the chorus of sailors to hold a speaking-trumpet in his hands, and to sing the first number through these devices.[30] Like the fingers that Mefistofele places between his lips, these speaking-trumpets both amplify sound and point toward its bodily origins. And, although she never smiles in the opera, Gioconda's name does serve to summon the most famous mouth in all of Western art. Surveying the crowd at La Scala before the work's premiere, one critic mused: «Gioconda! Where was Gioconda? At 7:45 I looked for her still. A sea of heads undulated in front of me; my thought, however, caressed Leonardo's *Mona Lisa*, with her adorable smile».[31]

These images of human vocality are further emphasized by repeated references to acts of listening: throughout the opera, characters rely on aural information much more than on visual evidence. The central figure here is of course La Cieca, Gioconda's blind mother, whose disability forces her to depend on ears alone. But Barnaba is also a master of eavesdropping, as is Gioconda, who hides behind a pillar in Act I to learn of his plot to ensnare her beloved Enzo. Further examples abound: Enzo first gleans the true identity of the masked Laura through the sound of her voice; the Doge's impotence is figured as an inability to be heard – for Barnaba he is nothing more than a «muto scheletro», a mute skeleton.

The opera's richest figuration of these tropes is the *bocca del leone* that focuses both the musical and the visual interest of the first act. A familiar icon of the Venetian state, the lion's mouth was essentially a wide slit carved into a stone block, a receptacle for anonymous denunciations: its name referred both to the mouth-like opening and to the power the stone wielded over the citizenry. Politics, however, do not alone account for the symbolic force with which Boito and Ponchielli invest this gruesome mailbox. After having his scribe Isepo prepare a secret condemnation, Barnaba addresses his chilling aria «O monumento» directly to the lion's mouth. At the climax of the aria, he commands the stone itself to speak:

> O monumento! Apri le tue latèbre,
> *vicino alla bocca del leone*
> spalanca la tua fauce di tenèbre,
> s'anco il sangue giungesse a soffocarla!
> Io son l'orecchio e tu la bocca: Parla!

---

[30] «All'alzarsi della tela, alcuni MARINAI sono seduti sulla tolda, altri in piedi aggruppati; tutti hanno un portavoce in mano; molti MOZZI sono arrampicati, o seduti, o sospesi alle sartie degli alberi e stanno cantando una marinaresca».

[31] «Gioconda! Ma dov'era Gioconda? Alle sette e quarantacinque minuti la cercavo ancora. Un mare di teste mi ondeggiava intorno; però il mio pensiero accarezzava la *Monna Lisa* di Leonardo, col suo adorabile sorriso, col suo sguardo in cui filtra un raggio di sole, colle sue chiome rutilanti più dell'oro». «Il fanfulla», reprinted in «Gazzetta musicale di Milano», 16 April 1876, p. 131.

[O monument! Open your throat, | *close to the lion's mouth* | open your shadowy jaws wide, | even if blood comes to suffocate them! | I am the ear and you the mouth: Speak!]

Ponchielli sets Barnaba's last word with a leap to a *fortissimo* high G, dramatically sustained over a final dominant. An awkward setting for the syllable «par», and the highest note the baritone sings in the opera, this fierce sound is intensified by its visual impact: with Barnaba's jaws agape, he seems a mirror image of his subject.

Barnaba's injunction to the lion's mouth – «Io son l'orecchio e tu la bocca: Parla!» – is a calculated echo of his previous instructions to Isepo:

> Io son la mano
> e tu la penna.
> Scrivi.

[I am the hand | and you the pen. | Write.]

While neither command is literally true, Barnaba's demonic power in the scene nonetheless derives from his seeming ability to disperse his energy into other agents. If Isepo's pen does indeed transcribe his message, then perhaps we must imagine the lion's mouth, like the sailors' speaking-horns, as also amplifying Barnaba's own voice. The *bocca del leone* thus shares a shadowy affinity with those other silent objects that Boito imagines giving rise to sound: the face in *Do, mi, sol* that repeats a song, the statue of Guido that intones lauds to itself.

As we have seen in *Iràm* and *Mefistofele*, this transcending of the natural limits of voice ultimately leads to incoherent sound. In the final moments of the opera, Barnaba, all his other machinations having failed, demands that Gioconda offer him her body in fulfillment of their previous contract. She concedes, but first asks for a moment to adorn herself, and uses the opportunity to commit suicide. Outraged at this deception, Barnaba curses her:

> Ah! ferma! irrïsion!... ebben... or tu...
> M'odi... e muori dannata:
> *curvandosi sul cadavere di Gioconda e gridandogli all'orecchio con voce furibonda*
> ier tua madre m'ha offeso! Io l'ho affogata!
> Non ode più!!

[Ah! stop! derision!... well then... now you... | hate me... and die damned *(bending over Gioconda's corpse and screaming with a furious voice in her ear)* | Yesterday your mother offended me! I drowned her! | She hears no more!!]

The dramatic situation here recalls Barnaba's previous one-sided colloquy with the lion's mouth, although now the roles have been both reversed and negated. Gioconda is the ear and he the mouth, her deafness contrasting with Barnaba's earlier auditory omnipotence, just as his voice has little of the mighty power he previously ascribed to the *bocca del leone*. Boito breaks the spy's lines down into stuttered, arbitrary phrases, and Ponchielli adds a final unpitched «Ah!!» into the score. Barnaba, like Mefistofele, disappears into empty sound.

VI

Boito's next major collaboration would also climax at the moment in which the voice of a maritime despot exceeds the normal limits of his body and is repeated by another. To quote the staging manual published for its first performance:

The Doge cries out, in a frightening manner, «Sia maledetto»; then suddenly, with his left hand, he grabs Paolo's right arm [and] darkly adds a command, «And, you, repeat the curse». Paolo is almost stricken dead by this anathema; his face denotes the greatest fright; he would like to refuse, but, subjugated by the Doge's eyes, frees himself, takes a step forward, and tremblingly cries out, «Sia maledetto»; he then instantly covers his face with his hands, whispering, «Orror! Orror!».[32]

Here, in the Council Chamber scene of Verdi's revised *Simon Boccanegra* (1881), speech is echoed not by some marble statue, but by another living being, and the ensemble will get caught up in the play of repetitions too, the stage becoming a dreadful acoustic hall of mirrors. Gary Tomlinson describes «an excess that rises up – that must rise up, given the transcending of subjective voice at stake – and carries with it both words and drama. Its terror originates in [the] broaching of a place beyond meaning».[33]

This is a brilliant description of the scene's mechanics, yet the 'terror' of its music may have less to do with the contradictions of German idealism (the context that interests Tomlinson) than with the fact that Boito seems to have found, for the first time, a composer inventive enough to respond to his peculiarly materialist vision. Related to this shift in emphasis, the asemantic scandal of Verdi's music might be located somewhat earlier than where Tomlinson finds it: not in the bombastic, quasi-Wagnerian orchestral peroration that concludes the scene, but rather in the wild, unpredictable, almost anti-musical chanting of the chorus. Their outbursts are not a response to the noumenal magic of curses in general; instead, they literalize the fact that the Doge himself cares less about the content of his malediction than the thunderous clang of his speech, a noise that is described as al-

---

[32] Quoted in GARY TOMLINSON, *Learning to Curse at Sixty-Seven*, «Cambridge Opera Journal», XIV, 2002, p. 232.

[33] TOMLINSON, *Learning to Curse*, p. 241.

most physical. «Piombare», the operative verb here, means «to swoop down upon», but also, more viscerally, «to cover or to seal with lead».

According to Tomlinson, an anti-semiotic excess rises up once more in Verdi's *oeuvre*, in the music that accompanies the Moor's repeated kisses at the conclusion of Verdi and Boito's *Otello*. It is hard to refrain from mentioning that, once again, the transcending of subjective voice is linked to a visceral image of a human mouth. Otello's necrophiliac kiss thus completes a thematic unfurled at the very beginning of the opera, when Iago mocks his antagonist as «quel selvaggio dalle gonfie labbra» (that savage with swollen lips). That line is easily dismissed as an unfortunate stereotype of racial difference, but it also calls attention to the dangerous physicality of Otello's mouth as such. Cassio's drunkenness, the device that will soon set the whole plot in motion, bespeaks a similarly risky inability to keep his lips shut. His disastrous *brindisi* – like Iràm's sacreligious song, like Barnaba's wild address to the *bocca del leone*, and like Otello's fatal, excessive *bacio* – paints the failure to control one's mouth as an almost moral weakness.[34]

Perhaps it should come as no surprise then that a collaboration launched with an opera named 'Simon Blackmouth' would culminate in one that featured a character whose swearing, lying, drunkenness, and obesity all suggest that he is not the master of his own lips. In this context, Boito's libretto for Verdi's *Falstaff* reads like a monument to earlier sonic obsessions. In addition to Falstaff's Mephistophelean degradation of the word «honor» as «aria che vola», quoted above, we might note his Act III monologue, which, like Iràm's *brindisi*, proposes an analogy between the state of drunkenness and a musical trill:

> Il buon vino sperde le tetre fole
> dello sconforto, accende l'occhio e il pensier, dal labbro
> sale al cervel e quivi risveglia il picciol fabbro
> dei trilli; un negro grillo che vibra entro l'uom brillo
> trilla ogni fibra in cor, l'allegro etere al trillo,
> guizza e il giocondo globo squilibra una demenza
> trillante! E il trillo invade il mondo!!!..

---

[34] In this context, it may also be worth noting a suggestive affinity between Barnaba's incoherent final lines and Iago's Credo as interpreted by Katherine Bergeron. For her, Iago's concluding gesture – a mute shrug – stages the ultimate undecidability of his 'creed': «[The shrug] acts instead more like a question, extending the influence of that unexpected and inconclusive 'E poi?' to the very end [...] Through this noncommittal sign, a shrug, the reader is faced with the one option he would have preferred to avoid – the suspension of his disbelief». KATHERINE BERGERON, *How to Avoid Believing (while Reading Iago's «Credo»)*, in *Reading Opera*, ed. by Arthur Groos and Roger Parker, Princeton, Princeton University Press, 1988, pp. 184-199: 198-199.

[Good wine dispels the grim nonsense | of dejection, kindles eye and thought, from the lips, | it rises to the brain and thus reawakens the little maker | of trills; a black cricket that vibrates within the man with a buzz | trills every fiber in his heart, at the trill the happy ether | flashes and the smiling globe unhinges with a trilling dementia! | And the trill invades the world!!!]

In *Iràm*, the extended metaphor leads to a chorus based on solfège syllables and the sound of a gurgling cask. Here no such progression is necessary: with its rich onomatopoeia, and its obsessive repetitions of double l's, the aria collapses the evocation and performance of phonic chaos.

It is tempting to note a further correspondence here, between the «trilling dementia» that invades the world and Mefistofele's superhuman whistle.[35] (Falstaff's attribution of the trill to a weird «black cricket» would help the case). It is not the only demonic allusion in the text. Boito's most astonishing self-borrowing involves a paraphrase of a passage in his bizarre early narrative poem *Re Orso*. In the section of that poem entitled *Litania*, a satanic monk and a toad enact a grotesque ritual over Orso's corpse, reciting a nearly meaningless chant that represents one of Boito's most extreme linguistic experiments:

FRATE	*Pape Satan.*	
ROSPO		*Ora pro eo.*
FRATE	*Pape Pluton.*	
ROSPO		*Ora pro eo.*
FRATE	*Pape Ariman*	
ROSPO		*Ora pro eo.*
FRATE	*Pape Caron.*	
ROSPO		*Ora pro eo.*
FRATE	*Chiron.*	
	Geryon.	
	Typhon.	
	Ophion.	
	Gorgon.	
	Demogorgon.	

Now compare both the rhythm (five three-syllable lines, followed by a final five-syllable line) and the rhyme of the monk's final outburst with this passage barked by the maskers – dressed as witches, fairies, and satyrs – in Act III, Scene 2 of *Falstaff*:

---

[35] For another (extremely insightful) discussion of connections between *Mefistofele* and *Falstaff*, see DANIEL ALBRIGHT, *Verdi*, in *Berlioz, Verdi, Wagner, Britten*, London, Bloomsbury Arden Shakespeare, 2014, pp. 125-134.

DR. CAJUS e FORD

Cialtron!

BARDOLFO e PISTOLA

Poltron!
Ghiotton!

TUTTI GLI UOMINI

Pancion!
Beòn!
Briccon!
In ginocchion!

Further parallels between *Re Orso*'s black ritual and *Falstaff*'s torture scene might also be adduced. The toad's repetition of the Latin formula «ora pro eo» resembles the wives' equally obsessive intoning of the faux-religious phrase «domine fallo guasto» later in the scene. And just as Boito's *Litania* mocks Catholic rites, Verdi's music for the scene (described by Budden as a «mock-litany») parodies two melodic fragments from his own Requiem.[36]

Above and beyond any specific echoes, though, the greatest affinity between these two texts is simply the extravagance of their word-play. The monk's resonant litany continues for another two pages, culminating in a meaningless sentence first spoken by one of the damned in Dante's *Inferno*: «*Rafel mai amech zabi àlmi*». Falstaff's tormentors indulge in an onomatopoetic frenzy of even greater proportions:

ALICE, MEG, QUICKLY

Pizzica, pizzica,
pizzica, stuzzica,
spizzica, spizzica,
pungi, spilluzzica. [...]

BARDOLFO

Sconquassa-letti!

QUICKLY

Spacca-farsetti!

PISTOLA

Vuota-barili!

MEG

Sfonda-sedili!

DR. CAJUS

Sfianca-giumenti!

FORD

Triplice mento!

---

[36] JULIAN BUDDEN, *The Operas of Verdi: From Don Carlos to Falstaff*, III, Oxford, Clarendon Press, 1992², p. 523.

One critic at the opera's premiere complained that this scene was composed «with strange and antiquated words, with clashing rhymes, with assonances, with *sdruccioli* and *tronchi*, with crowded repetitions, with extravagances and eccentricities [...] of every form, color and taste».[37] Another recoiled from the linguistic riot as if in terror, reporting that «Boito has collected and jumbled together obsolete and old-fashioned words that are horrifying [...] [words] that not even Ruscelli dared to put into his famous rhyming dictionary».[38] We might thus say that Falstaff's torture involves a specifically Dantean justice. Having attacked language throughout the opera, the glutton is now forced to eat his words.

VII

And yet, just how infernal is *Falstaff*? A number of recent studies have emphasized the comedy's darker dimensions. According to Michal Grover-Friedlander: «In *Falstaff*, voice is independent and detachable from its original operatic body, it is no longer pure voice but a voice that can migrate grotesquely from one body to another and acquire meaning through its different voicings».[39] Similarly, Emanuele Senici argues that, in the opera, «the body cannot make any sound that can be meaningfully translated into either words or music».[40] *Falstaff* thus represents «a deeply skeptical interrogation of the relationship both between words and music and song and aria, reality and opera, body and voice».[41] For Senici, these fissures are at root political; the separation of voice from body figures the distance between debased modern Italy and its glorious historical roots.[42]

Although sympathetic to Senici's path-breaking account, I would part company with it in two respects. First, as already suggested, I think *Falstaff*'s anxiety about voice may concern not only its detachability from human

---

[37] «E qui, preso l'aire, coi vocaboli antiquati ed eterocliti, con le rime bisbetiche, con le assonanze, con gli sdruccioli e i tronchi, con le ripetizioni accalcate, con le bizzarrie e le stranezze, insomma, d'ogni forma, d'ogni colore e d'ogni gusto, il Boito non la finisce più». B., *Il Falstaff di Giuseppe Verdi*, «Nuova antologia: rivista di scienze, lettere ed arti», 15 February 1893, pp. 750-758: 757.

[38] «La sera», 10 February 1893. Quoted in JAMES A. HEPOKOSKI, *Giuseppe Verdi: Falstaff*, Cambridge, Cambridge University Press, 1983, p. 30.

[39] MICHAL GROVER-FRIEDLANDER, *Vocal Apparitions: The Attraction of Cinema to Opera*, Princeton, Princeton University Press, 2005, p. 82.

[40] EMANUELE SENICI, *Verdi's «Falstaff» at Italy's Fin-de-Siècle*, «Musical Quarterly», LXXXV, 2001, pp. 274-310: 294. See also ANSELM GERHARD, *Ultimi baci nei «giardini del Decameron». Allusioni intertestuali nei libretti di Boito per Verdi*, in *L'opera prima dell'opera. Fonti, libretti, intertestualità*, ed. by Alessandro Grilli, Pisa, Plus, 2006, pp. 141-150.

[41] SENICI, *Verdi's «Falstaff»*, p. 295.

[42] For other studies of the opera's cultural politics, see ROGER PARKER, *Falstaff and Verdi's Final Narratives*, in *Leonora's Last Act*, pp. 100-125; and BASINI, *From Reverence to Rebus*, in *Reviving the Past*, pp. 130-180. Both Parker and Basini interpret *Falstaff* as a less ambivalently 'nationalist' text.

bodies, but also its bodily origins and all too physical presence. Second, I would argue that by eliding this distinction, Senici may underestimate a more utopian strain in the libretto, in which Boito attempts to enact a union between voice and body, language and song, and, ultimately, Italy's past and present. Our disagreement might be summarized by an interpretation of the opera's final couplet, which concludes the action and launches the famous fugue:

FALSTAFF

Un coro e terminiam la scena

FORD

E poi con Falstaff, tutti, andiamo a cena.

[FALSTAFF A chorus and we'll end the scene, | FORD and then, with Falstaff, let's all go to dinner.]

Senici is clearly right that the self-reflexive first line unsettles the conventional fictions of nineteenth-century opera, but it seems important that it is followed by an image of communal ritual – vaguely sacramental, and undeniably Italian – that proposes a socially constructive function for the mouth.

With these issues in mind, let us turn to Boito's famous 'sonnet' that opens Act III, Scene 2, a text that is also the centerpiece of Senici's analysis:

FENTON

Dal labbro il canto estasïato vola
pe' silenzi notturni e va lontano
e alfin ritrova un altro labbro umano
che gli risponde con la sua parola.

Allor la nota che non è più sola
vibra di gioia in un accordo arcano
e innamorando l'aer antelucano
con altra voce al suo fonte rivola.

Quivi ripiglia suon, ma la sua cura
tende sempre ad unir chi lo disuna.
Così baciai la disiata bocca!

Bocca baciata non perde ventura.

NANETTA

di dentro, lontana e avvicinandosi
Anzi rinnova come fa la luna.

FENTON

slanciandosi verso la parte dove udì la voce
Ma il canto muor nel bacio che lo tocca.

[Fenton From lips the ecstatic song flies | toward nocturnal silences and goes far away, | and at the end it finds another human lip | that responds to it with its own word. | Now the note that is no longer alone | vibrates with joy in an arcane accord, | and enchanting the antelucan air | flies back with another voice in turn. | There it regains sound, but its concern | tends always to unite who breaks it apart. | Thus I kissed the desired mouth! | Nanetta *from within, far off and coming nearer* | A kissed mouth doesn't lose its freshness | but renews itself as the moon does. | Fenton *running toward where the voice was heard* But the song dies in the kiss that touches it.]

Faced with the poem's convoluted syntax and archaic vocabulary, many critics have responded by looking for literary models in the poetry of the *Trecento* and in Shakespeare.[43] I will return to these arguments, but I would first stress that, in their search for origins, critics may have overlooked how much of the sonnet's meaning lies on the very surface of the text.

To begin, what precisely is the sound that moves from lip to lip? Although the first line identifies it, reasonably, as a «canto», the rest of the poem works to undermine this certainty, alternately describing it as a «parola», «nota», «voce», and «suono». These different terms blur any clear distinction between music and language, between an organized melody and a single pitch. The song's mysterious identity is amplified by the strange mechanics of its transfer: recalling Barnaba's dialogue with the *bocca del leone*, it moves directly from one mouth to another without any mediation of human ears.

In so doing, it strongly resembles the trill that takes leave of Falstaff's body to invade the world. The parallels between Falstaff's monologue and Fenton's sonnet are striking and numerous. Falstaff's phrase «dal labbro sale» is echoed by Fenton's «dal labbro [...] vola», and his line «quivi risveglia il picciol fabbro dei trilli» anticipates Fenton's more concise «quivi ripiglia suon». Falstaff's claim «L'allegro etere al trillo guizza» (the happy ether flashes at the trill) mirrors Fenton's description of sound «innamorando l'aer antelucano» (enchanting antelucan air), while his description of «un negro grillo che vibra entro l'uom brillo» (a black cricket that vibrates in the man with a buzz) has a parallel in Fenton's «la nota [...] vibra di gioia in un accordo arcano» (the note vibrates with joy in an arcane accord). Even the structural position of the two texts – Falstaff's monologue at the beginning of Act III, Scene 1; Fenton's sonnet at the beginning of Act III, Scene 2 – is similar.

---

[43] See Wolfgang Osthoff, *Il Sonetto nel Falstaff di Verdi*, in *Il melodramma italiano dell'Ottocento. Studi e ricerche per Massimo Mila*, ed. by Giorgio Pestelli, Turin, Einaudi, 1977, pp. 157-183. Senici also considers the sonnet in relation to its historical precedents.

These parallels serve to highlight the real differences between the texts. If Falstaff's monologue gives voice to all of Boito's nocturnal anxieties – about sound's ability to break down language, to escape from its origins – then Fenton's sonnet attempts to resolve these fears; imagining a mystical union of speech and song, it also seeks to restore sound to the sources of its production. If Falstaff's trill invades the world, in other words, Fenton's 'song' returns to human lips. But these lips are, crucially, more than just Nannetta's. Critics have long noted that the opening of the last tercet – «Bocca baciata non perde ventura» – quotes a line from the *Decameron*. I would add that the first syllables of the phrase – boc-ca (ba)-cia – themselves contain an 'arcane' echo of the author's name: Boccaccio. Given that Boccaccio's name literally translates as «naughty mouth», we might say that Fenton's song is restored not just to his lover's lips, but to those of the Florentine poet and, by extension, to the historical and geographic origins of Italian literature itself.

Nor is Boccaccio the only Tuscan writer invoked in Fenton's sonnet. Petrarch is there, most obviously, in the form of the text itself. Dante's presence is less directly advertised – at least until we remember that, for Boito, Dante's genius lay in the radical musicality of his language. «The process through which [Dante] chooses a word», he argued in a long letter to the French critic Camille Bellaigue,

the place that that word occupies, the mysterious connections between vocables, rhythms, assonances, the rhymes that precede and follow it, all this, and something even more arcane, give a Dantean tercet the value of a true composer's music. He operates with words with the same talent that your divine Mozart and my divine Bach operated with notes, and in the same manner.[44]

Mysterious sonic connections are the very subject of Fenton's sonnet, and I would argue that his poem is an attempt to bring the three members of the 'Holy Trinity' of Tuscan literature together in a single text: Boccaccio provides the words, Petrarch the form, and Dante the inspiration. Like *Per la celebrazione di Frate Guido*, but with much greater subtlety, the sounds of the Italian past are allowed to mingle, to vibrate joyously, in an arcane accord with the language of the present.

In Tuscany, of course, Dante's language actually was the language of the present. In the nineteenth century, it was easy to believe that vocab-

---

[44] «La divination par laquelle il choisit la parole, la place que cette parole occupe, les liens mystérieux avec les vocables, les rythmes, les assonances, les rimes qui précèdent et qui suivent, tout ceci, et quelque chose de plus arcane encore, donnent au tercet du Dante la valeur d'une véritable musique de musicien. Il opère avec les mots le même prodige que votre divin Mozart et mon divin J.S. Bach opéraient avec les notes, et de la même manière». Boito's essayistic letter of 1902 is reprinted as *Dante e la Musica*, in *TGS*, pp. 1320-1333: 1320.

ulary of the *Divina commedia* was still spoken, unawares, by farmers, and claims like the following, published in the «Illustrazione italiana», are not hard to come by:

What an enormous difference between the poor wife of the Apulian peasant and the gentle Tuscan farmer's wife, elegant and clean, well-groomed, with a smile on her lips and speaking the language of our poets, whose demeanor reveals such a different level of affluence and civilization![45]

This linguistic continuity was easily fetishized – as the invidious comparison between north and south makes clear – but in a fragmented (and largely illiterate) nation, it must have had real power. Similar fantasies of historical connection inspired many of the major cultural projects of post-Unification Italy: from the brief relocation of the nation's capital from industrial Turin to storied Florence, to the even more ambitious labor of replacing countless regional dialects with a single language explicitly modeled on Dante's vernacular. Drawing on the poet's belief, articulated in *De vulgari eloquentia*, that true language was imbibed with the wet nurse's milk, the government sent armies of Tuscan women to primary schools throughout the peninsula.[46]

Boito made his first visit to Tuscany in 1882, to celebrate the unveiling of Guido's monument, and by the time of *Falstaff* he seems to have become quite enamored of the place. The letters he wrote during the composition of the opera make repeated (if improbable) claims for the Tuscan sources of Shakespeare's narrative. In another letter to Bellaigue he moves beyond philological arguments, describing a synaesthetic vision quite similar to others we have encountered:

Where shall I begin? In your letter you touch with admirable clairvoyance and subtle intuition upon the very essence of the work. You say: Here is the true modern and Latin lyric drama (or comedy). But you cannot imagine the immense spiritual joy this Latin lyric comedy produces on the stage. It is a real outburst of grace, power, and gaiety. By the miracle of sounds, Shakespeare's sparkling farce is returned to its clear Tuscan source of «Ser Giovanni Fiorentino». Come, do

---

[45] A. Trevellini, «L'illustrazione italiana», 2 August 1874, quoted in Nelson Moe, *The View from Vesuvius: Italian Culture and the Southern Question*, Berkeley, University of California Press, 2002, p. 209.

[46] On the issues involved in Italian linguistic reform, see Brian Richardson, *Questions of Language*, in *The Cambridge to Modern Italian Culture*, ed. by Zygmunt G. Baranski and Rebecca J. West, Cambridge, Cambridge University Press, 2001, pp. 63-79; Tullio de Mauro, *Linguistic Consumption and Linguistic Minorities*, in *Italian Cultural Studies: An Introduction*, ed. by David Forgacs and Roger Lumley, Oxford, Oxford University Press, 1996, pp. 88-101; and Mark I. Choate, *The Language of Dante*, in *Emigrant Nation: The Making of Italy Abroad*, Cambridge, MA, Harvard University Press, 2008, pp. 101-128.

come, dear friend, come to hear this masterwork; come and live for two hours in the gardens of the Decameron, and breathe the flowers that are notes and the breezes that are sounds.[47]

Fenton's sonnet should be read in the context of this letter, as a similarly mystical attempt to connect with the Tuscan past through the redemptive power of pure sound.

VIII

How does Verdi's setting inflect these meanings? Although the composer is clearly (even unusually) respectful of the structure of Boito's text – Fenton's line cadences at the end of each quatrain and tercet – it would be hard to pinpoint anything specifically 'Tuscan', or even archaic, in the score. Fenton's song does stand out from its surroundings, though: lyrical, in an opera that is famously declamatory; leisurely, in a work that is often fragmented and propulsive. The blunt comic mimesis and the ironic historical allusions that are such a part of *Falstaff*'s sound world are not in evidence here. Bellaigue claimed that «Nowhere has a voice, an Italian voice, been more freely and purely displayed» than in this aria.[48] Hanslick thought it the one moment in *Falstaff* that «recall[ed] the earlier Verdi's sensual charm».[49] It might thus be argued that Boito's gestures to an idealized literary past are coupled with a return to a more naive musical style, that Verdi is evoking a moment when the voice could still luxuriate in its own Italian sensuality, free and pure. This combination of *Trecento* poetry and *primo Ottocento* opera could well be described as nationalist; it seems an attempt to collapse and resurrect two different highpoints of Italian art.

Nationalism, though, may be too blunt a word for Fenton's sonnet. Sparsely orchestrated and exquisitely fragile, Verdi's A-flat major aria slides through a series of increasingly remote tonalities – E-flat, E, B – before ending on the subdominant of the home key, avoiding any true sense of closure. And Boito's text is perhaps too obscure to be of any real political use. Had younger Italian composers been interested in the delicacy of Fenton's sonnet, they might well have gone on to develop a sort of local alternative to French symbolism; yet by the time of *Falstaff*, they were already at

---

[47] Boito to Camille Bellaigue, 16 February 1893, in HANS BUSCH, *Verdi's Falstaff in Letters and Contemporary Reviews*, Bloomington, Indiana University Press, 1997, pp. 362-363: 363. Compare Boito's strikingly similar claim about the *Paradiso* in his Dante essay: «vers la fin du poème *on respire des sons* et des chants qui pénètrent jusqu'au fond de l'âme». BOITO, *Dante e la musica*, p. 1321.

[48] CAMILLE BELLAIGUE, *The Lessons of Falstaff*, «Revue des deux mondes», 15 August 1924, pp. 935-943. Reprinted in BUSCH, *Verdi's Falstaff*, pp. 537-540: 538.

[49] EDUARD HANSLICK, *Memoirs of Verdi and Falstaff in Rome*, in BUSCH, *Verdi's Falstaff*, pp. 523-526: 525.

work transmogrifying Boito's materials into harsher stuff. As I will explore in Chapter Two, *verismo* composers share Boito's interest in acoustic materiality – especially as a means to evoke place and landscape – but not his sense of wonder at the sheer mystery of sound.

To introduce my discussion of the positivist acoustics of Italian realist opera, it may be instructive to point to one final (and, in the context of my study, prescient) reference to Guido d'Arezzo in Boito's *œuvre*. It occurs in the conclusion of *Re Orso*'s «Intermezzo storico», an enormously obscure ode to the progress made by civilization in the years around 1000 A.D., in which a variety of political and intellectual discoveries are described as bringing the Dark Ages to their close:

> Sorgeva il Sid purpureo
> come una calda aurora,
> simiglïante ad aquila,
> nel furïoso vol;
> e l'inspirato monaco
> che sul collo dell'ora
> carcava i pesi plumbei
> del suo primo orïuol.
>   Tutto era gloria! Il lezzo
> forbìa dei negri secoli
> la guerrïera età;
> e un fraticel d'Arezzo
> strillava in cima agli organi:
> ut, re, mi, fa, sol, la.

[Up rose El Cid, purple | like a warm dawn, | resembling the eagle | in its furious flight. | And the inspired monk | who on time's neck | hung the leaden weights | of his first clock. | All was glory! | The stench of black centuries cleansed by | the warlike age; | and a little bird from Arezzo | shrieked to the organs from on high: | Ut, re, mi, fa, sol, la.]

In this catalogue of military and scientific innovations, which celebrates the conquest of space (El Cid), time (the unnamed monastic clockmaker), and finally (in the figure of Guido d'Arezzo) sound itself, solfège syllables appear neither menacing nor magical; they are simply an abstract system of discipline and measurement, equivalent to the hours of the day. An untranslatable pun («fraticello» means «little monk», but also refers to a type of sea bird) further removes the syllables from the mysteries of language and the human voice. Incoherent sounds screeched by an uncomprehending animal, they sound like the battle cry of disenchantment.

VERISMO BELLS

Adopting the phraseology of a more polite generation of musicologists, we might describe Italian opera in the 1880s as a «period of transition».[1] Verdi spent much of the decade puttering around his farm, revising old texts, and the stars of the *giovane scuola* had not begun fully to shine. A decade that saw the premiere of *Otello* (1887) could hardly be considered lacking, yet no other operatic composition – neither Amilcare Ponchielli's Old-Testament drama *Il figliuol prodigo* (1880), nor Puccini's magical *Le Villi* (1884) – provoked much contemporary excitement, or achieved more than a marginal position in the repertoire. Indeed, it is telling that the most popular musical work created in 1880s Italy was not even an opera. That title goes to *Excelsior*, a ballet choreographed by Luigi Manzotti to a score by Romualdo Marenco, which debuted at La Scala in 1881, running for a hundred straight performances. It would prove to be a huge success throughout Europe, the United States, and South America, mounted frequently on three continents until the First World War.[2]

Excelsior has largely been written out of music history, yet it may be instructive to linger on its forgotten charms.[3] In its broadest outlines, the ballet narrated the victory of «progress» over the forces of «obscurantism»; its final tableau took place in the «Palace of Civilization», as all the nations of the world danced in honor of «Science, Progress, Brotherhood, and Love». This admittedly abstract allegory was enlivened by scenes that illustrated great moments in nineteenth-century industrial history. Denis Papin's invention of the steamboat, Alessandro Volta's discovery of the

---

[1] For one approach to the decade in these terms, see Jay Nicolaisen, *Italian Opera in Transition, 1871-1893*, Ann Arbor, UMI Research Press, 1980.

[2] For important background information on the ballet, see Flavia Pappacena, *Excelsior: Documenti e saggi/Documents and Essays*, Rome, Di Giacomo, 1998.

[3] One study that does include *Excelsior* within its framework is Alan Mallach, *The Autumn of Italian Opera: From Verismo to Modernism, 1890-1915*, Boston, Northeastern University Press, 2007, pp. 10-12.

electric battery, the building of the Suez Canal, the creation of a massive Alpine tunnel that linked France and Italy by train – all these were lovingly depicted. Incorporating national dramas of industrialization into a mythology of universal progress, *Excelsior* self-consciously imitated the narrative structure, as well as the visual style, of Italian World's Fairs.[4]

An ode to scientific reason on the stage of La Scala! Given opera's long-standing association with the «exotic and irrational», the popularity of *Excelsior* might be interpreted as a sign of the medium's incipient demise. Similarly, the fairground atmosphere of Manzotti's ballet, with its concrete representations of recent history, might seem a challenge to the more remote nature of operatic entertainment. One critic in 1882 described:

a ballet that destroys, annihilates all other ballets [...] where the real combines itself with the fantastic in most ingenious ways, where colors, lines, dances, and even the mimes' scenes follow one another with such harmony and such beauty that spectators are chained to their seats, stunned and confused for one and a half hours, and sent home wishing more than ever to come back and watch it again.[5]

Emphasizing realism and transfiguration, and an audience manipulated through techniques that sound quite a bit like suture and the montage of attractions, this passage comes close to imagining *Excelsior* as cinema, another of opera's familiar, «annihilating» demons.

Yet the presence of *Excelsior* at La Scala might also call attention to the surprising extent to which Italians were fascinated by the artistic potential of commercial mass spectacle. Wandering through Turin's Universal Exposition of 1884, no less a critic than Camillo Boito praised the superiority of its imitation medieval castles over their (inevitably more compromised) originals.[6] The ambitious painter Giovanni Segantini hoped to contribute a «multi-media installation» to the 1900 exposition in Paris, «a panorama of the Engadine in which gigantic paintings as well as water and sound machines would recreate the experience of the high mountains as realistically as possible».[7] The premiere of Verdi's *Don Carlos* was scheduled to correspond with the Paris *Exposition Universelle* of 1867, and the elaborate-

---

4 See CRISTINA DELLA COLETTA, *World's Fairs Italian Style: The Great Exhibitions in Turin and Their Narratives, 1860-1915*, Toronto, University of Toronto Press, 2006, pp. 65-78.

5 *Corrispondenze*, «L'Asmodeo», 11 November 1882, p. 8. Quoted in DELLA COLETTA, *World's Fairs Italian Style*, p. 72.

6 On Camillo Boito's response to the exposition, see DELLA COLETTA, *World's Fairs Italian Style*, pp. 40-41.

7 EMANUELE SENICI, *Landscape and Gender in Italian Opera: The Alpine Virgin from Bellini to Puccini*, Cambridge, Cambridge University Press, 2005, p. 220.

ly detailed national pavilions of that exposition arguably lurk behind the grandiose *tableaux* of his *Aida* (1871).[8]

Puccini's *Tosca* was not literally written for a World's Fair, but it would be difficult to think of another opera that embraces the late nineteenth-century vogue for «spectacular realities» more enthusiastically, or more completely.[9] The opera, created in Rome on 14 January 1900, is set in three of the city's iconic landmarks – the Jesuit basilica of Sant'Andrea della Valle, Michelangelo's Palazzo Farnese, and the Castel Sant'Angelo – and its much lauded «unity of time» lends a further aura of authenticity to the production. Equally important are the ways in which Puccini, like Segantini, attempted to enforce the visual spectacle through a specifically aural realism.[10] While working on the opera, the composer wrote frequently to priests and ethnographers, inquiring about the music that accompanied Catholic rites, about the pitch of Saint Peter's Bell, and the intricacies of local dialect. In the start of the third act, he used fourteen bells in eight different locations to reproduce, as faithfully as possible, the soundscape of the Eternal City as heard from a specific location at a specific time of day. Seen in this context, the premiere of *Tosca* at Rome's Teatro Costanzi might be interpreted as a deliberate provocation: an invitation for audiences to compare the sights and sounds of the stage world with the ambience of their own lives.

Many early critics were unimpressed. Romans were quick to point out a host of inaccuracies in the work, starting with the church in the first act, incorrectly named «Sant'Andrea *alla* Valle». More significantly, the opera's meticulous soundscape was found to be not only unmusical, but inimical to deeply held convictions about the nature of operatic representation. These early responses have largely been forgotten, a sign perhaps that Puccini's values are now more completely our own. Today, *Tosca*'s Rome occupies a comfortable, if hardly exalted, place within the operatic landscape, yet something important has been lost in this process of assimilation. By attempting to reconstruct some of the opera's early reception history, I aim to open up a lost avenue into the interpretation of the work, but also to raise larger questions about *Tosca*'s relationship with the culture of Italian positivism. I propose that Puccini's opera – not unlike Manzotti's ballet, if

---

[8] Relationships between Verdi's opera and the Paris exposition are explored in KATHERINE BERGERON, *Verdi's Egyptian Spectacle: On the Colonial Subject of «Aida»*, «Cambridge Opera Journal», XIV, 2002, pp. 149-159; and GABRIELLA CRUZ, *Aida's Flutes*, «Cambridge Opera Journal», XIV, 2002, pp. 177-200.

[9] I borrow this term from VANESSA R. SCHWARTZ, *Spectacular Realities: Early Mass Culture in Fin-de-Siècle Paris*, Berkeley, University of California Press, 1999.

[10] For a discussion of 'realistic' sound in earlier Italian opera, see LUCA ZOPPELLI, *«Stage Music» in Early Nineteenth-Century Opera*, trans. by Arthur Groos, «Cambridge Opera Journal», II, 1990, pp. 29-39.

less explicitly – stages the confrontation of empirical science with operatic tradition. To begin, however, it may be helpful to reexamine the relationship between *Tosca*'s hyper-realism and the phenomenon that scholars have identified, often with considerable discomfort, as musical *verismo*.

I

The term *verismo* refers primarily to Italian literature of the 1870s and 80s, where it describes the work of a number of writers, Giovanni Verga most prominently, who attempted to apply the 'scientific' and 'objective' techniques of French Naturalism to the depiction of their nation's rural poor. When, in 1890, the young composer Pietro Mascagni adapted one of Verga's Sicilian tales for his one-act opera *Cavalleria rusticana*, he set in motion a trend that would influence Italian opera for the next forty years. 1892 saw the premiere of two operas that closely followed *Cavalleria rusticana*'s model: Umberto Giordano's *Mala vita*, set in Neapolitan slums, and Ruggero Leoncavallo's *Pagliacci*, which unfolds in the backwaters of Calabria. Stefano Scardovi has catalogued some eighty operas written along similar lines between 1890 and 1933, works whose very titles – *Vendetta sarda, Vendetta zingaresca, Un mafioso, Tradita!* – testify to Mascagni's influence.[11] The interest in 'low' subjects extended to more exotic climes as well, including the Left Bank garrets depicted in Puccini's and Leoncavallo's versions of *La bohème* (premiered in 1896 and 1897 respectively), and the world of Japanese geishas and prostitutes imagined in Puccini's *Madama Butterfly* (1904) and Mascagni's *Iris* (1898). As they grab at alternatives to traditional operatic spectacle, some of these works come remarkably close to the modish excesses of the *Zeitopern* popular in the Weimar Republic. Giordano's *Fedora* (1898), to take an extreme example, features a plot involving anarchist assassinations, draws on the conventions of popular murder mysteries, and includes a scene where major characters enter the stage on bicycles.[12]

Verismo operas are easy to spot from their plots, but scholars have had more difficulty explaining how their musical language relates to their innovative dramaturgy. Although it is possible to isolate a number of stylistic features shared by the composers of the *giovane scuola* – jagged vocal decla-

---

[11] See STEFANO SCARDOVI, *L'opera dei bassifondi. Il melodramma 'plebeo' nel verismo musicale italiano*, Lucca, LIM, 1994.

[12] It is tempting to imagine Giordano's opera as a direct model for Kurt Weill's *Der Zar lässt sich photographieren* (1928), which also concerns anarchist assassinations of Russian aristocrats. The notorious scene in which Weill's characters listen to an on stage gramophone recording has a parallel in the second act of *Fedora*, where characters at a party delight in the virtuoso stylings of an onstage pianist. For a broader consideration of modernist irony in *Fedora*, see SENICI, *Landscape and Gender in Italian Opera*, pp. 181-227.

mation, a tendency to conclude acts with massive orchestral groundswells – it is harder to describe these techniques as shared responses to their subject matter. Composers did not write in an obviously different style when composing works with more conventionally aristocratic themes. What is more, the roots of their language can all be found in the far-from-adventurous music of Ponchielli, with whom many members of the *giovane scuola* had studied. Not surprisingly, many musicologists have urged caution in any use of the term *verismo* as applied to opera. Comparing Verga's programmatic preface to his story *L'amante di Gramigna* with the aesthetics of the *giovane scuola*, Egon Voss concluded that no significant affinity exists between the aims of literary and operatic realism.[13] More recent scholars – Virgilio Bernardoni, Andreas Giger – have by and large concurred.[14]

A different (and, to me, more suggestive) approach to the question is offered by Adriana Guarnieri Corazzol, who argues that *verismo* novels and operas do share «a poetics, as well as a practice, of anti-subjectivity».[15] In her view, both novelists and composers worked to undo assumptions about the proper relationship between an author and his characters; «lowering the linguistic level [of the work] to match the social level of the plot», they self-consciously adopted a «regressive» point of view.[16] Guarnieri Corazzol's notion of linguistic 'regression' resonates with a recent study by Noa Steimatsky, for whom «Verga's utopian notion of realist art points outside literary discourse, toward a spontaneous indexical tracing of the premises – or shall we say *referents* – of literature [...] in a nonverbal, nonsymbolic form of representation».[17] Steimatsky, in short, suggests that Verga attempted to remake literature in the image of photography. She calls attention to a suggestive passage in Verga's preface to *Gramigna* where he claims that:

when the hand of the artist will remain absolutely invisible, then the work will have the imprint of an actual happening; the work of art will seem to have made itself, to have matured and come into being spontaneously, like a fact of nature.[18]

---

[13] Egon Voss, *Il verismo nell'opera*, in *Cavalleria rusticana, 1890-1990: cento anni di un capolavoro*, ed. by Piero and Nandi Ostali, Milan, Sonzogno, 1990, pp. 47-55.

[14] See Virgilio Bernardoni, *Le 'tinte' del vero nel melodramma dell'Ottocento*, «Il saggiatore musicale», V, 1998, pp. 43-68; and Andreas Giger, *Verismo: Origin, Corruption, and Redemption of an Operatic Term*, «Journal of the American Musicological Society», LX, 2007, pp. 271-316. See also Carl Dahlhaus, *Realism in Nineteenth-Century Music*, trans. by Mary Whittall, Cambridge, Cambridge University Press, 1985, pp. 69-72.

[15] Adriana Guarnieri Corazzol, *Opera and Verismo: Regressive Points of View and the Artifice of Alienation*, trans. by Roger Parker, «Cambridge Opera Journal», V, 1993, pp. 39-53: 42.

[16] Guarnieri Corazzol, *Opera and Verismo*, p. 43.

[17] Noa Steimatsky, *Italian Locations: Reinhabiting the Past in Postwar Cinema*, Minneapolis, University of Minnesota Press, 2008, p. 93.

[18] Giovanni Verga, *Gramigna's Mistress*, in *The She-Wolf and Other Stories*, trans. by

Furthermore, she argues, it may have been this dream of the unmediated photographic 'tracing' of reality that led Verga to abandon novel-writing altogether around 1890. In an ultimate act of authorial regression, he left prose description behind and devoted the rest of his life to taking pictures of his native Sicily.

As a film historian, Steimatsky is primarily interested in the legacy of Verga's poetics for the neorealist movement. I wonder, though, if her emphasis on the visual dimension of *verismo* literature underplays an equally strong desire for acoustic precision. As Guarnieri Corazzol reminds us, two of Verga's most recognizable techniques – the all-pervasive use of free indirect discourse, and a related reliance on Sicilian dialect expressions – are both attempts to replace the 'voice' of the author with the less mediated speech of his characters. And Nelson Moe has suggested that acoustics are at the heart of Verga's attempt to replace a tradition of highly aestheticized representations of the Italian South with a more immediate realism. «It is specifically hearing that marks the shift from the picturesque to another form of perception», he writes, «hearing is the vehicle for the experience of proximity that runs counter to the distance required for the picturesque perspective».[19] Just as Verga flirted with the objectivity of the camera lens, it might be argued that he was also motivated by another technology for 'tracing' empirical reality: namely, the phonograph.

If we took the most salient feature of Verga's project to be neither an interest in the hardships of Sicilian life, nor in the 'sociological' determinants of human character, but rather a fascination with unmediated sound, then a new relationship between *verismo* literature and music might come into focus. Indeed, one thing that links the diverse works produced by young composers in the 1890s is an impulse to provide opera's basic fiction – that people express themselves through song, while an orchestra plays somewhere in the background – with a newly objective footing. This is most obviously true in the sudden vogue for plots featuring characters who are themselves professional performers. The trend began with the itinerant comedians in Leoncavallo's *Pagliacci*, and it continued with the cabaret singers in his *Zazà* (1900), the traveling performers in Mascagni's *Iris*, the professional actors in Franceso Cilea's *Adriana Lecouvreur* (1902), and of course the diva heroine of *Tosca* as well as the geisha heroine of *Butterfly*. Even in operas less overtly concerned with conflicts between life and art, performers make a remarkable number

---

Giovanni Cecchetti, Berkeley, University of California Press, 1962, pp. 86-88. Quoted in Steimatsky, *Italian Locations*, p. 93.

[19] Nelson Moe, *The View from Vesuvius: Italian Culture and the Southern Question*, Berkeley, University of California Press, 2002, pp. 269-270.

of cameo appearances: a group of madrigalists show up at the home of Puccini's *Manon Lescaut* (1893); a violin is performed onstage in Mascagni's *L'amico Fritz* (1891); onstage pianos are played by secondary characters in *Zazà*, Giordano's *Fedora*, and Puccini's *La rondine* (1917). Singing, in *verismo* opera, is no longer only a conventional means for expressing extreme emotional states. It is also an ordinary fact of characters' daily lives.

Yet even these works bear marks of unease about conventional operatic performance. Consider, for example, a scene from the first act of *Adriana Lecouvreur*, which is set in the wings backstage at the Comédie Française. Adriana, a famous actress, has just gone onstage (i.e., offstage as we in the audience see it) to deliver an important soliloquy in the evening's performance of Corneille. This soliloquy could easily have been the occasion for the sort of diegetic song that operatic composers had delighted in for centuries; instead, we hear not Adriana's voice, but that of the stage director Michonnet, as he describes the effects of her performance (Act I, Scene 8, «Ecco il monologo»).[20] The music Cilea writes for Michonnet is calculatedly mundane – declamatory, anti-melodic, barely accompanied by the orchestra – and instead of a virtuoso aria the audience is left with a chain of somewhat empty substitutions: off-stage for on-stage, absence for presence, narration for enactment, a man's voice for a woman's, and sentimental comedy instead of tragic drama.

Adriana's silence is extraordinary, but she is far from the only *verismo* character to move offstage at key moments. At the very end of the first-act love duet in Puccini's *La bohème*, Mimì and Rodolfo move into the wings to sing their climactic high notes. In that opera's third act, the lovers only intone their lush last phrase (including a high B-flat) after the curtain has fallen. The most extreme example of offstage singing in the decade is, without a doubt, *Cavalleria rusticana*, the prelude to which is interrupted by the principal tenor, who sings an entire aria behind the curtain. Turridu's classically poised *Siciliana* contrasts with his more rugged discourse elsewhere in the opera, much as Mimì's and Rodolfo's concluding phrases are flashes of pure song in an opera otherwise noteworthy for its 'realistically' discursive style. In moments like these, Mascagni and Puccini might be described as trying to find a place for conventional singing apart from the exigencies of realism. At the same time, though, their placement of singers offstage also extends the boundaries of the visual: sound is used to expand and delineate dramatic space, pushing its horizon beyond the

---

[20] For a classic study of operatic *mise-en-abyme* see Carolyn Abbate, *Unsung Voices: Opera and Musical Narrative in the Nineteenth Century*, Princeton, Princeton University Press, 1991. The qualities that Abbate celebrates in diegetic songs – most importantly, their ability to reflect on the power of live performance – are precisely those that *verismo* operas seem to call into question.

confines of the literal stage, and making characters, if briefly, into a sort of aural scenery.[21]

«Sounding architecture» might also be invoked to make one final point about *verismo* style: its tendency to make extravagant, excessive use of bells. Bells resounding from distant churches featured prominently in *Cavalleria rusticana*, where a simple tonic-dominant peal ushers in the opening chorus, and the techniques used by Mascagni in this piece («Gli aranci olezzano») would be closely imitated by Leoncavallo in the bell chorus («Don, din, don – suona vespero») of *Pagliacci*. Less mediated bells chime through a host of other works: *Tosca* and *Iris*, as well as later operas like Mascagni's *Isabeau* (1911) and Puccini's *La rondine* (1917) and *Suor Angelica* (1918). A good indication of the importance of bells for the style can be found by glancing at Jules Massenet's *La Navarraise*: the 1894 opera, written for Covent Garden, was widely considered to be a shameless imitation of the Italian style (Shaw quipped that Massenet had not so much written an opera as «made up a prescription») and in its final three minutes the singers are supported by almost no other sound. Like the conceit of performer-characters, the use of bells seems to have offered composers a way around opera's basic fiction: unlike song, unlike orchestral music, the sound of bells emanating from a source within the stage world required no elaborate justification. And yet, the limitations of the conceit are well captured in Guarnieri Corazzol's term «regression». If bells offered composers a promise of objectivity, they entailed an equally strong sacrifice of musical richness. Unable to sing or develop, bells in these operas are simply, stupidly, real.

II

«And they want to be realists», Giuseppe Samoggia complained in the «Rivista teatrale italiana» in 1901: «Mascagni with his scenes from peasant life, Giordano with his characters in evening dress, and Puccini with his use of *parlati* and of bells».[22] In this sentence, Samoggia anticipates standard musicological accounts of the *verismo* movement, as well as my own interest in auditory realism. In so doing, he belies recent assertions that there was no operative concept of operatic *verismo* in the late nineteenth century. More

---

[21] For a study of the uses of the offstage world in earlier Italian opera, see MARY ANN SMART, *Bellini's Unseen Voices*, in *Mimomania: Music and Gesture in Nineteenth-Century Opera*, Berkeley, University of California Press, 2004, pp. 69-100.

[22] «E realisti vogliono essere Mascagni coi suoi bozzetti paesani, Giordano coi suoi personaggi in frack, e Puccini coll'uso dei parlati e colle campane, sebbene tutto questo sia agli antipodi colle tendenze che la scuola tedesca ha sempre professate». GIUSEPPE SAMOGGIA, *Il realismo nel melodramma*, «Rivista teatrale italiana», 16 January 1901, pp. 73-76: 74.

important, though, are the ways in which Samoggia helps call attention to how strange and even menacing the concept of musical realism originally was.

Although the word «*verismo*» does not seem to have figured prominently in the first reviews of either *Cavalleria rusticana* or *Pagliacci*, by 1895 – after a rash of new works, and a significant interest on the part of foreign audiences – Italian writers realized they had a problem on their hands.[23] On 13 August 1896, the «Gazzetta musicale di Milano» published an essay by Alfredo Untersteiner written in the form of «an open letter to certain German music critics».[24] These critics, Untersteiner complained, had responded to the success of Mascagni and Leoncavallo's operas by dismissing them as «crass realism»; it was time to bring these arguments to a halt. «I confess that the whole question of the musical realism of the modern Italian school strikes me as a word without substance», he declared, «and I would be happy to hear even once, instead of idle chatter, a good definition of this *verismo*».[25] In the ensuing months six Italian writers published essays in response. Despite the appearance of a debate, however, the judgment of these critics was unanimous: music was an abstract and universalizing idiom, and the notion of any close affinity between the style of the *giovane scuola* and the subjects of their operas was simply absurd. The most overtly religious commentators were willing to allow for operatic *verismo* in a more eccentric sense: since humanity, they argued, was divided between divine and material essences, the dichotomy between noble music and base plot might be considered a sort of spiritual realism.[26] (Valeriano Valeriani, pushing this reasoning to its conclusion, argued that Palestrina might thus be considered the greatest realist of all). But, in general, critics insisted that the only type of musical realism was what they termed *musica descrittiva*, the imitation of thunderstorms and bird-calls, and this was hardly

---

[23] On the early reception of *verismo* opera, see MATTEO SANSONE, *Verga and Mascagni: The Critics' Response to «Cavalleria rusticana»*, «Music and Letters», LXXI, 1990, pp. 198-214; and SANSONE, *Giordano's «Mala vita»: A 'Verismo' Opera too True to Be Good*, «Music and Letters», LXXV, 1994, pp. 381-400.

[24] ALFREDO UNTERSTEINER, *Un'accusa ingiusta: lettera aperta a certi critici musicali tedeschi*, «Gazzetta musicale di Milano», 13 August 1896, pp. 556-558. Untersteiner's article, as well as the major responses to it, are reprinted (and here cited) in SERGIO VIGLINO, *La fortuna italiana della «Carmen» di Bizet (1879-1900)*, Turin, De Sono, 2003, pp. 119-146.

[25] «Alla musica drammatica italiana moderna viene, quasi senza eccezione, da musicisti e da non musicisti, rinfacciato il crasso realismo e fu ed è questo che le recò maggiormente danno. Io confesso che tutta la questione del realismo musicale della scuola italiana moderna mi sembra una parola vuota di sostanza e sarei contento di sentire una volta invece di lunghe chiacchiere una bella e buona definizione di questo verismo». UNTERSTEINER, *Un'accusa ingiusta*, p. 121.

[26] See ANTON GIULIO CORRIERI, *Pel verismo musicale*, pp. 125-128; and VALERIANO VALERIANI, *Del verismo nell'arte musicale*, pp. 129-131.

worth mentioning at all.[27] The whole discussion could be summarized with the words of the critic Arnaldo Bonaventura: «If music cannot signify, even less can it be realistic: and to be realistic it would have to cease being music».[28]

The unanimity of these writers should be taken with a grain of salt. Untersteiner's question was couched in explicitly nationalist rhetoric, and few official voices were willing to consider the possibility that the Italian tradition might be under threat. Smaller, more independent music journals wrote about *verismo* with a much greater sense of urgency, however, while still sharing many of the «Gazzetta's» key terms. A year before the Untersteiner debate, the Milanese journal «Il mondo artistico» had published a series of hyperbolic articles with titles like *Dangerous Tendencies* and *Opera's Decline*. Each was devoted to a new innovation of the *verismo* school – prose libretti, plebeian subject matter, modern dress – and each came to an identical conclusion: although all opera was based on the unsupportable fiction of human characters who sing, an increasingly realistic dramaturgy strained this long-standing convention to the point of mocking it.[29] In his essay in the «Rivista teatrale italiana», Samoggia went even further, claiming that the *verismo* imperative was leading to the very death of song:

for some time now, the music in new works has tended to eliminate itself, to slip away ever more: in the culminating points of the action it abdicates, it abstains, in order to cede its place to *parlati* and to the explosions of an orchestral artillery that intervenes to resolve dramatic situations of every genre in the same way: it is not rare to find entire scenes, of capital importance for the action, in which song is lacking and the orchestra fills the space, accompanying out of habit, a convention, that is to say, even worse than that which it intends to abolish.[30]

---

27 *Musica descrittiva* is touched on in ARNALDO BONAVENTURA, *Il realismo nella musica*, pp. 133-135; and CARMELO LO RE, *Sempre pel verismo*, pp. 137-139.

28 «La musica, se non può significare, tanto meno può essere verista; e per essere verista dovrebbe cessare di essere musica». BONVENTURA, *Il realismo nella musica*, p. 135.

29 See *Il dramma per musica: tendenze pericolose*, «Il mondo artistico», 31 March 1895, pp. 1-2; *La decadenza del melodramma*, «Il mondo artistico», 10 May 1895, pp. 1-2; and *Il costume borghese nel melodramma*, «Il mondo artistico», 31 January 1896, pp. 1-2.

30 «Il figurino cambierà presto, e non varrebbe la pena di discuterne, se non ci parve un fatto grave, un sintomo veramente allarmante; è cioè che da qualche tempo nei nuovi lavori la musica tende ad eliminarsi, ad ecclissarsi sempre di più: nei punti culminanti dell'azione essa abdica, si astiene, per lasciare il luogo ai *parlati* ed alle esplosioni di un'artiglieria orchestrale che interviene a risolvere nello stesso modo le situazioni di qualunque genere: non è raro trovare delle scene intere, di importanza capitale per l'azione, in cui il canto manca e l'orchestra fa l'effetto di un riempitivo, accompagna per consuetudine, vale a dire per una convenzione assai peggiore di quella che si intende abolire». SAMOGGIA, *Il realismo nel melodramma*, p. 75.

The critic concluded by noting that, «With the excuse of realism, the true musical substance becomes leaner and duller by the day».[31] It was as if Bonaventura's worry had finally been actualized: in the process of becoming realistic, music had gradually ceased to be.

III

It is tempting to interpret Puccini's *Tosca* in light of this journalistic discourse. Scarpia, after all, is an arch-realist – obsessed with signs of visual and verbal truth – and Tosca is an Italianate performer *par excellence*. Given his monstrosity, and her naïve goodness, the opera may seem a less than optimistic comment on the operatic reforms of the previous ten years. At the same time, though, it would be equally easy to describe *Tosca* as enthusiastically embracing all manner of *verismo* reforms.[32] For while the tropes I described above – the fascination with performer characters, the use of offstage singing, the recourse to non-orchestral sources of sound – are configured variously in different works from the 1890s, nowhere are they elaborated more extensively than in Puccini's opera. *Tosca* is littered with self-justifying performances, from the chants and Latin choruses of the first act to the shepherd's song of the third, and bells have a nearly ubiquitous presence: they toll the *Angelus* and they announce the *Te Deum*; as already mentioned, fourteen of them sound Matins in the third act; and an arsenal of sheep-bells even trails the shepherd and his flock. When, in the second act, Scarpia opens his window, allowing the sounds of Tosca's eighteenth-century cantata to waft onstage, he might be described as initiating a little allegory about the reversal of traditional operatic values in the work. Tosca's cantata, with its lyrical phrases, its sustained high B's and C's, is quite unlike anything she sings elsewhere in the opera; yet this moment of unapologetic singing is treated as mere scenery, the backdrop to Scarpia's more empirical pursuits.

This second interpretation – *Tosca* as an extreme example of *verismo* innovation – may be closer to how early critics heard the work.[33] Reviews of the premiere were harsh, critic after critic despairing that Puccini had pushed the anti-musical tendencies of *verismo* to a disastrous conclusion. A mild example of this line appears in the «Cosmorama pittorico». Com-

---

[31] «Colla scusa del realismo, la vera sostanza musicale diventa ogni giorno più scarsa ed incolore: è tempo di tornar indietro». SAMOGGIA, *Il realismo nel melodramma*, p. 76.

[32] For earlier considerations of *Tosca*'s relationship with *verismo*, see SIEGHART DÖHRING, *Musikalischer Realismus in Puccinis Tosca*, «Analecta Musicologica», XXII, 1984, pp. 249-295; and MOSCO CARNER, *Giacomo Puccini: «Tosca»*, Cambridge, Cambridge University Press, 1985, pp. 6-10.

[33] For another study of the opera's reception, see ALEXANDRA WILSON, *The Puccini Problem: Opera, Nationalism, and Modernity*, Cambridge, Cambridge University Press, 2007, pp. 69-96.

menting on the gavotte and cantata in the second act, Gustavo Macchi noted that, «It is the orchestra, the chorus that sing for themselves, more as a descriptive element of the action than as a musical interpretation of it». The moments struck him as among the «least interesting» in the score.[34] An article in «Avanti!» was more forceful:

At the mute scene which concludes the [second] act, a great void opened up in the orchestra as well, and the curtain descended on the coldness of the entire public [...] Their comments were disheartening, and among the greater part of the spectators there was an impression of stupor [...] One admired the elegance of the dialogue, one appreciated the scraps of melody that appeared here and there; but as for the drama, no one could find it. The public's coldness persisted in the first part of the third act, so that the prelude, the reawakening of Rome, with the sound of bells, the shepherd's interlude, and the Roman dialect refrain passed by in silence.[35]

This critic's sense of the opera as a succession of empty sounds, as a musical «void», would be echoed by the «Fanfulla della domenica», which provided an extravagant list of *Tosca*'s offenses. «The sonatinas and cantatas from the wings», they complained, «and the organ, and the Gregorian chant, and the drums that announce the march to the scaffold, and the bells, and the cow bells, and the rifle shots, and the cannon fire, which at times constitute essential elements in the development of the opera, are not enough to fill the holes left by the lack of music».[36]

Not surprisingly, given their critique of *verismo* quoted above, the «Rivista teatrale italiana» published the strongest denunciation of *Tosca*'s percussive sound world:

---

[34] «In altri punti – la *gavotte*, la *cantata interna*, per esempio – è l'orchestra, il coro che cantano per conto loro, come elemento descrittivo dell'azione, piuttostoché come interpretazione musicale di essa. Né sono questi i punti meno interessanti». Gustavo Macchi, *La Tosca del Maestro Giacomo Puccini al Teatro Costanzi di Roma: la musica*, «Il cosmorama pittorico», 3 February 1900, p. 2.

[35] «Alla scena muta che chiude l'atto, un gran vuoto si fa anche nell'orchestrale, e la tela scende sulla freddezza di tutto il pubblico. All'autore, agli esecutori ed al maestro Mugnone due chiamate sole. I commenti qui sono sconfortanti, nella maggior parte degli spettatori è una impressione di stupore per la delusione provata, dopo sì febbrile aspettativa. Si loda l'eleganza del dialogato, si apprezzano gli spunti melodici mostratisi qua e là; ma il dramma, il dramma non si trova. La freddezza del pubblico perdura nella prima parte dell'atto terzo, sì che il preludio, il risveglio di Roma, col suono delle campane, il passaggio del capraio e lo stornello romanesco, passano sotto silenzio». *La 'Tosca' del M. Puccini al Costanzi*, «Avanti!», 16 January 1900.

[36] «Ma è certo che le sonatine e le cantate dietro le quinte, e l'organo, e il canto gregoriano, e i tamburi che scandiscono la marcia al supplizio, e le campana, e i campanacci delle pecore, e le fucilate, e le cannonate che costituiscono talvolta elementi essenziali nello svolgimento dell'opera, non bastano a colmare i vuoti lasciati dalla deficienza di musica». Giorgio Barini, *'Tosca' Melodramma di G. Puccini*, «Fanfulla della domenica», 21 January 1900.

In thirty years, or – if there is a god watching our poor country – even before, *Tosca*, together with all the other operas of its type, will be an obscure and uncertain memory of a time of confusion in which music was subtracted, by the logic of history, from its own dominion, from its own laws, and from common sense [...] [and someone] will remember this about the third act of *Tosca*: a composition where there were the bells of various churches, the great bell of St. Peter's, cow bells, a voice in the distance [...] everything was there, except for music.[37]

Even as august and (one assumes) forward-looking a commentator as Gustav Mahler had difficulty hearing anything of substance in the work. Among his letters to his wife, we find this baffled account of one early performance:

Act 1. Papal pageantry with continual chiming of bells [...] Act 2. A man tortured; horrible cries. Another stabbed by a sharp bread knife. Act 3. More of the magnificent tintinnabulations and a view over all Rome from a Citadel. Followed by an entirely fresh onset of bell ringing. A man shot by a firing-squad.[38]

Mahler's comments could, of course, be dismissed as just one more instance of Germanic disdain for Italian exuberance, but, given the composer's own notorious interest in all manner of crude percussion, it may be more accurate to speak of a moment of shared recognition here, a worry that Puccini's music may have cut too close to home.[39]

The *Tosca* that emerges from these reviews is many things – urban soundscape, *musique concrète*, degree zero of musical meaning – but it is not the work loved by modern audiences for its lyricism and sentimental pathos. The arias and duets, the elaborate leitmotivic structure, everything in short that has interested today's scholars and audiences: all this was noted by *Tosca*'s early critics, but it is not what they found most

---

[37] «Fra trent'anni o – se esiste un Iddio superstite per questo nostro paese – anche prima, la *Tosca*, insieme con tutte le opere congeneri, sarà ricordo incerto ed oscuro di un periodo di confusione delle lingue in cui la musica fu sottratta, per fatalità storica, al dominio di se stessa, delle proprie leggi e del senso comune [...] E il nipote più erudito, a citare un esemplare tipico di nullaggine musicale, dopo il preludio al terzo atto di *Iris* che merita il primo posto, ricorderà quello al terzo atto di *Tosca*: "un pezzo dove erano le campane delle chiese minori, il campanone di San Pietro, il campanaccio delle vacche, una voce in lontananza, una violinata, una strombonata, un caprioleggiare di terzine [...] tutto c'era, fuorché la musica». ETTORE MARRONI, *'La Tosca' di Giacomo Puccini al 'San Carlo' di Napoli*, «Rivista teatrale italiana», 16 January 1901, pp. 86-89.

[38] Quoted in MICHELE GIRARDI, *Puccini: His International Art*, trans. by Laura Basini, Chicago, University of Chicago Press, 2000, p. 190, n. 47.

[39] Mahler's distaste is especially striking given how easily «Es sungen drei Engel», the fifth movement of his Symphony No. 3 (1893-96), could be described as a direct imitation of the bell choruses in *Cavalleria rusticana* and especially *Pagliacci*.

distinctive or important. The question, then, is how to account for these early responses without lapsing into their rhetoric of empty parataxis; how to describe in musicological detail an opera distinguished by its lack of music.

IV

One might begin by considering more closely those ubiquitous bells.[40] As mentioned above, Puccini took extraordinary interest in the specificity of Rome's sonic landscape, allegedly spending an evening atop the Castel Sant'Angelo waiting to observe the tolling of Matins, and corresponding with the Vatican – through the agency of his friend Don Pietro Panichelli – about the precise details of Saint Peter's bell. Panichelli's memoir of the composer narrates the latter story at some length:

But the most serious difficulty was finding the pitch of the great bell of Saint Peter's (called *er campanone*) that many had tried, and failed, to guess and to decipher. I asked my friend Orlando Virgili, who told me, «Do you know who would be able to give you precise information?». «Who?», I asked. «Old Maestro Meluzzi, who they tell me has carried out minute studies in this matter». I ran immediately to the elderly musician, a true celebrity in matters of religious music, a real Roman, and connected to the traditions of his time in the manner of [the early nineteenth-century church composer] Gaetano Capocci.[41]

Panichelli's conversation with Meluzzi was a success, as he reported in a letter to the composer:

Eureka! I have discovered it. Maestro Meluzzi was able to assure me that the pitch – indistinct, confused, elusive – of the great bell of Saint Peter's corresponds to an E natural. And he promised that I can inform you of this with confidence, and that he takes full responsibility in this matter.[42]

---

[40] For a helpful introduction to Puccini's use of bells in the opera, see GIRARDI, *Puccini*, pp. 165-167.

[41] «Ma la difficoltà più seria fu quella di trovare il tono della campana grossa di San Pietro (er campanone) che molti avevano tentato inutilmente di indovinare e di decifrare. Ne feci parola all'amico Orlando Virgili il quale mi disse: – Sai chi ti potrebbe dare informazioni precise? – Chi? – Il vecchio maestro Meluzzi, che mi dicono abbia fatto ricerche minuziose a tal proposito. Corsi immediatamente dal vecchio musicista, una vera celebrità in fatto di musica religiosa, romano di Roma, e attaccato alle tradizioni del suo tempo stile Gaetano Capocci». PIETRO PANICHELLI, *Il 'pretino' di Giacomo Puccini*, Pisa, Nistri-Lischi, 1962[4], p. 52.

[42] «Eureka! Ho trovato. Il maestro Meluzzi ha potuto assicurarmi che quel tono squarciato, indistinto, confuso, inafferrabile del campanone di San Pietro risponde ad un 'mi' naturale. E mi ha soggiunto che posso scriverlo con sicurezza a lei sotto la sua responsabilità». PANICHELLI, *Il pretino*, p. 52.

With its delight in clerical intrigue, Panichelli's narrative makes for an entertaining read, but it also reveals a more suggestive tension: on the one hand, the bell is described as mysterious and inscrutable; on the other hand, it is reduced to an empirical object, an instrument whose exact pitch can be ascertained with confidence.

In their quest to 'decipher' the mysteries of the great bell, Puccini and Panichelli were participating in a late nineteenth-century craze for studying church bells, a historically specific 'campanomania' that has been discussed in Alain Corbin's influential study *Village Bells*.[43] According to Corbin, bells had been objects of fascination for local communities through the early nineteenth century: sites of magical power, but also of civic pride and intense affection. (A good example is the Roman dialect name, *er campanone*, given to Saint Peter's bell itself). By the 1870s, this mysticism had largely ceded to more positivist pursuits: in place of Romantic poets writing odes to sonic ineffability, «specialists attended conferences on the subject and contributed to specialist journals».[44] Bells had, in short, become another object of academic discipline, with much of their original fascination lost in the process. As Corbin writes, «The disenchantment of the world and the desacralizing of life and the environment somehow disqualified the act of listening to bells».[45]

Corbin's history might prompt us to revisit a few familiar moments in nineteenth-century Italian opera. A good illustration of his earlier, enchanted paradigm appears in the last act of Verdi's *Rigoletto*, where a bell announces midnight, the time that Rigoletto has appointed to retrieve his gruesome package.[46] Verdi casually notates the bell's strokes within the space of a single measure, and does not bother to support its chiming with any other orchestral sound. Verdi's scene may seem almost naïve in its simplicity, but perhaps this is a sign that the composer assumed his audience would react to the bell's raw force. Like the musical thunder and lightning effects, the wordless offstage chorus, and the weird pastoral chords – all the agents, in short, of the uncanny magic that Gary Tomlinson has argued was originally at work in *Rigoletto* – the bell contributes its archaic power to the mystery and terror of the scene.[47]

A bell has a similar agency in the last scene of Verdi's *Falstaff*, where the twelve strokes of midnight mark the transition to the dangerous fairy

---

[43] ALAIN CORBIN, *Village Bells: Sound and Meaning in the Nineteenth-Century French Countryside*, trans. by Martin Thom, New York, Columbia University Press, 1998, pp. 293-298.

[44] CORBIN, *Village Bells*, p. 296.

[45] CORBIN, *Village Bells*, p. 307.

[46] For another, quite similar example, see «Ma dall'arida stella divulsa», Amelia's aria in Act II of Verdi's *Un ballo in maschera* (1859).

[47] See GARY TOMLINSON, *Metaphysical Song: An Essay on Opera*, Princeton, Princeton University Press, 1999, pp. 101-102.

world of Windsor Park. In contrast to *Rigoletto*, though, the *Falstaff* bell is accompanied by a series of strangely shifting string chords. Although the sheer beauty of this latter scene, along with its palpable delight in harmonic ingenuity, reflect all that Verdi had learned in the forty years between these two passages, one also suspects that the elaborate chromatic harmonies were there for a reason: greater resources were needed in 1893 to give bells the same numinous force they had in 1851.

Certainly the early reception of *Tosca* contains ample evidence that bells had lost much of their former charm. The critics cited earlier regard the sound of bells as just one unpleasant sound among many – equivalent to drum rolls, or (for Mahler) brutal cries – an equation that would have been impossible in the earlier auditory discourse. And, hearing nothing but distracting noise in the opera's bells, critics were also echoing a widespread unease with bells in metropolitan centers. As the modern city developed, its independent rhythms were increasingly found to be incompatible with the enchanted notion of communal time that church bells had long solidified. Urban reformers complained about «torture by bells» and argued that modern workers needed uninterrupted sleep.[48] In contrast to the sense of local attachment captured in the name *er campanone*, one might quote the «Fanfulla della domenica»: «But if, at the beginning of the century, Rome had really been so atrociously infested with the sounds of bells, it would have been quickly depopulated. Who, except for a few deaf people, would have been able to live there?».[49]

Attempting to seal the case for the disenchanting of the sonic landscape, Corbin describes at length a passage from naturalist fiction:

Zola, the author of *Le Rêve*, gave a precise description of the range of sensations and sentiments aroused by the din of bell ringing: the anticipation of the divine sacrifice, the manner in which the vibrations of the tenor bell from Bourges cathedral permeated the Hubert's house, the collective rejoicing, and Augustine's enraptured state followed by her flight in response to the heavenly call of the angel, which is also that of the wedding bell. Yet the analysis has a distant feel to it as if it were a clinical record. The emotional power of the bell, laid bare and desacralized, is simply the agency that produces the dream; it is intrinsically linked to hallucination.[50]

A similar case could be made for the depiction of the dawn in the third act of *Tosca*. Despite, or rather because of, the massive empirical effort expended on realistic scene painting, the final result is curiously unmoving, dead.

---

[48] Corbin discusses the rise of urban intolerance for bells in *Village Bells*, pp. 298-308.

[49] «Ma se al principio del secolo, Roma fosse stata davvero così atrocemente infestata dal suono delle campane, si sarebbe in breve spopolata. Chi, se non qualche sordo, avrebbe potuto resistervi?». BARINI, *Tosca*.

[50] CORBIN, *Village Bells*, p. 305.

V

And yet, there is a vast distance between a literary depiction of bells and an actual reproduction of them within the space of a musical work. When another critic for the «Gazzetta teatrale italiana» argued that *Tosca* «represents the hegemony of materialism over music», he gave some sense of what this distance entails: the incursion of a foreign sound world, and an alien set of aesthetic criteria, into the conventional languages of Italian opera.[51] Drawing an opposition between Puccini's empiricist obsessions and a more traditional notion of Italian lyricism («this Latin substance in which music is music»), the journal also anticipated an argument about realist opera that would be made in 1948 by W. H. Auden.[52] In an essay entitled *Cav & Pag*, Auden noted that «the difficulty for the naturalistic writer is that he cannot hold consistently to his principles without ceasing to be an artist and becoming a statistician, for an artist is by definition interested in uniqueness».[53] This difficulty, he continued, was even more attenuated when naturalist fiction was remade into opera:

The role of impersonal necessity, the necessities of nature or the necessities of the social order in its totality upon the human person can be presented in fiction, in epic poetry and, better still, in the movies, because these media can verbally describe or visually picture that nature and that order; but in drama, where they are forced to remain offstage [...] this is very difficult. And in opera it is impossible, firstly, because music is in its essence dynamic, an expression of will and self-affirmation and, secondly, because opera, like ballet, is a virtuoso art; whatever his role, an actor who sings is an uncommon man, more a master of his fate, even as a self-destroyer, than an actor who speaks. Passivity or collapse of will cannot be expressed in song.[54]

Auden's definition of music as «an expression of will and self-affirmation» seems to me a good description of the values that Puccini's liberal-democratic audiences would have ascribed to singing, values to which Cavaradossi and Tosca themselves give voice. What is most striking about *Tosca* in this context, though, is that – despite its apparent political program – its music often seems to perform the «collapse of will» that Auden found impossible.

---

[51] «*Tosca*, astrazion fatta dai pochi fronzoli melodici che Puccini vi ha sparsi qua e là come per una estrema nostalgia di musicista, rappresenta l'egemonia del materialismo sulla musica». Roberto Bracco, *Del teatro lirico italiano: sintomi di decadenza*, «Gazzetta teatrale italiana», 19 January 1901, pp. 54-59.

[52] «Ebbene, proprio questa essenza, proprio questa sostanza latina per la quale la musica è la musica, proprio quest'anima d'ogni organismo musicale è ciò che i nostri giovani operisti tendono a rinnegare». Bracco, *Del teatro lirico italiano*, p. 59.

[53] W.H. Auden, *Cav & Pag*, in *The Dyer's Hand and Other Essays*, New York, Vintage Books, 1968, pp. 475-482: 477.

[54] Auden, *Cav & Pag*, pp. 477-478.

The opera's bells are threatening not only because of their ubiquity, not only because of their deadness, but also because of their 'hegemonic' power over the musical action, which at times makes the characters into singing puppets.

The first time that a bell sounds in *Tosca* is near the beginning of Act One (see I, 13[+186-201]).[55] The Sacristan has been strutting around the stage, accompanied by his comic 6/8 theme, when an offstage bell announces the Angelus, suddenly shifting the musical discourse into a more dignified cut time (marked «Andante religioso» in the score). The bell sounds a single note (an F below middle C) and the Sacristan repeats this note at pitch, using it as the reciting tone for his subsequent prayer, during which the bell functions as a constant pedal point. The sacred mood persists until Cavaradossi appears on stage, restoring a freer style of vocal declamation, and the opera's typically restless chromatic motion. The Angelus episode is short, but it introduces a number of devices – a bell slowing time, halting harmonic movement, dictating the melodic vocabulary of the characters – which will be developed more extensively later in the opera.

Bells make their second appearance during Tosca's and Scarpia's first meeting (see Ex. 2.1). Once again, a metrically and harmonically shifting musical

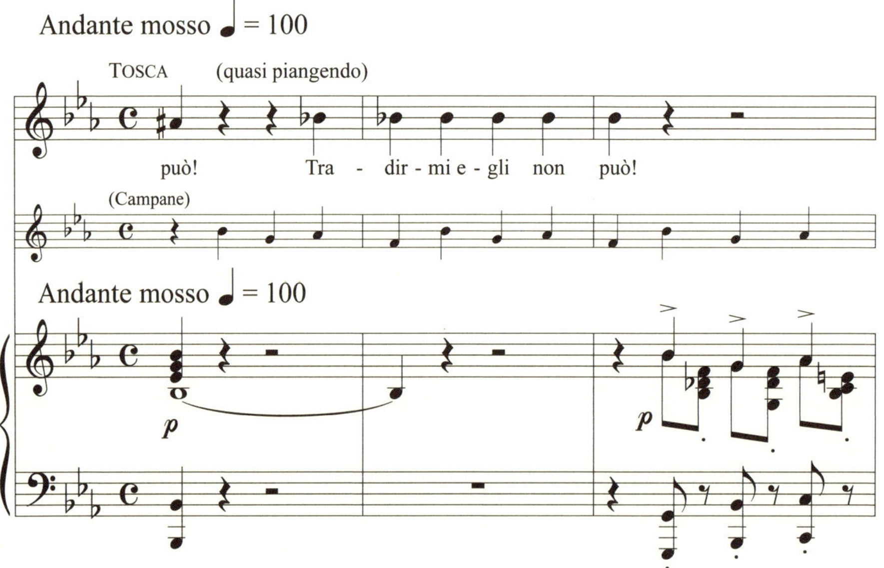

Ex. 2.1. PUCCINI, *Tosca*, I[+1085-1096].

(continues)

---

[55] All citations of both the score and the libretto refer to the edition of the piano-vocal score, ed. by ROGER PARKER (Milan, Ricordi, 1995).

Ex. 2.1. *(conclusion)*

texture is immediately replaced by a stable one; the bells first pull the music into E-flat (reinterpreting Tosca's A-sharp as a B-flat), and then keep it there, their measured four-note ostinato underlining the action with a steady quarter-note pulse. Even the adversaries are overtaken by an eerie sort of stasis. At the beginning of the scene Tosca twice exclaims «Tradirmi egli non può!» (He cannot betray me!), and it is immediately before her second iteration that the evening bells begin to chime. Puccini's first setting of Tosca's line is naturalistic, carefully following the rhythms and inflections of the verse. The second time, however, Tosca's voice is subtly forced into conformity with the rhythm of the bells: syllables are squeezed together, and natural speech patterns stretched out, producing a line that is both stranger and less dynamic. When Scarpia enters the ensemble his melody is even more exaggeratedly pinned to the bells: first stuck on their opening pitch of B-flat, and then following the texture in mock first species counterpoint. Imitating both the rhythm of the bells and their distinctive off-beat phrase structure, Scarpia's line is awkward, breathless, and weirdly incantatory. Opportunities for (knowing) pauses after phrases like «Tosca divina» and «piccola manina» are studiously avoided.

It is credible, perhaps, that the Sacristan would unconsciously respond to the sound of a single bell resonating in the church; Tosca's and Scarpia's possession is more difficult to explain. In terms of dramatic logic, the first act finale is even more demonically mysterious. The finale begins with bells sounding the pitches F and B-flat – majestically, in whole notes – and the two-bar pattern will serve as a massive ostinato in the scene, underlying a full 175 bars of music. The scene begins with a rushed dialogue in which Scarpia and Spoletta intone only the pitch F, and Scarpia's ensuing monologue is elaborately tied to the bells' pitches: his thrice repeated command «Va! Tosca!» is set each time to the falling fourth B-flat/F, and the majority of his longer phrases either begin or end on those notes. Meanwhile, the orchestra also takes its cues from the bells. The conversation between Scarpia and Spoletta is underpinned with a series of two-bar phrases that rise and fall as the bells do, and the rest of the music in the scene – the orchestral part, the diegetic organ, the onstage chorus – will also be constructed out of oscillating two-bar fragments.[56] What Puccini has written, in other words, is a crude passacaglia, with the bells serving as an unusually primal bass. Most commentary on the finale has focused on the contrast between Scarpia's indecent sentiments and the piety of the chorus's *Te Deum*, but it is also possible to hear a darker message: good and evil marching together, united behind an irrational, archaic force.[57]

VI

The first act of *Tosca* unfolds like a series of increasingly complex variations of the theme of the power and strange agency of bells. Yet none of these

---

[56] For a discussion of the motivic structure of this scene, see DÖHRING, *Musikalischer Realismus*, p. 271.

[57] For an extensive survey of different ways of reading the psychology of this scene, see SUSAN VANDIVER NICASSIO, *Tosca's Rome: The Play and the Opera in Historical Perspective*, Chicago, University of Chicago Press, 1999, pp. 155-168. Girardi is perhaps unique in his claim that the fusion of different sentiments is part of Puccini's point. See *Puccini*, p. 183.

scenes quite prepares the listener for the ambition with which Puccini evokes the great bell of Saint Peter's in the third act. The bell's pitch, we recall, was a low E, and its sound dominates the opening of the act, well before the tolling of the *campanone* itself. The first 127 measures of the act are written entirely in E, rarely straying far from its harmonic orbit, and at three points the texture is underscored with simple ostinatos on E and B. When, at the end of the depiction of the dawn, and after a hushed dominant preparation, the *campanone* finally sounds, with its tone supported by the double basses, the harp, and the contrabassoon, we cannot but feel its grim inevitability.[58]

We might also hear the bell's E as having been prepared in a much more elaborate sense. *Tosca* opens, famously, with three triads constructed from the bass notes B-flat, A-flat, and E. Puccini does not notate these chords in any key, and it is hard to imagine any diatonic context in which they would make sense. The three chords will be repeated throughout the opera – always in the same order, and rarely transposed – and they are clearly linked to Scarpia: critics have referred to them as the Scarpia theme, or as a leitmotiv associated with a related but more general concept like 'tyranny'.[59] Without disagreeing with this interpretation, I would also suggest that the chords function on a level less bound to semantic meaning, as an anticipation of Saint Peter's bell. In its first iteration, 'Scarpia's' E chord sounds at the same low pitch level as the *campanone*, and it is harmonized with an open fifth, an interval that Puccini associates with bells throughout the opera. More strikingly, the three chords appear at two points in the third act that have little connection with Scarpia (who is dead by this point in the drama) but are explicitly linked to the sound of bells. The orchestral introduction to Act III concludes with a repeated oscillation of the B-flat and A-flat chords; the E chord only sounds, after a bar and a half of silence, at the beginning of the shepherd's song, where it both initiates an ostinato on the pitches E and B and marks the first sounding of the sheep bells (see III, 2[+40-44]). The three chords sound again at the conclusion of the shepherd's first strophe, where they signal a slowing of the ostinato rhythm (from quarter note triplets to half notes), accompanied by a stage direction that «*le oscillazioni delle campanelle dell'armento si estinguono in lontananza*» (*the tinkling of the sheep-bells dies away in the distance*) (see III, 3[+58-63]). Just as Scarpia's presence fades from the drama, so too does 'his' theme as it

---

[58] For an analytic discussion of *Tosca* that emphasizes the importance of E for the opera, see DEBORAH BURTON, *Structural Symmetries and Reversals in «Tosca»*, in *Recondite Harmony: Essays on Puccini's Operas*, Hillsdale, NY, Pendragon Press, 2012, pp. 169-183. See also GIRARDI, *Puccini*, p. 167.

[59] For one discussion of the use of the chords and their dramatic meaning, see GIRARDI, *Puccini*, pp. 160-163.

is transformed from triple *forte* to *pianissimo*, gradually integrated into an harmonic context, and, most importantly, made polyvalent, loosened further from its initial connotations.

While Scarpia's theme vanishes into Saint Peter's bell, a strange alchemy also allows the bell to give birth to one of the opera's other central motives. The *campanone*'s entrance is accompanied by the first statement of the opera's most famous melody: structured around the pitches E and B, making prominent use of 'chiming' fourths and fifths, and always supported by a pedal tone, it seems to arise from the partials of the bell itself (see Ex. 2.2).

Ex. 2.2. PUCCINI, *Tosca*, III[+125-133].

This melody, of course, is usually associated with its later appearance in Cavaradossi's aria «E lucevan le stelle», where it appears three times, first as a setting for the words «Oh! dolci baci, o languide carezze» (Oh! sweet kisses, oh languid caresses). Because of this coincidence of words and music, it is tempting to describe the melody as something like Cavaradossi's love theme, but other evidence mitigates against this. The melody is elaborated extensively by the orchestra before entering the tenor's orbit, and its simple outlining of an E-minor scale is not obviously languid. Much like Scarpia's chords, the melody is linked with the character of Cavaradossi without ever becoming his exclusive property.

This point is worth stressing because the final appearance of the theme is routinely attacked by critics, the evidence used to seal the case for Puccini's crass opportunism.[60] As Tosca jumps from the Castel Sant'Angelo – «*si getta nel vuoto*» (throws herself into the void), as the libretto puts it – the full orchestra plays the melody one last time, now at full volume. If we associate the theme with Cavaradossi, this reprise makes little sense: there is no reason to be reminded of his erotic reverie during Tosca's suicide. If, however, we associate the melody with Saint Peter's bell, and, by extension, the entire sonic landscape of Rome, then Puccini's use of the tune seems rather more appropriate. Disappearing into the scenery – into the void, you might say, left by the lack of music – Tosca fulfills the tendency of all characters in the opera to be overtaken by primal sound, and the bell theme rises up in the final moments to place its grim seal on the process.

VII

The best description of *Tosca* that I have come across appears – somewhat improbably, and certainly unintentionally – in Adorno's book *In Search of Wagner*. Attempting to describe Wagner's 'regressive' style, Adorno writes:

the really productive element in Wagner is seen at the moments when the subject abdicates sovereignty and passively abandons itself to the archaic, the instinctual – the element which, precisely because it has been emancipated, renounces its now unattainable claim to give meaningful shape to the passage of time. This element, with its two dimensions of harmony and colour, is sonority. Through sonority time seems transfixed in space, and while as harmony it «fills» space, the notion

---

⁶⁰ Especially forceful statements of this position include Joseph Kerman, *Opera as Drama*, Berkeley, University of California Press, 1988², p. 19; Mosco Carner, *Puccini: A Critical Biography*, New York, Knopf, 1959, pp. 377-378; and Charles Osborne, *The Complete Operas of Puccini: A Critical Guide*, London, Gollancz, 1981, p. 143. Typically more fair-minded is Julian Budden, *Puccini: His Life and Works*, Oxford, Oxford University Press, 2002, pp. 221-222.

of colour, for which musical theory has no better name, is directly borrowed from the realm of visual space. At the same it is mere sonority which actually represents that unarticulated natural state into which Wagner dissolves.[61]

What Adorno seems to have in mind here is Wagner's use of piquant but non-functional harmonic complexes, but his description of «mere sonority» could be applied, with remarkably little violence, to Puccini's bells. This is most obviously true in Adorno's evocation of an archaic sound which interrupts the normal flow of time, drawing music into an undifferentiated stasis, and his other observations – that, suspended in motion, sound becomes a sort of space; that the freeing of sonority is linked to a renunciation of subjective autonomy – seem equally apt.

What interests me most about Adorno's argument, though, is his attempt to connect Wagner's attraction to pure sonority with later developments in twentieth-century music. At one point he notes that Wagner's style «immortalizes the moment between the death of Romanticism and the birth of realism», and at another he attempts to link Wagner's primal sounds to the more brutal ones that would erupt in Stravinsky's *Le Sacre du printemps*.[62] Putting these two observations together, we might describe *Tosca* as a realist stopping point between Wagner's Romantic archaism and the primitivism of Stravinsky: as empirical objects, Puccini's bells look back to the faded magic of Wagner's mythic worlds, while also pointing the way to the dark biologism that would soon fascinate European culture. More specifically, Puccini's interest in pure sonority might be pointed to as an essential link between Boito's nostalgic celebration of linguistic sound (in *Falstaff*) and the more aggressive sonic experiments of the Italian Futurists. In 1901 the young Filippo Tommaso Marinetti could complain, in a review of *Tosca*, that «Gingerbread fairs (drums, accordions, organs of breathless barbarism) would never surpass the discordant hubbub and the deafening chanting that the heroes of Sardou-Illica-Giacosa shriek over an orchestration of negroes!».[63] Only a few years later, just this primal and discordant hubbub would become the centerpiece of his own aesthetic.

---

[61] Theodor W. Adorno, *In Search of Wagner*, trans. by Rodney Livingstone, London, Verso, 2005[2], p. 52.

[62] See Adorno, *In Search of Wagner*, pp. 80 and 51. «Despite a profound affinity in their concern with the prehistoric, or perhaps even because of it, Stravinsky regards himself as the complete antipode of Wagner. Stravinsky is inexhaustible in finding new forms for regression; in his aesthetic ideology, as in the ideology of Fascism, the concept of progress is repudiated. Wagner, however, living a century earlier and rooted in a liberalism whose own atavism he anticipated, would like to present the regressive element as progress, the static as the dynamic».

[63] «Jamais les foires aux pains d'épices (tambours, accordéons, orgues de barbarie essoufflés) ne surpasseront le discordant brouhaha et les mélopées abrutissantes que les héros de

Friedrich Kittler has argued that a move away from Romanticism, with its fantasies of an intimate connection between writing and orality, and toward the modernist discovery of sound *an sich*, was motivated by the invention of the gramophone – a technology, he writes, that «does not hear as do ears that have been trained immediately to filter voices, words, and sounds out of noise».[64] No one would accuse Kittler of being overly interested in geographic specificity, but it is striking how many of his best examples of artists articulating the shift from meaning to noise come from Italy. He points to Futurism – to Luigi Russolo's *intonarumori* and to the acts of semantic decomposition that Marinetti referred to as «*parole in libertà*» – but also to Ottorino Respighi's orchestral suite *I pini di Roma* (1924): the first work in music history to include a phonographic record in its score. Another one of Kittler's central texts – Rainer Maria Rilke's 1919 essay *Primal Sound* – was written in the Piedmontese city of Soglio, during the feast of the Assumption. Sitting at his desk, thinking about the uncanny nature of phonographic transcription, Rilke would have been haunted by the sound of Italian church bells in the distance.

As the poet may have recognized, the connection between bells and phonographs is actually quite complex. Like phonographs preserving long dead voices, bells too contain sounds from a distant past, producing (or so we like to think) exactly the same noise as they did hundreds of years before. Like phonographs, but unlike traditional instruments, bells short-circuit the relationship between performer and score: since they both inscribe and play back sound, striking a bell is more like dropping a needle on a record than the infinitely variable act of dragging a bow across the strings of a violin. Finally, bells and phonographs are both agents of musical repetition: reproducing the same sounds endlessly, and without change. These observations return us to my earlier discussion of Verga and the 'technologies' of realist literature. They suggest that, for *verismo* composers, bells may not have been only a readily available example of environmental sound, they may also have been a way of thinking through the mechanism of sound recording itself.

I want to stop short of claiming that *Tosca* self-consciously thematizes the fate of opera in an age of mechanical reproduction. I am also wary of subjecting Puccini's work to the political readings that have dominated recent discussions of Marinetti and Respighi – to say nothing of Wagner and Stravinsky. Nonetheless, I would note that a horror of mechanism, and

---

Sardou-Illica-Giacosa glapissent sur une orchestration de négres!». Filippo Tommaso Marinetti, *Teatro Dal Verme*, «La Revue d'art dramatique», November 1901, p. 118. This review is also discussed in WILSON, *The Puccini Problem*, p. 171.

[64] FRIEDRICH A. KITTLER, *Gramophone, Film, Typewriter*, trans. by Geoffrey Winthrop-Young and Michael Wutz, Stanford, Stanford University Press, 1999, p. 23.

a related defense of subjective autonomy, does seem to be at the root of one of the most notorious attacks ever launched against Puccini's opera. Joseph Kerman may not have had the look of a phonograph record in mind when he described *Tosca* as an «excellently oiled wheel». But his strange and oft-cited claim that, «*Tosca* leaps, and the orchestra screams the first thing that comes into its head», does seem close to imagining a work in which human singing succumbs to another force – impersonal, noisy, mysterious, irrational.[65] In the preface to his revised edition of *Opera as Drama*, Kerman asked, more pointedly, «What, then, does Puccini's score accomplish that would not be accomplished by literal folksongs and Sunday-morning tape recordings?».[66] I am not sure if Puccini had an answer in 1900, but, as I will argue in the ensuing chapters, questions about the relationship between technology and traditional singing – as well as the larger aesthetic and political issues they entail – would continue to haunt the composition of his later operas.

---

[65] KERMAN, *Opera and Drama*, p. 15.

[66] KERMAN, *Opera and Drama*, p. XIII.

VERISMO ECHOES

What happened to *verismo*? It is easy enough to narrate the origins of the movement: the Sonzogno competition of 1888, the triumphant premiere of *Cavalleria rusticana* that resulted two years later, the rash of imitations that exploded in its wake. It is much harder, though, to pinpoint the moment when the excitement faded. In part, this is because Italian composers produced no «next big thing», no coherent, internationally successful movement to unseat the premises of realist opera. Another reason is that many stars of the *giovane scuola* remained haunted by their first successes, watching their works become canonical – indeed, watching themselves become monuments – as they experimented with new themes and styles and then returned, inevitably and with what often sounds like increasing desperation, to the ideas that made them famous.[1] *Verismo*, like so many relics of the Italian liberal state, persisted, however unnaturally, throughout the fascist period.

Nonetheless, a certain modulation in the reception of *verismo* can be observed in two notorious attacks on Puccini that were published in Italy in the years immediately before World War One.[2] In 1911, the rising composer Ildebrando Pizzetti (1880-1968) published a vicious essay on Puccini that he later expanded into a chapter of his 1914 book *Musicisti contemporanei*.[3] And in 1912, Fausto Torrefranca (1880-1955) unleashed his *Giacomo Puccini e l'opera internazionale*, an extraordinary 130-page assault.[4] These

---

[1] For a nuanced recent history of the fortunes of Italian music during this period, see ALAN MALLACH, *The Autumn of Italian Opera: From Verismo to Modernism, 1890-1915*, Lebanon, NH, Northeastern University Press, 2007.

[2] For two, rather different, attempts to contextualize these attacks, see ALEXANDRA WILSON, *The Puccini Problem: Opera, Nationalism, and Modernity*, Cambridge, Cambridge University Press, 2007, *passim*; and BEN EARLE, *Luigi Dallapiccola and Musical Modernism in Fascist Italy*, Cambridge, Cambridge University Press, 2013, pp. 41-42.

[3] See ILDEBRANDO PIZZETTI, *Musicisti contemporanei: saggi critici*, Milan, Treves, 1914. The essay was originally published as *Giacomo Puccini*, «La voce», III, 1911.

[4] See FAUSTO TORREFRANCA, *Giacomo Puccini e l'opera internazionale*, Turin, Bocca, 1912.

writers found much to hate: Puccini was too bourgeois, too feminine, too cosmopolitan, his range too limited. In the context of the present study, though, Pizzetti and Torrefranca's critiques are equally striking for what they overlook. Unlike so many critics in the 1890s and early 1900s, Pizzetti and Torrefranca were not upset by Puccini's interest in unmediated sound. True, Pizzetti complained about the presence of «rumori amusicali» (amusical noises) in *Tosca*, and argued that the opera tended to privilege empty scenic effects over psychological development.[5] But he also admired the third act depiction of the dawn, whose arsenal of bells had caused so much outrage only ten years before. It was «a page of extremely delicate and suggestive music».[6] Comparing this passage to the opening of the third act of *La bohème* and the 'lamplighter' scene in the third act of *Manon Lescaut*, Pizzetti suggested that Puccini's soundscape scenes «want to be admired as little things, perfect in their genre».[7] This is guarded praise, but it is also evidence that an earlier source of concern had begun to seem benign. Given how many aspects of Puccini's style disgusted Torrefranca, the critic's lack of interest in the composer's use of «amusical noises» is even more telling.

A shifting attitude toward realistic sound can also be detected within Puccini's scores. To begin thinking in more detail about the afterlife of the *verismo* movement, it may be instructive to consider *Il tabarro* – the first 'panel' in Puccini's triptych of one-act operas, premiered at the Metropolitan Opera in 1918 – a work that is often described as an *envoi* or homage to the *giovane scuola*. The connection is usually viewed in terms of dramaturgy: the grim, working-class milieu in which the plot unfolds, the gruesome and sadistic denouement. More striking, though, are the ways in which Puccini reconfigures a variety of realist musical techniques that he and his contemporaries had developed some thirty years before. All of the techniques described in the previous chapter – offstage singing, diegetic performance, non-orchestral sources of sound – are present in *Il tabarro*. This may also be the place to introduce a fourth device, not yet discussed, which might be termed spatialization – the reduction of all musical parameters to a cold and eerie stasis. It is a kind of negative *ekphrasis* in which music, instead of enlivening the painted backdrop, aspires to its stillness. The unrelenting ostinato that, as we have seen, structures the first act finale of *Tosca* is a good example of the device. So too is the 112-bar long pedal point that supports what Eduard Hanslick described, despairingly, as «columns of

---

[5] Pizzetti, *Musicisti*, pp. 91 and 92-93.

[6] «È una pagina di musica delicatissima e suggestiva». Pizzetti, *Musicisti*, p. 94.

[7] «E vogliono essere ammirate come piccole cose, nel loro genere, perfette». See Pizzetti, *Musicisti*, p. 94.

ascending and descending parallel fifths», «ghastly fifth-rods» that beat the characters into submission, during the start of the third act of *La bohème*.[8]

The first eight bars of *Il tabarro* employ similar techniques: obsessively ticking eighth-notes, parallel fourths and fifths, and a melody, full of internal repetitions, that floats in some modal netherworld, suggesting but never quite settling on a tonal center. Encouraged by the compound meter and barcarolle-like affect, commentators have described this passage as painting the ebb and flow of the Seine; but in so doing they miss something of the music's stasis. Puccini repeats this eight-bar unit twice more during the opening moments of the opera, at rehearsal numbers 1 and 2. And, while he allows himself a little climax halfway through the process, this glimmer of conventional development and forward motion does little more than enforce the underlying sameness of the passage as a whole.

The most striking aspect of this acoustic backcloth is what Puccini layers on top of it: two long tugboat whistles – carefully located at different distances from the audience – and a staccato car horn. Realistic sound was, of course, a major feature of Puccini's ambient style in the 1890s: *Tosca*'s ostinati support a riot of church bells, organs, and 'authentic' plainsong, and the voices of distant workers echo through the hollows of *La bohème*'s *Barrière d'Enfer*. As we have seen, this combination of repetitive and inexpressive orchestral music with 'objective' diegetic noise was designed to support a fiction of authorial abdication, inviting us to believe that we are hearing nothing more – and nothing less – than the unmediated resonance of the fictional world. This dream of facticity seems inseparable from the documentary claims of early sound recording; it also brings to mind Jonathan Sterne's description of the strange temporality of an Edison cylinder, «a little piece of repeatable time within a carefully bounded frame».[9]

Reviewing *Tosca*'s American premiere, «Life» magazine complained (as already mentioned in the Introduction) about the opera's «ultra modern style, with bells and cannons thrown in left and right».[10] But those bells, however new, were still pitched and carefully integrated into the harmonic and melodic fabric: not thrown in at all. In contrast, the industrial sounds of *Il tabarro* stand out, almost bathetically, from their more delicate surroundings. They resemble less the visceral noise-music prophesied by the Italian futurists and more the poignantly inarticulate typewriters in Satie's

---

8 Hanslick's 1897 review is excerpted, and here cited, in ARTHUR GROOS and ROGER PARKER, *Giacomo Puccini: «La bohème»*, Cambridge, Cambridge University Press, 1986, pp. 133-135: 135.

9 JONATHAN STERNE, *The Audible Past: Cultural Origins of Sound Reproduction*, Durham, Duke University Press, 2003, p. 310.

10 MONSECRET, *La Tosca*, «Life», XXXVII, 1901, p. 173.

Parade, premiered one year before. If Puccini was indeed looking back to his earlier style, it was with a note of skepticism, an almost melancholy acknowledgement that the aims of empiricist realism and operatic composition would never quite add up.

Il tabarro's opening music returns some twenty minutes later. The music is nearly identical, save for a change of key and one other difference: two wordless, offstage voices accompany the tune (see 56^{+1-11}). It should be stressed that these are only voices: although numerous characters enter and exit the stage while singing, the 'sopranino' and 'tenorino' are not amongst them. One could invent a variety of explanations for this effect – Rhine maidens, the ineffable magic of Paris, a fantasy projection of the protagonists' prohibited affair – but all would unsettle the realist pretensions of the opera as a whole. Up to this point, the offstage world has functioned as an extension of the visible one – the car horn is there, after all, to insist on a reality beyond the confines of the stage. Now, in contrast, the space beyond the flats appears mysterious and inscrutable. You can have tugboat sirens or you can have Homeric sirens; but in a work of realist theater you should not have both.

Wordless offstage singing is a feature of all of Puccini's later operas. The humming chorus in *Madama Butterfly* is the first and most famous example of the device; the penumbra of sound added by 15 tenors to the final measures of the first act of *La fanciulla del West* is perhaps the strangest.[11] These mysterious sounds suggest the existence of a second, only dimly perceptible acoustic reality, one inconceivable in Puccini's earlier style. His new fascination with musical effects of echoing and distance is refracted on multiple thematic planes. Most obvious is a move away from the familiar urban locales of *Manon Lescaut*, *La bohème* and *Tosca*, and toward remote, exotic landscapes: Meiji Japan, Gold Rush California, ancient China. This large-scale interest in temporal and geographic distance is restaged, within Puccini's operas, in numerous songs of nostalgic longing: for the elusive 'lontano' of *La fanciulla del West* and the Florence of *Gianni Schicchi*; for suburban Belleville in *Il tabarro* and rural Hunan in *Turandot*. Equally relevant here is a sense in which many of Puccini's later works are themselves echoes of distant masterpieces: *La rondine* updates and rewrites the plot of *La traviata* (to say nothing of his own, already-citational, *Manon Lescaut*); *Gianni Schicchi* is modeled on Verdi's *Falstaff*; and, as Emanuele Senici has shown, *La Fanciulla* is a disillusioned look back at the pastoral mountain

---

[11] Also worth mentioning are the final measures of *La rondine*, where Magda moves offstage to intone a mysterious high A, and the onstage humming chorus (to be discussed in more detail in Chapter Five) that accompanies the offstage children's choir during the first appearance of the «Mo-li-hua» theme in *Turandot*, Act I.

operas of Donizetti and Bellini.[12] It may also be worth mentioning a new element of wearily ironic parody within Puccini's music itself – seen in the knowing quotations of «Mi chiamano Mimì» in *Il tabarro* and of *Salome* in *La rondine*. Finally, we might observe that Puccini considered incorporating quite original scenic effects of distance into his *mise-en-scène*. Discussing the staging of *Il tabarro* with Tito Ricordi, the composer suggested, «And even in a theater with a large proscenium, it wouldn't strike me as a great misfortune if the action remained in the distance. It's only for one act. And it could be an original idea. Think about it».[13] If Puccini's operas from the 1890s aspire to a phonographic objectivity, his later works approach reality more circumspectly, as if through a cloak.

This admittedly breathless survey of Puccini's *seconda prattica* has avoided mention of one work – *Suor Angelica*, the second panel of *Il trittico*. In many ways it fits awkwardly into the story told above. The opera is not especially exotic, overtly nostalgic, or based on any clear operatic precedent.[14] Indeed, its world of oppressively cloistered ritual seems designed to efface all specificities of geography and history. However, of all Puccini's operas *Suor Angelica* is the most indebted to both his realist experiments of the 1890s and to the poetics of distance explored in his later works. It might in this sense be described as an attempt to thematize and so work through a crisis in Puccini's style, a crisis that speaks to a ripple of sorts within modernity, one that musicological accounts of modernism have largely overlooked.

I

Puccini approached *Suor Angelica* with the same positivist zeal that had been his trademark since the time of *Tosca*. He wrote to the priest and scholar Don Pietro Panichelli asking for appropriate litanies, and petitioned his sister, the mother superior at an Augustinian convent outside Lucca, for access to its secret rites.[15] While no one would describe the resulting work as documentary, its opening scene does contain the most explicit catalogue

---

[12] See EMANUELE SENICI, *Landscape and Gender in Italian Opera: The Alpine Virgin from Bellini to Puccini*, Cambridge University Press, 2005.

[13] «E anche con teatro a gran proscenio, non mi pare gran male che l'azione rimanga a distanza. È solo per un atto. E può essere un'idea originale. Pensaci». GIACOMO PUCCINI to Tito Ricordi (23 July 1918); in *Carteggi Pucciniani*, ed. by Eugenio Gara, Milan, Ricordi, 1986, pp. 463-464 (no. 724).

[14] It has been suggested, however, that the Grand Inquisitor scene in Verdi's *Don Carlos* may have served as a model for the central duet between Angelica and the Zia Principessa. See HELEN M. GREENWALD, *Verdi's Patriarch and Puccini's Matriarch: «Through the Looking Glass and What Puccini Found There»*, «19th-Century Music», XVII, 1994, pp. 220-236.

[15] See PIETRO PANICHELLI, *Il pretino di Giacomo Puccini*, Pisa, Pisa University Press, 1962[4], pp. 168-173.

of *verismo* musical devices the composer ever wrote. Before the curtain even rises, the audience is greeted by the sound of offstage bells, playing a simple four-bar melody. Then, as the stage is revealed, this tune transforms into an unceasing ostinato figure, played by the strings and celesta, a static effect intensified, as in *Il tabarro*, by improper voice-leading, quasi-modal harmony, and internal melodic repetitions. One by one, a parade of offstage, diegetic noises enter the texture: the sisters in their chapel, a bird in the trees, a church organ, and finally Angelica herself. For the first three minutes of the opera, the audience does not see a single person singing. The normal priorities of operatic spectacle are submerged behind the *mise-en-scène*.

But then, as in *Il tabarro*, the opera's closing scene presents an effect of magical distance that utterly contradicts these realist expectations:

Suor Angelica vede il miracolo compiersi: la chiesetta sfolgora di mistica luce, la porta si apre: apparisce la Regina del conforto, solenne, dolcissima e, avanti a Lei, un bimbo biondo, tutto bianco ... la Vergine sospinge, con dolce gesto, il bimbo verso la moribonda.[16]

[*Suor Angelica sees the miracle achieved: the chapel blazes with mystic light, the door is opened: the Queen of Solace appears, solemn, very sweet, and, in front of her, a blond little boy, all in white ... the Virgin pushes, with a gentle gesture, the child toward the dying woman.*]

The music that accompanies this apparition emanates from behind the flats, just like the opening music, and uses many of the same forces: choir, organ, bells. After having been taught that these offstage sounds signified a concrete place within the fictional world, we are now asked to believe that they are echoing from another place entirely.

It is very difficult to bring this last scene off. Gary Tomlinson has claimed that Puccini's operas «bring us face to face with a force we can believe only through a willfully nostalgic engagement», and, at least in the case of *Suor Angelica*, most critics have agreed with him that «a part of us knows better [...] than to trust a pushy salesman».[17] «The apparition is an illuminated Christmas card», cried James Huenecker after the premiere, sounding quite a bit like Tomlinson in his anxious conflation of Puccini's miracle with the commodified circuitry of mass culture.[18] A critic at the work's first Italian

---

[16] Unless otherwise noted, all quotations from the libretto are taken from the edition of the first published libretto of *Il trittico* that has been edited by Eduardo Rescigno (Milan, Ricordi, 1997).

[17] GARY TOMLINSON, *Metaphysical Song: An Essay on Opera*, Princeton, Princeton University Press, 1999, p. 149.

[18] JAMES GIBBONS HUENEKER, *A World Premier [sic] of Puccini Operas*, «New York Times», 15 December 1918.

performances made a similar point when he suggested that *Suor Angelica* was «more cinematographic than mystical».[19]

More recently, it has become common to defend the apparition, but only by redefining it as a hallucination, the product of Angelica's fevered mind. There are problems with this psychological approach, though, including the fact that the event is unambiguously labeled «IL MIRACOLO» in the libretto. In the most nuanced discussion of the issue, James Hepokoski proposes that the events of *Suor Angelica* can only be made sense of within the context of *Il trittico* as a whole. *Il tabarro*, he notes, «had presented the gritty, urban material world already fallen away from spiritual illusions and securities. There had been no *deus ex machina* in that brittle arena of things now abandoned by the once-held comforts of religion».[20] With this contemporary framework in mind, listeners can choose either to interpret Angelica's vision as madness, or – through that act of willfully nostalgic engagement – participate in her self-deception. To make his argument, Hepokoski, like Tomlinson, relies on a characterization of Puccini's era as one in which «the once-held comforts of religion» were located firmly in the past. But is it fair to assume that listeners in 1918 would have understood their world as one bereft of magic?

At least from an anthropological perspective, the Virgin Mary was in fact appearing with increasing frequency throughout the nineteenth century. While the eighteenth century has been described as the one true lull in the history of Marian apparitions, something began to change after the Revolution. First there was the miracle at Rue du Bac in 1830, and it was followed by apparitions at La Salette in 1846, Lourdes in 1858, and Pontmain in 1870. The trend seems to have culminated with the six apparitions of the Virgin at Fatima, in Portugal – the last witnessed by a crowd of 70,000 spectators – in 1917, one year before the premiere of *Suor Angelica*.[21] These apparitions fueled a vogue for monasteries and miracles on the European

---

[19] ALASTOR, *Le tre nuove opere di Giacomo Puccini*, «Musica», 15 January 1919. Quoted in WILSON, *The Puccini Problem*, p. 180.

[20] JAMES HEPOKOSKI, *Structure, Implication, and the End of «Suor Angelica»*, «Studi pucciniani», 3, 2004, pp. 241-264: 259-260.

[21] Studies of nineteenth- and early twentieth-century Marian apparitions include SANDRA ZIMDARS-SWARTZ, *Encountering Mary: From La Salette to Medjugorje*, Princeton, Princeton University Press, 1991; DAVID BLACKBOURN, *Marpingen: Apparitions of the Virgin Mary in a Nineteenth-Century German Village*, New York, Vintage, 1993; WILLIAM CHRISTIAN, *Visionaries: The Spanish Republic and the Reign of Christ*, Berkeley, University of California Press, 1996; and SUZANNE K. KAUFMAN, *Consuming Visions: Mass Culture and the Lourdes Shrine*, Ithaca, Cornell University Press, 2004. Also relevant is PAOLO APOLITO, *The Internet and the Madonna*, Chicago, University of Chicago Press, 2005. Many thanks to Deirdre de la Cruz for pointing me in the direction of these texts.

stage, as evidenced by works like Jules Massenet's *Le jongleur de Notre Dame* (1902); Maurice Maeterlinck's *Soeur Béatrice* (1901), itself the subject of four operatic adaptations between 1912 and 1944;[22] and Max Reinhardt's «grand pageant» *The Miracle*, with music by Engelbert Humperdinck, described by the «New York Times» as «the most profoundly moving thing ever seen in London» when it was presented to rapturous crowds in 1912.[23] None of this is to say that Marian apparitions were not debated, discredited, experienced and interpreted differently by different parties, nor that Puccini, an arch-cynic, would have believed them. Nonetheless, it would be a mistake to cordon off the world of Catholic credulity, safely placing it in some distant moment prior to the opera's composition.

Furthermore, many prominent members of Puccini's world – sober men, operating in the brittle arena of things – were demonstrably interested in the occult. The names of distinguished scientists and thinkers drawn to the spiritualist movement at the turn of the century are legion but it will be most instructive to concentrate on two.[24] The first is Cesare Lombroso (1835-1909), the militantly positivist criminologist whose conversion to spiritualism is documented in his final book, a nearly five-hundred-page tome published in English in 1909 under the title *After Death – What?*[25] In it, he describes, clearly and dispassionately, a series of transformative meetings with the Neapolitan medium Eusapia Palladino, which began in 1891. Hands appeared, a mandolin flew across the room and started to play, and in one of «the most important and significant of the occurrences», Palladino «was lifted up in her chair bodily, amid groans and lamentations on her part, and placed (still seated) on the table, then returned to the same position as before».[26] Alessandra Violi suggests that Lombroso's embrace of Palladino represents less a rejection of positivism than its triumph, de-

---

[22] See Michele Girardi, *Puccini: His International Art*, trans. by Laura Basini, Chicago, University of Chicago Press, 2000, p. 396.

[23] *Reinhardt's New Spectacle*, «New York Times», 14 January 1912.

[24] Major studies of occultism on which I draw include Alex Thomas, *The Place of Enchantment: British Occultism and the Culture of the Modern*, Chicago, University of Chicago Press, 2004; Roger Luckhurst, *The Invention of Telepathy, 1870-1901*, Oxford: Oxford University Press, 2001; and Jeffrey Sconce, *Haunted Media: Electronic Presence from Telegraphy to Television*, Durham, Duke University Press, 2000. For a discussion of these issues in a specifically Italian context, see Luciano Chessa, *Luigi Russolo, Futurist: Noise, Visual Arts, and the Occult*, Berkeley, University of California Press, 2012.

[25] For a reading of this text in the context of Lombroso's earlier writings, and of post-Unification discourse more generally, see Suzane Stewart-Steinberg, *In a Dark Continent: Cesare Lombroso's Other Italy*, in *The Pinocchio Effect: On Making Italians, 1860-1920*, Chicago, University of Chicago Press, 2007, pp. 229-288.

[26] Cesare Lombroso, *After Death – What?: Spiritistic Phenomena and their Interpretation*, trans. by William Sloane Kennedy, Boston, Small, Maynard, and Company, 1909, p. 49.

scribing the «emergence of an imaginary that is already inscribed in the project of the positivist sciences, an imaginary that Lombroso pushes to its extreme consequences, rendering unto it the contours and character of a phantasmatic revelation».[27]

Lombroso's new interests also brought him into contact with my second figure, the novelist Luigi Capuana (1839-1915).[28] Along with Giovanni Verga, Capuana had been one of the lions of the *verismo* movement until he too underwent a conversion of sorts. The advocate of narrative *impersonalità* and what he termed the «science of literature» now began to conduct more practical experiments, building a laboratory in his home and hypnotizing local peasants (hoping, in one case, to contact spirits that would help him complete a biography of Ugo Foscolo). Capuana's research also signaled the beginning of a second literary practice, one that critics have politely labeled «originale e segreto» and have allowed to languish at the margins of the canon.[29] Those attempting to rehabilitate these texts have, like Violi, stressed their 'phantasmatic' relationship with Capuana's earlier project. Paul Barnaby reads his novel *Profumo* as allegorizing the proposition that «the institutional positivism of post-*Risorgimento* Italy is itself haunted by the self-torturing asceticism of the medieval Church».[30]

Barnaby and Violi's emphasis on the uncanny underside of Italian positivism offers a new way to think about the place of *Suor Angelica* within the larger framework of *Il trittico* and the place of *Il trittico* within the larger context of Italian liberalism. Poised awkwardly between the gritty realism of *Il tabarro* and the equally authenticist historicism of *Gianni Schicchi*, this perennially maligned opera is itself a sort of phantom. The aesthetic discomfort it provokes may also inscribe a political dilemma. Considered (like *Profumo*) as an intervention into the ideology of post-Unification Italy, *Il trittico* seems to imagine two futures for the fledgling nation: either the nightmare of urban disenchantment presented in *Il tabarro* or a return to the glories of *trecento* Florence evoked in

---

[27] ALESSANDRA VIOLI, *Storie di fantasmi per adulti: Lombroso e le tecnologie dello spettrale*, in *Locus Solus: Lombroso e la fotografia*, ed. by Silvana Turzio, Renzo Villa, and Alessandra Violi, Milan, Mondadori, 2005, pp. 43-69. Quoted and translated in STEWART-STEINBERG, *The Pinocchio Effect*, p. 269.

[28] In this paragraph I follow the illuminating discussion of Capuana and Lombroso in JONATHAN ROBERT HILLER, *Bodies that Tell: Physiognomy, Criminology, Race, and Gender in Late Nineteenth- and Early Twentieth-Century Italian Literature and Opera*, Ph.D. Dissertation, University of California, Los Angeles, 2009, pp. 167-217.

[29] The phrase derives from CORRADO DI BLASI, *Luigi Capuana: originale e segreto*, Catania, Giannotta, 1968.

[30] PAUL BARNABY, *The Haunted Monastery: Capuana's «Profumo» and the Ghosts of the «Nuova Italia»*, «Romance Studies», XIX, 2001, pp. 109-121: 110.

Gianni Schicchi. These were compelling fantasies – the ideology of *Gianni Schicchi* will be explored in more detail in the subsequent chapter – yet *Suor Angelica* emerges as a symptomatic remainder of the unassimilated legacies of official and popular Catholicism, repressed and left unresolved by both.

II

A specter lingering at the margins of realist dramaturgy, *Suor Angelica* is itself a haunted work. At three moments there emerge strong occultist undercurrents, ones that have never been described as such. When taken together, these moments help tug the opera away from the pieties of sentimental Catholicism, and ground it firmly in the world of Lombroso and Capuana.

The first and simplest of the three scenes occurs early in the opera, when the nuns' thoughts turn to a departed sister:

Un silenzio doloroso è nel chiostro; le suore assorte in un atteggiamento di muta preghiera sembrano rievocare l'immagine della sorella che non è più.[31]

[*A dolorous silence is in the cloister; the sisters, pensive in an attitude of silent prayer, seem to summon up the image of the sister that is no more.*]

The tempo slows dramatically to mark this action, and a series of parallel seventh chords, played on the bridge by muted strings, adds to the sense of mystery. A simple melodic figure that had accompanied the nuns' earlier conversation suddenly appears as strange and luminous (see Ex. 3.1).

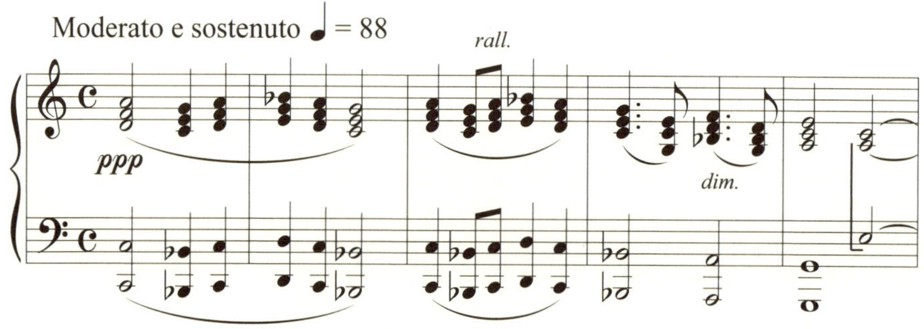

Ex. 3.1. Puccini, *Suor Angelica*, 14[+1-5].

---

[31] This is how the stage direction appears in the published score. In the first published libretto, it reads, more simply, «*Le suore, assorte, sembrano rievocare l'immagine della sorella che non è più*».

There is nothing unduly weird about this passage – no ghost appears on stage – but Puccini would invoke a similar soundworld during a more disturbing scene of conjuring later in his work. At the heart of the great duet between Suor Angelica and her imposing aunt, the Zia Principessa describes a series of colloquies she held with her dead sister:

> Di frequente, la sera,
> là, nel nostro oratorio,
> io mi raccolgo...
>
> Nel silenzio di quei raccoglimenti,
> il mio spirito par che s'allontani
> e s'incontri con quel di vostra madre
> in colloquî eterei e arcani!
>
> Com'è penoso, com'è penoso
> udire i morti dolorare e piangere!
> Quando l'estasi mistica scompare,
> per voi serbata ho una parola sola:
> espiare! Espiare!...
>
> Offritela alla Vergine
> la mia giustizia!

[Often, in the evening, | there, in our chapel, | I meditate. | In the silence of those meditations, | my spirit seems to move off | and meet that of your mother | in ethereal, mysterious conversations! | How painful it is, how painful it is, | to hear the dead suffer and weep! | When the mystic ecstasy disappears, | I have retained for you only one word: | Expiate! Expiate! | Offer to the Virgin | my justice!]

This monologue reads like a textbook account of fin-de-siècle séances: the domestic interior, the out of body experience, the contact with a departed family member, the physical manifestations of cries and sobs, the prophetic message from the beyond. While the Zia Principessa's vocabulary of meditation and ecstasy might seem to draw on a longer tradition of Catholic visions, it is striking that none of the actual nuns in the opera use anything like this language. This is one of the most telling ironies of *Suor Angelica*: the opera's most credulous account of mystical experience is placed in the mouth of its sole representative of secular society.

Puccini's music for this scene draws on many techniques encountered earlier. Here, too, are the muted, *ponticello* strings, now made more mysterious through the addition of muted brass, a celesta doubled by a ghostly piccolo, and a remarkably low harp. The clearest echo of the earlier scene comes in the form of three, just-barely functional, parallel triads (F-sharp minor, B major, C-sharp minor: IV–VII–I in the home key) that sound at the beginning, climax, and conclusion of the monologue (see Ex. 3.2). (If Puccini had previously re-

Ex. 3.2. PUCCINI, *Suor Angelica*, 50⁺⁴⁻⁷.

served 'impressionist' voice-leading for ekphrastic landscape music, in *Suor Angelica* he seems to associate it with visions of a different sort). Against this spectral backdrop, the contralto's line leaps by fourths from the lowest to the highest extremes of its range. It would be hard to think of a melodic style further removed from the little declamatory arcs through which Puccini normally constructs his vocal lines. In many performances, it sounds as if the Zia Principessa's voice is being pulled upwards by a magnetism beyond its control.

The parallel triads that structure «Di frequente la sera» will return once more after the conclusion of the duet, as an ostinato that accompanies the opening section of Angelica's aria «Senza mamma» (see Ex. 3.3).[32] Although the tonality has been shifted from C-sharp minor to A minor, and the meter from 4/4 to 3/4, the connection between the two passages is highly audible and alerts us to other resonances between the scenes.

Ex. 3.3. Puccini, *Suor Angelica*, 60[+1-5].

---

[32] This connection is noted, if interpreted somewhat differently, in Girardi, *Puccini*, p. 406.

The Zia Principessa's phrase «estasi mistica» is echoed in a stage direction that describes Angelica's «*esaltazione mistica*», and the Gothic ambience of her narration anticipates another stage direction, which calls for an effect that would not have been out of place at one of Palladino's séances:

I lumi del cimitero sono tutti accesi; il chiostro è ormai quasi oscuro. Le suore escono dal cimitero e si avviano verso Suor Angelica che è come in estasi. Il gruppo delle suore si avvicina in silenzio. Nella semioscurità sembra che le figure bianche, camminando, non tocchino terra.

[*The lights of the cemetery are all illuminated; the cloister is now almost dark. The nuns come from the cemetery and head for Suor Angelica, who is as if in ecstasy. The group of nuns approaches in silence. In the semi-darkness it seems that the white forms, as they walk, do not touch the ground.*]

This occult backdrop – flickering candles, levitating nuns – is of a piece with the climax of «Senza mamma», where Angelica initiates a mystical conversation of her own:

> Ora che sei un angelo del cielo,
> ora tu puoi vederla la tua mamma,
> tu puoi scendere giù pel firmamento
> ed aleggiare intorno a me, ti sento.
> Sei qui, sei qui, mi baci e m'accarezzi.
> Ah! dimmi, quando in ciel con te potrò vederti?
> Quando potrò baciarti? [...]
> Parlami, parlami, amore, amore, amor![33]

[Now that you are an angel in heaven, | now you can see her, your mother, | and you can come down from the firmament | and hover about me. I feel you. | You're here, you're here, you kiss and caress me. | Ah! tell me: when will I be able to see you in heaven? | When will I be able to kiss you? | Speak to me, speak to me, my love, love, love!]

These lines have been interpreted as marking the onset of Angelica's derangement, and their overt eroticism and desperate demand for prophetic knowledge are certainly unnerving. If Angelica is mad, however, the connections between «Senza mamma», «Di frequente la sera», and the nuns'

---

[33] This is how the text appears in the published score (and, hence, how it is always performed). Forzano's original text read, more simply: «Ora che tutto sai, | angelo bello, | dimmi | quando potrò volar con te nel cielo? | Quando potrò vederti? | Dimmi! Dimmi!... | Quando potrò baciarti? | Baciarti!... Amor mio santo!!». The spiritualist rhetoric is, if anything, even blunter in the original.

earlier scene suggest that there is nothing singular about her condition. Indeed, it seems a default mode for women in this opera.[34]

III

Although Suor Angelica and the Zia Principessa draw on the discourse of fin-de-siècle spiritualism, they part company with it in one important regard: both women imagine the dead contacting them directly, without the aid of a medium. Jeffery Sconce has suggested that, as a cultural fantasy, the idea of unmediated auditory contact with the beyond emerged only at the beginning of the twentieth century, where it helped make sense of a fundamental shift in mass communication technology. Victorian spiritualists, he argues, imagined «streams» and «wires» that linked mundane and transcendental spheres – one way of thinking through the networked cables of Morse's telegraph. With the advent of Marconi (whose first overseas transmission was broadcast in 1897), however:

Wireless replaced this comforting and often utopian ideal of extraordinary interconnection with a more bittersweet presence, one that evoked a no less marvelous yet somehow more melancholy realm of abandoned bodies and dispersed consciousness. In this respect, wireless was not a technology that stood as an analog to the body, but an apparatus that possessed the power to atomize and disperse both body and consciousness across the vast expanses of the universe.[35]

This more ethereal, mysterious form of communication gave rise to an unsettling new soundscape, «a lonely realm of distant and estranged consciousnesses, a vast ocean where the very act of communication reminded the operator of his or her profound isolation». They also inspired the emergence of a peculiar narrative genre: «tales [that] frequently centered on lovers separated by death but reunited through wireless [communication]».[36]

So much of the world of *Suor Angelica* is present in Sconce's essay: from the opera's basic narrative structure and pervasive emphasis on alienation and the impossibility of physical contact to its vocabulary of ether and disembodiment. Furthermore, a convent – or, at least, this convent – provides

---

[34] Given the pervasive gendering of mediums at the *fin-de-siècle*, it is perhaps no surprise that these themes emerge most fully in Puccini's one all-female opera. For more on occultism and gender see, in addition to the texts by Luckhurst and Sconce already cited, ALEX THOMAS, *The Darkened Room: Women, Power, and Spiritualism in Late Victorian England*, Chicago, University of Chicago Press, 2004.

[35] SCONCE, *Haunted Media*, p. 14. The influence of Marconi's invention on Italian literature of the period is discussed in TIMOTHY CAMPBELL, *Wireless Writing in the Age of Marconi*, Minneapolis, University of Minnesota Press, 2006.

[36] SCONCE, *Haunted Media*, p. 15.

a remarkably useful figure for thinking about the «realm of distant and estranged consciousnesses» described by Sconce: not an intimate community as much as an atomized field of solitary women, all waiting anxiously for messages from beyond their cells. This is a feeling that Puccini would have encountered firsthand in his sister's convent. As one nun there later recounted:

He came many times here to Vicopelago. I've been here for 47 years and I remember it well. One day he arrived and sat right there at the harmonium – that very one, it's still the same – and he began to play. We sisters stood listening from behind the grates of the cloister.[37]

The narrative breaks off here, although other versions of the story report the sisters all bursting into tears.[38] I wonder if this experience – the experience of playing for countless hidden ears, ears that would carry the memory with them decades after the event – left a greater mark on *Suor Angelica* than any specific prayer or ritual.

At the center of the convent's aural architecture sits Mary, silently. «Ogni parola è udita dalla Vergine Pia» (Every word is heard by the Blessed Virgin), the Abbess warns Angelica before her fateful reunion with her aunt. «La Vergine m'ascolti» (May the Virgin listen to me), Angelica responds. Later, she will repeat this warning to the Zia Principessa:

> Perché tacete?
> Perché tacete?
> Un altro istante di questo silenzio
> e vi dannate per l'eternità!
> La Vergine vi ascolta e Lei vi giudica![39]

[Why are you silent? | Why are you silent? | Another moment of this silence | and you damn yourself for eternity! | The Virgin hears you and she judges you!]

These lines seem to imagine the Virgin as the ultimate radio operator – a figure of «electronic omniscience», in Sconce's formulation – and the with-

---

[37] «Veniva tante volte qui a Vicopelago. Sono 47 anni che sono qui e lo ricordo bene. Un giorno arrivò, si mise seduto proprio lì all'armonium. È sempre quello, il solito. E cominciò a suonare. Noi sorelle si stava a sentirlo dietro le grate della clausura». The interview appears in the film *Ricordi pucciniani* (1958), directed by Giorgio Ferroni.

[38] See, for example, DANTE DEL FIORENTINO, *Immortal Bohemian: An Intimate Memoir of Giacomo Puccini*, New York, Prentice Hall, 1952, pp. 168-169. Panichelli further notes that «quando il maestro mi parlava di quelle 'Cuffie' era esilarante e nello stesso tempo commosso». See *Il pretino*, p. 169.

[39] The published score alters this line, suggestively in the present context, from «La Vergine vi ascolta» to «La Vergine ci ascolta».

holding of sound as the gravest sin.[40] Their fantasy of divine audition also brings to mind a recent claim by Emanuele Senici:

What Puccini attempts in *La fanciulla*, and specifically in the man-hunt scene, is an expansion and internal articulation of the fixed space of the theatre by means of a multiplication and strategic placement of the sound sources. In the impossibility of moving the ear to follow the sources of sound as a way of substituting for a movable eye, *Puccini tries to create a particularly powerful ear, a giant one, capable of hearing the action beyond the fixed field of visibility* – an ear capable of 'seeing' the action that the eye cannot see.[41]

Senici connects *La fanciulla*'s staging of an impossibly vast acoustic terrain to Italian fantasies of the American landscape, «the sonic equivalent of what is known as the "big sky" of the West».[42] The affinity between his image of a giant, all-powerful ear and the terms through which the Virgin is described in *Suor Angelica* might also direct our attention beyond the immediate purview of *La fanciulla*, though, suggesting the contours of a broader poetics of radiophonic listening in Puccini's later style.

IV

Although musicologists have devoted considerable effort in the last ten years to exploring the influence of the phonograph on modernist composition, they have paid significantly less attention to the impact of the wireless.[43] But are there any distinctive tropes – analogues to mechanicity, deadness, and other signifiers of the phonographic uncanny – that might alert us to the presence of a competing radio discourse in early twentieth-century music?

When national broadcasting networks began to take form in the 1920s (the BBC was founded in 1922, the Unione Radiofonica Italiana, a precursor to RAI, in 1924), many musicians embraced the possibilities promised by the «new electronic community» of mass communication. Edgard Varèse began drafting a global successor to Beethoven's Ninth Symphony, which «would be timed precisely in seconds so that choral entries in Paris, Moscow, Peking, or New York could be exactly synchronized, creating a vast song of liberation for all the peoples of the world».[44] Leopold Stokowski

---

[40] Sconce, *Haunted Media*, p. 63.

[41] Senici, *Landscape and Gender*, p. 255. Emphasis mine.

[42] Senici, *Landscape and Gender*, p. 258.

[43] See Carolyn Abbate, *Outside the Tomb*, in *In Search of Opera*, Princeton, Princeton University Press, 2001, pp. 185-248; and Alexander Rehding, *On the Record*, «Cambridge Opera Journal», XVIII, 2006, pp. 59-82.

[44] Malcom MacDonald, *Varèse: Astronomer in Sound*, London, Kahn and Averill, 2003, p. 304.

anticipated the construction of vast pleasure gardens devoted to electric listening:

In one part of the gardens might be a high tower from which at night colored light would be diffused, which in time would create a new art of color in motion and form. From this tower music of several kinds might be sent out over this part of the gardens. [...] Perhaps every day two periods of jazz for dancing, both open-air and under cover; about three times a week the finest symphony concerts; at other times singers, violinists, pianists of the highest order.[45]

These dreams of cohesion are reflected in the music Kurt Weill wrote for Bertolt Brecht's radio play *Der Lindberghflug* (1929), a work in which Charles Lindbergh's literal transversal of physical space is conflated with the radio's more metaphoric powers. Although the recalcitrant natural elements in the story, personifications of fog and wind, are assigned neo-Bachian fugues, what would seem to be the actual polyphonic voices in the drama – isolated wireless operators in New York and at sea, dispersed communities of newspaper readers in America and Paris – sing in a style that is unremittingly homophonic.

A similar optimism motivated musical experiments before the 1920s, but it was often undermined by the material realities of wireless transmission. When the Metropolitan Opera attempted their first live operatic broadcast in 1910 (a double-bill of *Cavalleria rusticana* and *Pagliacci*, perhaps not incidentally), they promised an acoustic miracle – the voices of Caruso and Destinn «borne by wireless Hertzian waves over the turbulent waters of the sea to transcontinental and coastwise ships, and over the mountainous peaks and undulating valleys of the country». But, as the «New York Times» reported, «the homeless song waves were kept from finding themselves by constant interruptions said to come from the Manhattan Beach station».[46] The only voice the reporters could make out seemed to be talking about beer. As even Stokowski conceded: «physicists have not found a way to protect music that is conveyed by space radio against these extraneous sounds [...] fading, static, and disturbances of every kind».[47]

Static, fading, voices coming in and out of focus: these are the new structural principles that organize the prelude to Joaquin Turina's piano suite *Radio Madrid* (1931), one of the first pieces written explicitly for a

---

[45] Leopold Stokowski, *New Vistas in Radio*, «The Atlantic Monthly», CLV, 1935, pp. 1-16: 15.

[46] *Wireless Melody Jarred*, «New York Times», 14 January 1910. A similar modulation between the utopian promise and prosaic reality of the wireless is described in Hans-Ulrich Gumbrecht, *In 1926: Living at the Edge of Time*, Cambridge, MA, Harvard University Press, 1997, pp. 242-243.

[47] Stokowski, *New Vistas in Radio*, p. 7.

wireless broadcast. Glancing at it may give us insight into how disorienting the new medium was. The piece opens with three 'uncanny' parallel triads (B-flat minor, E major, C minor), sounded slowly;[48] this unholy chorale then comes into conflict with a series of genuinely dissonant improvisatory flourishes: arpeggios, accented appoggiaturas, trills. Out of this music of mystery and interference, a Satie-like waltz (*ppp* and marked «lontano») emerges, only to pause on a dominant-seventh chord, at which point the opening music returns. A loud galop is sounded – the result of a stronger signal, perhaps – until it too vanishes into the ether; the chorale theme and the appoggiatura gesture return once more. Now a staccato fugal exposition (identified as «los locutores de la Radio», the radio announcers) begins but, quickly and surprisingly, it bleeds back into the earlier waltz tune. Finally, and as before, the waltz breaks apart on a dominant-seventh chord and the opening chorale, now hushed, reemerges as the substitute for a clear conclusion. We are used to hearing splices, fade-outs, and 'white noise' effects like these in the compositions for radio of a later generation: John Cage's *Williams Mix*, Luciano Berio's *Visage*. But to encounter them in an obscure and unassuming character piece by a composer known more for Sevillian grace than modernist fragmentation is even more remarkable. *Radio Madrid* reminds us that the unsettling implications of new technologies were not only a subject for the avant-garde.

Puccini produced no composition as schematic as Turina's prelude (the closest he came was *Scossa elettrica* – Electric Shock – a jaunty march commissioned in 1899 by a committee of telegraph operators in the occasion of an exhibition in Como that celebrated the centennial of Alessandro Volta's invention of the electric battery). Nonetheless, what might be described as the two musics of the wireless imagination – sounds that transcend the normal limits of the human body and fragile, unmoored voices that emerge like phantoms – both leave a mark on Puccini's later operas. On the one hand, as we have seen, they give rise to fantasies of aural omniscience: *Suor Angelica's* all-hearing Virgin, *La fanciulla's* giant ear. On the other hand, they motivate the strange passages of wordless, offstage singing discussed at the beginning of this chapter: moments in which we seem suddenly to 'tune in' to voices – indistinct, bodiless, dispersed, ethereal – that will soon fade away. Nor are Puccini's works the only operas of their time that engage these themes. For an example of listening to «homeless song waves», think of the protagonist of Franz Schreker's *Der ferne Klang*, grasping at a melody

---

[48] On the use of similar triadic juxtapositions as a signifier of the uncanny, see Rick Cohn, *Uncanny Resemblances: Tonal Signification in the Freudian Age*, «Journal of the American Musicological Society», LVII, 2004, pp. 285-324.

forever just out of reach. For an example of omnipotent hearing, recall those notorious lines given to Strauss and Hofmannstahl's Elektra: «Ob ich nicht höre? Ob ich die Musik nicht höre? Sie kommt doch aus mir!» (How should I not hear? How should I not hear the music? It comes from me).

The aural effects in Strauss and Schreker have been described as 'post-Wagnerian', in the sense that they thematize the 'phantasmagoric' occlusion of time and space that Theodor Adorno identified as one of the more dubious features of music drama.[49] For Adorno, however, the real inheritor of Wagner's phantasmagoria – acoustic tricks in which «the near and the far are deceptively merged, like the comforting Fata Morgana that brings the mirage of cities and caravans within reach» – was the wireless itself.[50] What radio accomplished, he suggested, was the creation of a truly invisible orchestra, one that produced music that sounded neither identical to a live performance nor like a second-order, phonographic reproduction of it. The result was a sort of acoustic dizziness:

The listener feels as if presented with something totally familiar, and familiar it may be indeed, yet in such a manner that it assumes an air of strangeness [...] The strangeness of the phenomenon expresses itself in the somewhat vague and half-conscious awareness of being at home with it and yet quite far away.[51]

Searching for a metaphor to describe this paradox of proximity and distance, Adorno proposed the echo, a sound that «possesses not only the characteristic of remoteness but also of derivation».[52]

Adorno's notion of echoic estrangement might be used to describe, quite precisely, the relationship between the two passages in *Il tabarro* discussed at the beginning of this chapter. The first is an example of 'realistic' aural presence, the second sounds both «totally familiar» and, at the same time, mysterious, oblique. We listen to the first passage the way we listen to any music in the opera house. The second, however, invites us to step outside normal theatrical space, listening as if from a distance, or at home. Perhaps this explains

---

[49] See CAROLYN ABBATE, *Elektra's Voice: Music and Language in Strauss's Opera*, in *Richard Strauss: «Elektra»*, ed. by Derrick Puffett, Cambridge, Cambridge University Press, 1989, pp. 107-127; and SHERRY D. LEE, *A Minstrel in a World without Minstrels: Adorno and the Case of Schreker*, «Journal of the American Musicological Society», LVIII, 2005, pp. 639-696. For Adorno's own attempt to connect Wagnerian phantasmagoria to Schreker's style, see his radio lecture *Schreker*, in *Quasi una fantasia: Essays on Modern Music*, trans. by Rodney Livingstone, London, Verso, 1992, pp. 130-144.

[50] THEODOR ADORNO, *In Search of Wagner*, trans. by Rodney Livingstone, London, Verso, 2005, p. 75.

[51] ADORNO, *The Radio Voice*, in *Current of Music*, ed. Robert Hullot-Kentor, Cambridge, Polity Press, 2009, pp. 345-391: 348-349.

[52] ADORNO, *Radio Voice*, p. 349.

why Puccini's first wordless, offstage chorus was invented to depict Cio-Cio San as she sat waiting for Pinkerton's ship to arrive at port. In this scene she appears like one of the nuns in *Suor Angelica* (or one of the bereaved wireless operators described by Sconce): lonely, isolated, ears trained on the beyond.

V

A process of rehearing similar to the one in *Il tabarro* is at play, much more elaborately, in *Suor Angelica*. As Hepokoski has argued, the last fifteen minutes of Puccini's opera are structured around two «rotational cycles», in which four distinct musical ideas – each assigned a fixed tonality, harmonization, and melodic profile – appear twice, in the same order.[53] (These «full rotations» are preceded by a third, «partial» rotation, in which only the first three elements appear). For Hepokoski, this formal conceit, which he describes as «ceremonial» and «churning», performs an essentially symbolic function: Angelica's increasing alienation from the world around her is depicted through her progressive separation from the normal flow of Western music. Although his analysis is compelling, there may be other ways to account for Puccini's use of this technique. Adorno's theory of wireless listening allows us to explore a less hermeneutic question: not what does rotational form 'mean' in *Suor Angelica*, but what effect might its highly audible repetitions have on an audience in the theater?

Let us begin by focusing on the first of the four elements identified by Hepokoski.[54] We hear this music for the first time in a short scene that immediately precedes the central duet, as Angelica presses an alms-collector for information on the carriage that has just arrived (see Ex 3.4):

> Ah! ditemi, sorella,
> com'era la berlina?
> Non aveva uno stemma?
> Uno stemma d'avorio?...

[Ah! tell me, sister, | what was the carriage like? | Didn't it have a coat-of-arms? | An ivory coat-of-arms?...]

If the simple F-major melody suggests the alms-collector's naivety, her obliviousness to the tragedy that is about to unfold, the frequent shifts between duple and triple meter capture something of Angelica's anxiety.

---

[53] Hepokoski, *Structure, Implication*. The interaction of «rotational form» with other more conventional formal structures is explored in Andrew Davis, *Formal Multivalence in «Suor Angelica»*, in «Il trittico», «Turandot», and Puccini's Late Style, Bloomington, Indiana University Press, 2010, pp. 108-137.

[54] For Hepokoski's own description, see *Structure, Implication*, p. 245. For a different analysis of the same motivic material see Girardi, *Puccini*, pp. 399-400.

Ex. 3.4. Puccini, *Suor Angelica*, 36[+2-7].

At the climax of «Senza mamma» – the moment that signals the begin-ning of Angelica's mystical conversation or, for other critics, the onset of her madness – Angelica sings this music again, initiating the second (and first complete) rotational cycle (see Ex. 3.5). The melody and harmoniza-tion are unchanged, although the tempo has been slowed drastically and the jumpy meter smoothed out into a more even duple, alterations that serve to make the music calmer, more incantatory, and less physical. The orchestration is more distant also, a conventional battery of strings and winds replaced by a more ethereal palette of muted stings, muted horns, and harp.

Ex. 3.5. Puccini, *Suor Angelica*, 61[+1-5].

(continues)

Ex. 3.5. *(conclusion)*

The libretto suggests an intriguing link between these passages. The first occurrence of the F-major melody accompanies an image of mundane human connection: the arrival of the carriage at the convent. The second, in contrast, describes a rather more impressive scene of transportation: «Ora che sei un angelo del cielo, [...] tu puoi scendere giù pel firmamento» (Now that you are an angel in heaven, you can come down from the firmament). Fittingly, then, the third rotational cycle begins with the most miraculous moment of contact yet. «La grazia è discesa dal cielo» (Grace has descended from heaven), Angelica proclaims, before falling silent, for the last iteration of the F-major melody is purely instrumental (see $6^{+3\text{-}13}$). Just as the three visitors that greet Angelica – the carriage, the angel, grace itself – have less and less purchase on physical reality, so too is her melody made to sound ever more disembodied and distant from the world on stage. The orchestration of the third, instrumental version of the F-major melody is identical to its previous iteration in «Senza mamma». It is as if we were looking at Angelica's shadow, but now without Angelica herself.

Hepokoski imagines rotational form as the gradual clarification of a structural process, a move from obscurity to light. But, as the preceding discussion suggests, Puccini's use of the technique might alternatively be described as a process of dematerialization, of echoing and freeing. From this perspective, the real model for Puccini's use of rotational form in *Suor Angelica* might be something more modest than late nineteenth-century symphonic music: it might be that hackneyed strategy, inherited from Amilcare Ponchielli and late Verdi, of reiterating a readily identifiable sung melody in purely instrumental form at the conclusion of an act. Or, then again, maybe not so hackneyed. Gary Tomlinson has suggested that there

Ex. 3.6. PUCCINI, *Suor Angelica*, 64[+1-7].

is an almost Nietzchean dimension to orchestral groundswells in late Romantic Italian opera – Dionysiac moments when music breaks free from the words that had confined it. To describe these passages, Tomlinson invokes a series of astronomical metaphors that could not be more relevant to the subject of *Suor Angelica*: «Verdi uncovered in his new practice a potential leverage of Archimedean dimensions [...] one that could move the whole opera, wrenching it out of one orbit and into a new one». And again, quoting Franco Faccio: «Heaven seems to open up».[55]

---

[55] GARY TOMLINSON, *Learning to Curse at Sixty-Seven*, «Cambridge Opera Journal», XIV, 2002, pp. 229-241: 240.

VI

When heaven opens up at the end of *Suor Angelica*, we are greeted not, as one might have expected, with the voice of absolute acoustic alterity, but instead with sounds already heard in human form.[56] The music intoned by the angelic choir during the climactic miracle is based on the fourth (and final) element in the rotational cycle. The first time we heard this music was immediately after the conclusion of «Senza mamma» (see Ex. 3.6). «La grazia è discesa dal cielo», Angelica sang, anticipating the line that would soon mark the start of the third cycle, accompanied by an offstage chorus of nuns intoning hymns to the Virgin. Puccini's music for this passage – much more elaborate than the F-major melody that begins the cycles – is constructed from three parallel triads that are sequenced up by thirds – a «non-progression», in Hepokoski's phrase, giving rise to a «ritualized, circular processional».[57] The sequence is then itself cycled through two more times; cadences are deferred again and again until we finally settle into the implied tonic of C major.[58]

Nothing changes during the miracle scene except the orchestration and the placement of the sound source. The music previously assigned to Angelica and the orchestra is now taken over by an offstage ensemble: children's voices supported by sopranos and later a full choir (including the only male voices we hear in this opera) plus a coldly virginal instrumental group: two pianos playing arpeggios in their highest register, organ, hushed cymbals, muted trumpets (see 81$^{+1\text{-}7}$). Angelica remains silent during the start of the miracle music, and the orchestra drops out too, save for a few plucked string chords. This decision emphasizes the remoteness of the new sound world but it also suggests that Angelica's voice has quite literally been taken away from her, wrested from her body and allowed to echo through the atmosphere. When Angelica reenters the texture at the start of the second iteration of the sequence, she may be able to muster the force for a final high C, but she is also no longer singing 'her' melody, only one of the inner voices of its harmonization (see 82$^{+1\text{-}8}$). At the start of the third iteration, she emits two horrible unpitched moans. They are, to return to Sconce's formulation, the sounds of a body being atomized and dispersed and (unless you count the chilling, wordless high C the offstage sopranos unleash in the final four measures: chilling because it is calibrated

---

[56] It seems to be this lack of difference («the note of transfiguration that the event requires») that leads Julian Budden to conclude that, «The exalted regions open to Verdi and Wagner were closed to Puccini». See *Puccini*, p. 405.

[57] Hepokoski, *Structure, Implication*, p. 252.

[58] *Ibid.*, pp. 252-256.

so precisely to echo – or, as if by some electric force, prolong – the voice of a now dead woman) the last ones she will ever make. (See 84$^{+7\text{-}9}$).

VII

There are, then, two new ways one might describe this final miracle. On the one hand, it seems to appropriate both the actual sound of early wireless transmissions and the magical effect they had on many listeners. On the other hand, remembering that radiophonic communication was still, in the early twentieth-century, a two-way process, we can also hear the protagonist desperately broadcasting her own voice into the ether as we listen to the ever-more-distant echo of her cry. Choosing between these options is less important than observing how far, in either case, we have moved from the aims of realist opera.

And so, to return to our initial question, what happened to *verismo*? What Puccini's later career suggests – and *Suor Angelica* narrativizes, in its move from convent bells to heavenly ones – is that a phonographic regime ceded to, or came into conflict with, a radiophonic one. A movement founded on objective transcription and unmediated presence became haunted by echoes, unreal voices, distant sounds. This shift was noted by Ferruccio Busoni, who made it the subject of a short fable published as an April Fool's Day joke (the author is listed as «Aprilus Fischer») in 1911. (That year also saw the publication of Pizzetti's essay on Puccini, discussed at the beginning of this chapter. Busoni's tale is further evidence that a critical reevaluation of *verismo* was beginning to take hold).

Framed as an urgent dispatch from New York, Busoni's story centers on one Kennelton Humphrey Happenziegh, a conscientious positivist who «has devoted the greatest part of his studies to the experimental criticism of acoustic phenomena». His great invention is a «super-sensitive apparatus (intended for phonographic discs)», a device that can record sounds beyond the range of normal human hearing.[59] As the story begins, Happenziegh has accidentally left his device turned on and, after a short nap, has returned to discover «certain impressions which he could not account for [...] an accumulation of obscure diagrams which were systematic, complicated, and at first unintelligible».[60] Has Happenziegh's disc recorded sounds from the surrounding area? All restaurants were closed, no parties hosted, and yet the disc, when played back, seems to have transcribed the sounds of music. There is only one explanation:

---

[59] FERUCCIO BUSONI, *A Fairy-like Invention*, in *The Essence of Music and Other Papers*, trans. by Rosamond Ley, London, Rockliff, 1957, pp. 190-193: 190. The story originally appeared in the magazine «Signale für die muskalische Welt».

[60] BUSONI, *Invention*, p. 191.

As the air needs an instrument to make its vibrations perceptible to our ear, so the air itself is only an instrument which transmits the not yet fully fathomed wave-lengths. These original wave-lengths [...] have the characteristic quality of being similarly effective in a time-sphere, as, for instance, wireless telegraphy in that of space. [...] Thus, through a chance not yet cleared up, a demonstration of music in the future seems to have found its way on to the super-sensitive disc and to have impressed itself there.[61]

That is to say: just as the wireless can tune into sounds from far-flung locations, Happenziegh's device has picked up the noise of some future epoch. (The years around 2050 are presented as a plausible point of origin). Seemingly objective and impersonal recording techniques have yielded results that defy all logic. In a concrete demonstration of Adorno's theory of phantasmagoria, time and space have fused.

As for the music itself, it sounds not unlike the final miracle in *Suor Angelica*: «One might almost suppose that all the instruments, which one knows of or can guess at, play *muted* and that in addition to this the space in which they are placed is sharply separated from the listener».[62] The implication here – that we are not just listening to an orchestra from the future, but to an offstage orchestra from the future – is astonishing, and suggests how elaborate fantasies of musical disembodiment had become in the aftermath of Wagner and Marconi. It is telling, though, that Busoni himself would soon flee from this world of dangerous enchantments, embracing the cooler verities of neo-classicism (a stylistic shift marked, as it was for Puccini in the years following *Suor Angelica*, by a new interest in *commedia dell'arte* and Carlo Gozzi's *Turandot*). Neo-classicism, of course, is the movement that is usually associated with the impersonality of the phonograph. The triumph of musical objectivity in the 1920s should not, however, be understood as the inevitable byproduct of technological innovation, but rather as the return to an earlier dream of acoustic certainty, one that had been unsettled, if only briefly, by the amorphous voices of the wireless and the even more haunting music of the First World War. The extent to which Puccini's final operas were able to banish these unnerving sounds will the subject of the next two chapters.

---

61 BUSONI, *Invention*, p. 192.

62 BUSONI, *Invention*, p. 193. Original emphasis.

GIANNI SCHICCHI, TUSCAN REVIVALISM, WAR

The First World War lurked somewhere in the background of the preceding chapter. Although its horrors contributed to a resurgence of the spiritualist practices that, I suggested, informed the poetics of *Suor Angelica*, and although that opera's depiction of a woman desperate to connect with an absent child may have been more poignant and more pointed than is often assumed, the noise and fury of the war itself did not erupt directly onto the surface of Puccini's gentle score. Nor did it cast much shade over *Suor Angelica*'s reception. Indeed, the world premiere of *Il trittico* at the Metropolitan Opera on 14 December 1918 (only one month after the ceasefire) appears to have been a festive occasion. Newspapers noted the presence of Astors, Vanderbilts, and French aristocrats, «laughing, chattering people, talking more or less inanely about the new works».[1] Although these same publications were positively overflowing with stories of the war's aftermath, such concerns must have seemed blissfully remote from the gala in New York.

Yes, the composer was prevented from attending. And, yes, the «New York Times» spoke of an «orchestral trench» in which Roberto Moranzoni «conducted his forces with skill and enthusiasm», deserving «the highest ecominnis [sic] for the masterly manner in which he kept his army off and on the stage in action».[2] In general, though, Puccini seems to have inspired more nostalgic thoughts. *Il tabarro* reminded Sylvester Rawling of the sort of thing «one could see before the war at the Grand Guignol in Paris».[3] James Gibbons Huneker found *Gianni Schicchi* «as frothing and as exhilarating as champagne (before-the-war champagne, of course)».[4]

---

[1] Sylvester Rawling, *Puccini's Three New Works Make Gala Opera Night*, «The Evening World», 16 December 1918, p. 19. Notable audience members are listed in *Triple Premiers at Metropolitan*, unsigned, «The Sun», 15 December 1918, p. 11.

[2] James Gibbons Huneker, *A World Premier of Puccini Operas*, «The New York Times», 15 December 1918.

[3] Rawling, *Puccini's Three New Works*.

[4] Huneker, *A World Premier*.

Gianni Schicchi, as is often noted, was the frothiest and most successful of the three operas; heard in the context of 1918 New York, it seems almost wilfully benign. Eight years earlier, Puccini had arrived at the Met with an ambitious new opera based on a recent American play, set during the American Gold Rush, and featuring a noisily up-to-date harmonic language. Now he offered a domestic farce, loosely inspired by Dante's *Inferno*, which drew heavily on the conventions of *commedia dell'arte* and the style of Verdi's *Falstaff*. The Florentine setting would have been familiar to many in the audience. The year of the action, 1299, was comfortably remote. And as for the characters – bickering relatives, passionate lovers, a dodgy but fundamentally well-meaning father figure – were they not, well, just so 'Italian'? For American audiences wary of their ally's new-found territorial ambitions, and horrified by the slaughter of its people (at least one million dead and almost as many wounded), *Gianni Schicchi* presented the nation as it should have been: a timeless and beautiful landscape, populated by a race that may not have been especially trustworthy, but was also not especially serious.

Less than one month after its New York premiere, *Il trittico* debuted in Italy at Rome's Teatro Costanzi, and the reaction was rather different.[5] American critics were largely dismissive of *Gianni Schicchi*'s literary inspiration («Dante did nothing more for the opera than supply it with a name», according to the «New York Tribune»), but Italians took it seriously, and adduced a host of other great names (Boccaccio and Ariosto, Rossini and Verdi) in their celebrations of the work.[6] New York critics treated Puccini's opera as a nostalgic respite from political anxieties, but Italians referred to the war explicitly in their reviews, and incorporated the opera into a narrative of national struggle and rebirth:

But with *Gianni Schicchi*, the new Italian opera has rediscovered its ancient heights. Youth welcome it as an admonishment now that Italian civilization is setting out for a new path. [...] Oh, ancient Italy who now rises again from blood and sacrifice, you know how to rediscover your divinely sunny smile! It was bound to happen. After the Napoleonic storm – *The Barber of Seville*! After the terrible tragedies of Carso and Piave – *Gianni Schicchi*![7]

---

[5] For another discussion of the American and Italian reception of *Gianni Schicchi*, see ALEXANDRA WILSON, *The Puccini Problem: Opera, Nationalism, and Modernity*, Cambridge, Cambridge University Press, 2007, pp. 178-184.

[6] H.E. KREHBIEL, *First Performance of Three New Operas by Puccini at the Metropolitan*, «New York Tribune», 15 December 1918, p. 12.

[7] «Ma col *Gianni Schicchi* la nuova opera italiana ha ritrovato le antiche altezze. Lo accolgano i giovani come un ammonimento ora che l'Italia sta incamminandosi verso un nuovo cammino di civiltà. [...] O vecchia Italia che ora che risorgi dal sangue e dal sacrificio, sai ri-

These words were written by Giannotto Bastianelli (1883-1927), a Florentine critic who had moved in Futurist circles, edited a journal named «Dissonanza», and been an early Italian advocate for Schoenberg. He was no fan of Puccini – or, indeed, of the other operas in *Il trittico*. What made *Gianni Schicchi* new?

For Bastianelli, however paradoxically, the opera's originality resided in its return to 'timeless' Tuscan values: balance, gaiety, autochthony: «From Tuscany there comes a new masterpiece of equilibrium and laughing wisdom. Youth welcome it like the purest word of the race».[8] Given that Puccini was Tuscan, as was his librettist (and, of course, Dante), the opera had all the poignancy and mythic power of the return of a Prodigal Son. Or, to use a more specifically Tuscan concept, *Gianni Schicchi* represented a Renaissance. The words «rediscover» and «rise again» resound throughout Bastianelli's review. In his terms, Puccini's Florentine opera might be described as a sort of double resurgence, a rebirth of the Renaissance itself.

Similar claims were made even more hyperbolically by an anonymous critic for the ultranationalist daily «L'idea nazionale». «Many, almost all say: Bravo *Gianni Schicchi*», he observed:

What they mean is: Bravo to our ancient Florence! Bravo to our dear and tasty Tuscany, after so much French, Dutch, American, and Japanese exoticism![9] Bravo Forzano who finally has thought of us and repaid our good old Italy [...] And bravo Puccini, who has opened a window of serene comedy, of pleasing wit, of clear feeling, in this almost always cruel or sad or inconsistently tragic melopoeia that is modern opera![10]

It is one thing to assert that *Gianni Schicchi* was a stylistic response to postwar anxieties, but critics went further than this, imagining it as an actual

---

trovare il tuo divin solare sorriso! Come è fatale tutto questo. Dopo la bufera napoleonica – il *Barbiere di Siviglia*! Dopo la tragedia immane del Carso e della [sic] Piave – *Gianni Schicchi*!». Giannotto Bastianelli, *La prima rappresentazione delle nuove opere di Puccini*, «La Nazione», 11 January 1919.

8 «Dalla Toscana ci viene un nuovo capolavoro d'equilibrio e di saggezza ridente. Lo accolgano i giovani come il verbo più puro della razza». *Ibid.*

9 By «Dutch exoticism», the critic is presumably referring to the setting of Puccini's early opera *Edgar*.

10 «Moltissimi, quasi tutti dicevano: – Bravo *Gianni Schicchi*! E intendevano dire: – Brava la nostra antica Firenze! Brava la nostra cara e saporosa toscanità, dopo tanto esotismo francese, olandese, americano, giapponese! Bravo Forzano che finalmente ci ha pensato e la buona vecchia Italia lo ha ripagato facendogli fare il suo più bel libretto e, quel che conta più, uno dei più belli libretti d'opera! E bravo Puccini che ha aperto una finestra di comicità serena, di arguzia piacevole, di chiaro sentimento, in questa quasi sempre truce o triste o inconsistentemente tragica melopea che è l'opera musicale moderna». "Uno del pubblico", *Il successo di Puccini al Costanzi*, «L'idea nazionale», 13 January 1919.

allegory of cultural renewal. For Bastianelli, the character of Rinuccio – young, proud, and optimistic – was «symbolic» of Florence itself.[11] «L'idea nazionale», again, was more explicit:

Bravo, bravo to *Gianni Schicchi*, who, dressing up in clothes that were not his own, makes a good will, giving the petulant relatives what they deserve, giving the better and more just share to the happy couple of young lovers, entirely unlike the honourable Bissolati, who also dressed up in clothes that were not his own and made a fake will, disinheriting Italy in favor of its evil relatives, hungry and insatiable.[12]

Leonida Bissolati (1857-1920), about whom we shall hear more below, was a recently deposed government minister, much scorned by the right wing. In late 1918 and early 1919 he was actively trying to convince Italians to abandon their claims to Dalmatia and South Tyrol and support Woodrow Wilson and the League of Nations. In the journal's allegorical reading of the opera's plot, the Donati occupy the place of Italy's former allies. The young lovers Rinuccio and Lauretta represent (as Rinuccio did for Bastianelli) local Italian interests. Lacking conventional legal authority, but cunning and willing to do what is necessary to make things right for his people, Gianni Schicchi takes on a role that would soon be occupied by Gabriele d'Annunzio (who invaded Fiume, in violation of both national and international law, in September 1919) and Benito Mussolini.

No previous opera by Puccini had inspired such overtly political interpretations. The Italian response to *Gianni Schicchi* signals a turning point, not just in the composer's career, but in the larger history of Italian culture. Right-wing critics were beginning to articulate a new set of values – and, more haltingly, a new style of hermeneutics – that would remain in place until the end of the next World War. Some eight years after *Gianni Schicchi* debuted in Rome, Domenico Venturini published *Dante Alighieri e Benito Mussolini*, a book whose thesis, advanced through detailed allegorical readings, was that the thirteenth-century poet was already «exquisitely fascist» and, as such, an early advocate for the regime. «The political and moral renaissance that the Duce wanted is that which Dante desired», Venturini wrote.[13] His technique of «retrospective prophecy» was characteristic of a

---

[11] «Esso ci dice, per la bocca rosata di Rinuccio giovane simbolico di Firenze: *Guarda... Firenze è d'oro...Fiesole è bella!*». BASTIANELLI, *La prima rappresentazione*.

[12] «Bravo, bravo *Gianni Schicchi* che, disponendo di roba non sua, fa il buon testamento, dando quel che si merita ai parenti petulanti, dando il meglio e il giusto alla coppia felice del giovani amanti tutt'al contrario dell'on. Bissolati, che, disponendo anch'egli di roba non sua, ha fatto il falso testamento, diseredando l'Italia a favore di tutta la mala parentela insaziata e insaziabile». *Il successo di Puccini*, «L'idea nazionale».

[13] «Dante, ripeto, è squisitamente fascista. La rinascita politica e morale voluta dal Duce

regime that sought to legitimate itself by appropriating all aspects of Italian history.[14] It could have taken some degree of inspiration from Italian criticism of Puccini's Dantean opera.

The more complicated question, and the one I aim to explore in this chapter, is to what extent *Gianni Schicchi*'s own appropriation of Tuscan history should be described as participating in a proto-fascist discourse. To put the matter bluntly: Were American critics right when they treated the opera's celebration of Florence as an escapist fantasy? Or did Italians correctly identify a more bellicose and urgent message? Most scholarship on the opera has seemed to repeat the former position. For Alexandra Wilson, Puccini «was famously a composer who steered clear of making overt political statements and we might, therefore, interpret his insistence upon historical fidelity in the first staging of *Gianni Schicchi* (as of his other operas) as being guided by an impulse that was more theatrical than nationalistic».[15] Her claim, however, sits awkwardly with a letter Puccini mailed Carlo Vanbianchi on 10 October 1915:

Although I recognize great merit in these French musicians, the direct followers of the Russians, yet I say that our art is, must be, and has been the ruler of the world, and I insist that we Italians are [not so cruel] as foreigners. Italian geniality, even if it is less rich in technique, imposes itself on the world. And [should] we seek to depreciate it by accepting, desiring, and encouraging conglomerations and intrigues of notes? No, no, no! Clear Italian light must restore our [strength.][16]

Furthermore, if Puccini had wanted to «steer clear» of politics, Dante would have provided him with a far from perfect vehicle. Indeed, it is hard to overestimate the symbolic importance of the poet in Italy before and during World War One. Patriots carried copies of the *Divina commedia* with them into the trenches, and named their most important battleship the *Dante Alighieri*. Two famous lines in the *Inferno* – «a Pola, presso del Carnaro | ch'Italia chiude e suoi termini bagna» (at Pola, by the Carnaro, | which hems in Italy and bathes her borders) – had long been taken as key justification for expansion along the Adriatic coast, and the fact that Italian

---

è quella desiderata da Dante». DOMENICO VENTURINI, *Dante Alighieri e Benito Mussolini*, Rome, Casa Editrice «Nuova Italia», 1927, p. 315.

[14] On retrospective prophecy in the early twentieth century, see CATHY GERE, *Knossos and the Prophets of Modernism*, Chicago, University of Chicago Press, 2009, especially pp. 7-11.

[15] ALEXANDRA WILSON, *Golden Age Thinking: Updated Stagings of «Gianni Schicchi» and the Popular Historical Imagination*, «Cambridge Opera Journal», XXV, 2013, p. 191.

[16] Unpublished letter, quoted in MARY JANE PHILLIPS-MATZ, *Puccini: A Biography*, Boston, Northeastern University Press, 2002, p. 239. The original Italian version of this letter is not currently available to scholars.

citizens of the Austrian-occupied city of Trento had recently built a monument to the poet seemed to present further evidence for the necessity of intervention.[17] A 1911 Italian film adaptation of the *Inferno* concluded with a shot of that monument, an image considered so incendiary that censors removed it in 1914, lest it unsettle the nation's still-declared neutrality. Puccini may not have seen the (widely disseminated) film, but he was surely aware of Riccardo Zandonai and d'Annunzio's Dante-inspired opera *Francesca da Rimini* (1914), a work whose success with Italian audiences was partially attributed to irredentist feeling.[18]

The *Inferno* also took on darker meanings. In a 1915 letter to Ezra Pound, Henri Gaudier-Brzeska described the trenches as «a sight worthy of Dante». «There was at the bottom a foot deep of liquid mud in which we had to stand two days and two nights».[19] Gaudier-Brzeska's account brings to mind Dante's description of the deep trench-like hole to which Gianni Schicchi himself has been confined:

> Qual dolor fora, se de li spedali
> di Valdichiana tra 'l luglio e 'l settembre
> e di Maremma e di Sardigna, i mali
>   fossero in una fossa tutti 'nsembre,
> tal era quivi, e tal puzzo n'usciva
> qual suol venir de le marcite membre. (XXIX, 46-51)

[If the contagion of every hospital | in Vadichiana, from July until September, | and in the Maremma and Sardegna, were amassed | in one malarial ditch, just such suffering | was in that place. And from it rose | the stench of festering limbs.][20]

Creating a light entertainment out of these materials was never going to be a straightforward project. In his review of the New York premiere,

---

17 These anecdotes are discussed in MARK THOMPSON, *The White War: Life and Death on the Italian Front, 1915-1919*, London, Faber and Faber, 2008, *passim*.

18 For a discussion of the both the 1911 film and Zandonai's opera in the context of Italian irredentism, see ANTONELLA BRAIDA, *Dante's «Inferno» in the 1900s: from Drama to Film*, in *Dante on View: The Reception of Dante in the Visual and Performing Arts*, ed. by Antonella Braida and Luisa Calè, Aldershot, UK, Ashgate, 2007, pp. 39-52. See also NICK HAVELY, *Dante and Early Italian Cinema: The 1911 Milano-Films «Inferno» and Italian Nationalism*, in *Dante in the Long Nineteenth Century: Nationality, Identity, and Appropriation*, ed. by Aida Audeh and Nick Havely, Oxford, Oxford University Press, 2012, pp. 353-371.

19 Quoted in HUGH KENNER, *The Pound Era*, Berkeley, University of California Press, 1971, p. 202.

20 All translations and direct quotations from the *Inferno* are taken from Robert Hollander and Jean Hollander's translation (New York, Anchor Books, 2002), which also reproduces Dante's original Italian-language text as established in Giorgio Petrocchi's edition.

S. Foster Damon captured something of the strangeness when he described *Il trittico* as «a tragedy, a romance, and a comedy, all centered about death».[21]

And not just death, Damon might well have added, but more specifically exhumation and disinterment. *Il tabarro* ends with a corpse ripped from its shroud and forced into the eyes of the living. *Suor Angelica*, as we have seen, concerns a woman's attempts to communicate with her long-dead son. The central dramatic problem of *Gianni Schicchi*, meanwhile, is how a dead man can be made to dictate a new will. In Chapter Three, I examined how the climactic apparition in *Suor Angelica* called into question the premises of realist opera. Here I build on this discussion, exploring how the mechanics – and, more precisely, the acoustics – of resurrection in *Gianni Schicchi* inflect both its «nationalistic» and its «theatrical» revivalism. Emphasizing an uncanny underside to what Wilson terms the opera's «insistence upon historical fidelity» – and keeping in mind the more perfect union between Dantean poetry and lyric comedy enacted in Verdi and Boito's *Falstaff* – I attempt to ground both the politics and the aesthetics of *Gianni Schicchi* more fully within the Italian experience of the First World War.

I

To begin exploring the relationship between *Gianni Schicchi* and World War One in more detail, it may be helpful to look more closely at what Italian nationalists seem to have heard when they listened to the work. As mentioned above, both Bastianelli and the critic for «L'idea nazionale» gravitated toward the character of Rinuccio. For the former, he was «symbolic» of Florence; for the latter, he seemed to represent the hopes of Italy in general. The character's name may have been chosen to evoke associations with Rinuccio d'Arezzo, an important Renaissance humanist and translator, or with Rinuccio Della Rocca, a bellicose Corsican (and collector of Renaissance art) who led several successful battles against Genoa. Alternately, it may have been inspired by Boccaccio's hapless Rinuccio Palermini, tricked into stealing the body of a dead man who turns out to be his rival in disguise.[22] *Gianni Schicchi*'s Renaissance is full of geniuses and warriors, but it is also haunted by sham artists and uncanny doubles.

Bastianelli was especially taken with Rinuccio's lines «Guarda! Firenze è d'oro! Fiesole è bella!» (Look! Florence is golden! Fiesole is beautiful!). He quoted them at the culminating point in his review, and praised Puccini's setting as «a divine, incredibly sweet melody, of a spontaneity that wraps

---

[21] S. FOSTER DAMON, *The New Work of Puccini*, «The Dial», 11 January 1919, pp. 25-26.

[22] Rinuccio's tale is recounted in the first story of Day Nine in the *Decameron*.

us with hopes and with faith in our great, eternal land».[23] The critic was referring to a scene at the very end of *Gianni Schicchi*, where the young lovers finally find themselves alone in their new home:

Dal fondo apre di dentro le impannate del finestrone; appare Firenze inondata dal sole; i due innamorati restano sul terrazzo.

RINUCCIO

Lauretta, mia Lauretta!
Staremo sempre qui!
Guarda! Firenze è d'oro!
Fiesole è bella!

LAURETTA

Là mi giurasti amore!

RINUCCIO

Ti chiesi un bacio!

LAURETTA

Il primo bacio!

RINUCCIO

Tremante e bianca
volgesti il viso...

LAURETTA *e* RINUCCIO

Firenze da lontano
ci parve il Paradiso!...[24]

[*From the back of the stage the window curtains open inward; Florence appears bathed in light; the two lovers remain on the terrace.*
RINUCCIO Lauretta, my Lauretta! | We'll stay here always! | Look! Florence is golden! | Fiesole is beautiful! | LAURETTA There you swore your love to me! | RINUCCIO I asked you for a kiss! | LAURETTA The first kiss! | RINUCCIO Trembling and white | you turned your face... | LAURETTA *and* RINUCCIO Florence from the distance | seemed like Paradise to us!...]

This is the only love duet (indeed, the only duet) in *Gianni Schicchi*, and Puccini's music is more lush, and leisurely, than at any other point in the score (see 84$^{+1\text{-}14}$). The final two lines are sung in octaves, doubled by the strings, and rise to a climactic high B-flat. We could be listening to Tosca and Cavaradossi, Mimì and Rodolfo.

---

[23] «E una divina melodia dolcissima di spontaneità ci avvolge di speranze e di fede nel nostro grande eterno paese». BASTIANELLI, *La prima rappresentazione.*

[24] Unless otherwise noted, all quotations from the libretto are taken from Eduardo Rescigno's edition of the first published edition of the libretto (Milan, Ricordi, 1997).

And yet, as Bastianelli surely noticed, this is less a duet than a trio, for Lauretta and Rinuccio are not really singing to each other, but rather to Tuscany itself. The magical name of «Florence» encircles their declarations and gives them added meaning; in a reversal of the pathetic fallacy, their love is presented as an illustration of the golden landscape, and not the other way around. And it is surely no accident, in an opera based on Dante, that the characters describe their city as «Paradiso». For them, the poet's heaven has come down to earth.

«From the large central window, Florence rises in a poetic vision», noted a critic for the «Giornale d'Italia» of this moment.[25] Given that the action of *Gianni Schicchi* had taken place within a single room, and that this room had been «*semi-oscura*» (semi-dark) for the second half of the opera, the surprise opening of the curtains to reveal a sunbathed vista would have been especially striking. And the libretto is quite specific about what the «poetic vision» entails: «*Nel fondo a sinistra un finestrone da cui si scorge la torre di Arnolfo*» (*On the rear left of the stage, a large window through which Arnolfo's tower rises*). The so-called Torre d'Arnolfo, a 308-foot-high tower crowning the Palazzo Vecchio, Florence's historical town hall, was one of the great symbols of the city, familiar from countless photographic reproductions. But it stood for much more than mass tourism. As D. Medina Lasansky has noted, Tuscan civic halls were an object of considerable fantasy in early twentieth-century Italy: «the symbolic center of civic government, the heart of every medieval city, and the one structure that could arguably be said to represent the Italian *popolo*», these halls spoke to an image of medieval Tuscany as robust, participatory, and independent of the church.[26] Furthermore, their native, muscular style (which Lasansky names «virile architecture») contrasted favorably with other national styles – whether the feminized confections of the Italian Baroque, or the broken-down (and, in any case, Greek-inspired) ruins of ancient Rome.[27] The Palazzo Vecchio was the largest and most virile of these buildings; imitated on a smaller scale throughout the province, it suggested a symbolic geography with Florence at its centre. Of course, its celebrated tower had not yet been built in 1299, the year in which *Gianni Schicchi* is set. But the fact that Puc-

---

[25] «Dal finestrone centrale si scorge Firenze in una visione poetica». *Le nuove opere di Puccini al Teatro Costanzi*, «Giornale d'Italia», 12 January 1919.

[26] See D. MEDINA LASANSKY, *Towers and Tourists: The Cinematic City of San Gimignano*, in *Donatello Among the Blackshirts: History and Modernity in the Visual Culture of Fascist Italy*, ed. by Claudio Lazzaro and Roger J. Crum, Ithaca, Cornell University Press, 2005, p. 125. For a fuller presentation of Lasansky's ideas, on which I draw in the following paragraphs, see *The Renaissance Perfected: Architecture, Spectacle, and Tourism in Fascist Italy*, University Park, PA, The Pennsylvania State University Press, 2004.

[27] See LASANSKY, *Renaissance Perfected*, pp. 174-176.

cini and Forzano felt the need to include it anyway says much about their conception of the opera.

The values that Tuscan civic halls were thought to represent – populism, secularism, independence, masculinity – would be championed and reaffirmed by the Fascist government. Indeed, if Italian fascism looked to Rome for a model for its imperial ambitions, it turned to Tuscany for an image of what a renewed national culture might resemble. Town halls were rebuilt extensively during the 1920s and 30s, then made the subject of popular films, promoted as sites for patriotic tourism, and repurposed for the needs of a new people. To similar ends, ancient Tuscan civic rituals (the *palio* in Siena, the *calcio* in Florence) were reinstated and reimagined, so that contemporary Tuscans could make contact with the great traditions of the past. This Tuscan revivalism was a hallmark of Mussolini's dictatorship, but he did not create it out of nowhere. Lasansky points to the 1921 celebrations of Dante's six-hundredth birthday in Florence as «a dress rehearsal for subsequent Fascist-period projects that exploited the city as a stage for politicized history lessons».[28] Buildings were restored; passages from the *Divina commedia* that mentioned specific Florentine locations were placed on plaques throughout the city; speeches praised the poet as an «eternal symbol of the inexhaustible fecundity of the great country that is Italy».[29] And if the organisers of the 1921 Dante celebrations attempted to return Florence to the poet, so to speak, other Italian patriots worked in the opposite direction. In 1911, Vincenzo Peruggia, a former guard at the Louvre, stole the Mona Lisa from Paris, later claiming he hoped to restore the painting to the city of its origin. His crime was greeted enthusiastically by d'Annunzio and other Italian nationalists. It even inspired an opera: Max von Schillings' once-popular *Mona Lisa*, which premiered in Stuttgart in 1915. Like *Gianni Schicchi*, it is set in an ancient Florentine villa; but, in marked contrast to Puccini's comedy, it shuttles back and forth between the Renaissance and the present day. *Mona Lisa* is framed by two scenes which depict tourists visiting the home of Leonardo's subject, and finding scant evidence of its former glory. Compared to *Mona Lisa*, *Gianni Schicchi* may seem the more naive and less ironic work. But its innocence is wilful. Like one of Mussolini's overzealous restoration projects, it aims to present the glories of the past without the intervening patina of time.

Gianni Schicchi's unvarnished fantasy of Tuscan history is presented most explicitly in Rinuccio's aria «Firenze è come un albero fiorito», and

---

[28] LASANSKY, *Renaissance Perfected*, p. 58.

[29] These words were spoken by the Italian minister of public instruction during the festival's inauguration. See LASANSKY, *Renaissance Perfected*, p. 62.

in the formal recitative («Avete torto!») that precedes it. The aria occurs at a dramatic crux in the opera as a whole. We are some fifteen minutes into the story, and the wealthy Donati clan is in a state of crisis. Buoso, their patriarch, has died and unexpectedly disinherited his relatives. No one is more upset by this news than Rinuccio himself; he needs the money in order to obtain his family's permission to marry Lauretta, the daughter of the more plebeian Gianni Schicchi. Rinuccio suggests that, despite his low status as a member of the *gente nova*, Schicchi is the only person clever enough to find a way out of the will, but the Donati will hear nothing of it:

SIMONE

Un Donati sposare la figlia d'un villano!

ZITA

D'uno sceso a Firenze dal contado!
Imparentarsi colla gente nova!...
Io non voglio che venga!

[SIMONE A Donati marry the daughter of a peasant! | ZITA Of a man who came down to Florence from the country! | Become related to the *gente nova*!... | I don't want him to come!]

Now a messenger arrives: Schicchi is already on his way to the villa! Rinuccio launches a defence, not just of his prospective father-in-law, but of the entire social class he represents. It is cast in the form of a *stornello toscano*, an improvised poetic genre that conventionally began with a simile involving flowers:

Vien dal contado? Ebbene? E che vuol dire?
Basta con queste ubbie grette e piccine!

Firenze è come un albero fiorito
che in piazza dei Signori ha tronco e fronde,
ma le radici forze nuove apportano
dalle convalli limpide e feconde;
e Firenze germoglia ed alle stelle
salgon palagi saldi e torri snelle!

L'Arno, prima di correre alla foce,
canta, baciando piazza Santa Croce,
e il suo canto è sì dolce e sì sonoro
che a lui son scesi i ruscelletti in coro!...
Così scendano i dotti in arti e scienze
a far più ricca e splendida Firenze!

E di Val d'Elsa giù dalle castella
ben venga Arnolfo a far la torre bella!
E venga Giotto dal Mugel selvoso,

> e il Medici mercante coraggioso!...
> Basta con gli odi gretti e coi ripicchi!
> Viva la gente nova e Gianni Schicchi!

[He comes from the country? Well? What does that mean? Enough of these narrow and petty prejudices! | Florence is like a tree in blossom | Which has its trunk and branches in the Piazza dei Signori | But its roots bring new strength | From the limpid and fertile valleys! | And Florence sprouts and to the stars | Rise solid buildings and slender towers! | The Arno, before running to its mouth, | Sings, kissing Piazza Santa Croce, | And its song is so sweet and so sonorous | That the little streams have come down to it in chorus. | Thus descend men learned in the arts and sciences | To make Florence more rich and splendid! | And down from the castles of the Val d'Elsa | May Arnolfo come to make his beautiful tower! | And may Giotto come from the wooded Mugello, | And Medici, the brave merchant! | Enough with petty hatreds and spites! | Long live the *gente nova* and Gianni Schicchi!]

Framed by parallel exhortations against «pettiness» and disunity («Basta con queste ubbie grette e piccine!», «Basta con gli odi gretti e coi ripicchi!»), Rinuccio's aria may sound less like an appeal to his family members and more like a speech directed to the contemporary audience. His catalogue of Tuscany's great men, buildings, and natural beauties might seem strange directed at a group of selfish Florentines in 1299, but it did speak powerfully to those Italians in 1919 who had been schooled in the value of such things. A second review published in «L'idea nazionale» described «Firenze è come un albero fiorito» as «a hymn to Florence, to the Arno, and to the *gente nova*».[30] And surely it was this aria – part harangue, part hymn – that led Bastianelli to interpret Rinuccio as the opera's allegorical embodiment of the Tuscan capital.

Rinuccio mentions the great towers of Tuscany at two points in his aria, reveling in their virile and patriotic connotations. First, he describes Florence's «solid buildings and slender towers» rising «to the stars». Later, he cries out, «May Arnolfo come to make his beautiful tower!». Even more telling is a moment in the preceding recitative, where he connects these structures with Gianni Schicchi himself:

> Gli occhi furbi gli illuminan di riso
> lo strano viso,
> ombreggiato da quel suo gran nasone
> che pare un torracchione
> per così!

[His sly eyes illuminate with laughter | His strange face, | Shadowed by that great big nose of his | Which seems like an enormous tower | set on its side!]

---

30 *Il «trittico» di Puccini*, «L'idea nazionale», 12 January 1919.

These lines present Schicchi's body as a mirror of the Tuscan landscape, while also associating the trickster with the famously large and virile nose of Dante. Culture and geography, past and present, are collapsed into an almost mystic whole.

This is not the only allusion to Dante in Rinuccio's aria. Its central stanza, which describes «ruscelletti» running down to the Arno from fertile valleys, echoes a lovely tercet in the *Inferno*:

> Li ruscelletti che d'i verdi colli
> del Casentin discendon giuso in Arno,
> faccendo i lor canali freddi e molli [...] (XXX, 64-66)

[The streams that, from the green hills | of the Casentino run down to the Arno, | keeping their channels cool and moist]

In Dante's poem, these words occur a mere 18 lines after the story of Gianni Schicchi, and they were discussed extensively in the commentary by «Anonimo Fiorentino» on which Forzano based his libretto.[31] By combining a high-literary allusion with a lower poetic style, Forzano exemplified his populist vision of the province as a whole.

And yet, the reference to the *Inferno* also raises a more awkward point. Simply put, Dante hated the *gente nova*. A true patrician, he blamed the new social class for many of Tuscany's travails, and railed against them throughout his poem. One of his most virulent attacks occurs in Canto XIV of *Purgatorio*. Like «Firenze è come un albero fiorito», it uses an image of the Arno running its course from hills to sea:

> [...] ma degno
> ben è che 'l nome di tal valle pèra;
> ché dal principio suo [...]
> infin là 've si rende per ristoro
> di quel che 'l ciel de la marina asciuga,
> ond' hanno i fiumi ciò che va con loro,
> vertù così per nimica si fuga
> da tutti come biscia [...] (XIV, 29-38)

[It is only fitting | that the name of such a valley perish, | for from its source | down to where it surrenders to restore | what the sky draws from the sea, | so that the rivers are supplied in turn, | all flee from virtue as if it were a snake][32]

---

[31] *Commento alla Divina Commedia d'Anonimo Fiorentino del secolo XIV*, ed. by Pietro Fanfani, Bologna, G. Romagnoli, 1866, p. 641.

[32] All quotations from *Purgatorio* are taken from Jean and Robert Hollander's translation (New York, Anchor Books, 2004).

If Rinuccio's aria imagines the Arno happily drawing Tuscans from periphery to center, Dante's poem describes the river as twisting angrily to avoid them:

> Tra brutti porci, più degni di galle
> che d'altro cibo fatto in uman uso,
> dirizza prima il suo povero calle.
>   Botoli trova poi, venendo giuso,
> ringhiosi più che non chiede lor possa,
> e da lor disdegnosa torce il muso.
>   Vassi caggendo; e quant'ella più 'ngrossa,
> tanto più trova di can farsi lupi
> la maladetta e sventura fossa. (XIV, 43-51)

[Among filthy hogs | more fit to feed on acorns | than on any food that is prepared for men, | the water first directs its feeble course. | Then, coming lower, it finds whelps that snarl | more than their powers warrant, | and so in scorn the river turns its snout from them. | It goes on falling and the more it swells | the more does the accursed, ill-omened ditch | find that these dogs have been transformed to wolves.]

«Firenze è come un albero fiorito» might well be described as a creative misreading (or optimistic rewriting) of this passage. Forzano has often been praised for the historical verisimilitude of his libretto, but he was more than willing to sacrifice inconvenient facts when necessary. His text says less about thirteenth-century Florence than it does about the revivalist politics of his own time.

It seems telling, then, that Puccini's setting of Rinuccio's «stornello toscano» makes no attempt to recreate the sound of early Tuscan music. The suggestion is not as fanciful as it might seem. In his «azione storica» *I Medici* (1893), Leoncavallo had lovingly evoked recherché Tuscan genres. Even Franz von Suppé had managed to work a recognizably Tuscan melodic style into one of the waltz duets in his operetta *Boccaccio* (1879), set in fourteenth-century Florence. In 1919, Sir Thomas Beecham offered to provide Puccini with Elizabethan popular songs that might serve as musical models for a new project inspired by *The Taming of the Shrew*, so the composer clearly wasn't averse to the sound of early music.[33] And yet, not only does «Firenze è come un albero fiorito» avoid historicism, it is written in the style of a contemporary march (see Ex. 4.1). The largely diatonic vocal line unfolds through clearly delimited four-bar phrases. Persistent dotted rhythms propel the melody through a series of arpeggiated tonic triads, and the orchestra's chorale-like block chords and persistent military

---

[33] See BUDDEN, *Puccini*, p. 421.

Ex. 4.1. PUCCINI, *Gianni Schicchi*, 30$^{+1\text{-}9}$.

(continues)

Ex. 4.1. *(conclusion)*

tattoos magnify Rinuccio's message. Most of Puccini's tenor arias (including the anthemic «Nessun Dorma») begin with declamatory sections and keep their lyric outbursts in reserve. In contrast, the vocal style of «Firenze è come un albero fiorito» never changes, and Rinuccio has already reached his first high B-flat by the end of the first strophe.

Puccini's setting of «Firenze è come un albero fiorito» has no clear precedents in his corpus, but it does have one suggestive antecedent.[34] On 1 June 1919, less than six months after the Italian premiere of *Gianni Schicchi*, the composer debuted a bombastic *Inno a Roma* to commemorate the end of the war and the mythic anniversary of the city's founding.[35] Written for a chorus identified as the «canto del popolo» in the original score, its martial style, triadic melody, and omnipresent dotted-rhythms recall Rinuccio's aria (see Ex. 4.2). Similarly, Fausto Salvatori's text, originally written to celebrate Italian military conquests in spring 1918, recasts many of the tropes of Forzano's text in a more aggressive register.

> Roma divina, a te sul Campidoglio
> dove eterno verdeggia il sacro alloro,
> a te, nostra fortezza e nostro orgoglio,
> ascende il coro.

[Divine Roma, to you on the Campidoglio | where the sacred laurel is eternally green | to you, our fortress and our pride, | ascends the chorus.]

---

[34] A similar connection is drawn in Carolyn Abbate and Roger Parker, *A History of Opera*, New York, W. W. Norton and Company, 2012, p. 454.

[35] The premiere was originally scheduled for 21 April 1919. The hymn was to have been performed by some 4,000 students, veterans, and professional choristers, supported by an array of civic and military bands; for better or worse, the even ran afoul of bad weather.

Ex. 4.2. Puccini, *Inno a Roma*[+4-13].

Often dismissed as an occasional work, Puccini's hymn did nonetheless live on in the totalitarian canon, performed throughout fascist Italy and, in translation, Nazi Germany. In 1938, it was recorded by no less an artist than Beniamino Gigli. While it has been claimed that sentimental Italian lyricism fell out of favor during Mussolini's rule, replaced by the collective discipline of orchestral music, Gigli's performance, all slides and sobs, tells a different story.[36] Like *Gianni Schicchi*, it suggests how easily the traditional resources of Italian opera could be mobilized to serve the cause of national renewal.

II

And yet, a comparison of «Firenze è come un albero fiorito» with the *Inno a Roma* also suggests the former's limitations as propaganda. During the triumphant climax of Rinuccio's first strophe, the orchestra interrupts him with an anticipation of Lauretta's «O mio babbino caro», played at a much slower tempo (see 3^{+1-4}). Even for an audience member not yet familiar with her aria (a situation now virtually impossible), it is an oddly feminizing gesture, and sounds as if Rinuccio has briefly forgotten his own call to duty. At the very conclusion of the aria, Puccini demurs again. The orchestra reduces to a pregnant tremolo, Rinuccio's final exhortations («Basta con gli odi gretti e coi ripicchi! Viva la gente nova e Gianni Schicchi!») rise freely to a powerful pair of high B-flats, and then a postlude intervenes (see 32^{+11}-33^{+7}). The orchestra echoes his melody – softer and softer, lower and lower – as if absorbing and deflecting its power. The audience in the hall is denied an easy opportunity for applause, and the audience on stage remains silent. Forzano's libretto, normally so fastidious, provides no indication about how Rinuccio's relatives should respond to his hectoring, but it is clear that they are unmoved. After his performance has ended, they exhibit the same petty narrowness as they did before.

Italian critics were disappointed. Alberto Gasco, writing for «La tribuna», noted ambivalently that the aria «expands with a polite solemnity».[37] «L'idea nazionale» suggested that although Forzano's poem was «lively and straightforward», Puccini's setting exhibited «the same old useless overemphasized melodiousness». Even worse, the composer «unleashes a sugariness in the style of Lehár, reminding us of the sin of *La rondine*».[38]

---

36 See RICHARD TARUSKIN, *The Oxford History of Western Music*, IV, Oxford, Oxford University Press, 2005, p. 750.

37 «Il largo canto del tenore, *Firenze è come un albero fiorito*, che si espande con una garbata solennità». ALBERTO GASCO, *Le nuove opere di Puccini al 'Costanzi'*, «La tribuna», 13 January 1919.

38 «C'è un momento in cui purtroppo spunta una sdolcinatura alla Lehar, per farci ricor-

Given the Tuscan Renaissance promised by Forzano's text, the persistence of Puccini's worst habits (sentimentality, self-indulgence, internationalism) must have been especially disappointing. If there was one moment in *Gianni Schicchi* to avoid evoking the style of the hated Austrians, surely it was this.

Indeed, any interpretation of *Gianni Schicchi* that emphasizes bellicosity and nationalism will run up against an obvious problem. Puccini, unlike so many prominent members of his generation, was no supporter of the war.[39] When Germany bombed the Reims cathedral on 20 September 1914, Puccini refused to join other artists in a public statement condemning the destruction. «You know my feelings», he explained to Tito Ricordi, «and you also know that, even though I am a Germanophile, I have never wanted to express myself publicly, neither for one side or the other, always deploring that the war projects its torments into the world, and also because I want to remain hidden in my shell, behind my reserve, following the neutrality that our land has imposed on itself».[40] Puccini's refusal led to vicious attacks in the French press. But two months later, invited to add his name – alongside those of Debussy, Saint-Saëns, Elgar, Paderewski, and Leoncavallo – to another anti-German publication (Hall Caine's *King Albert's Book*), Puccini demurred again.

Nor did the composer's sentiments change when Italy entered the war in 1915. Arturo Toscanini conducted daring mid-battle concerts on the front, and d'Annunzio dropped his poetry from fighter planes, but Puccini retreated to his estates in Tuscany, entertaining his German lover and working on his Viennese operetta. If Leoncavallo wrote a bombastic *Hymne à la France*, Puccini's only wartime commissions are melancholy, domestic works. In 1916, he wrote a fragmentary, sixteen-bar *Pezzo per pianoforte* to raise funds for the wounded. That same year, he also penned a short song for a volume published by Ricordi to benefit the Italian Red Cross. (All the other leading Italian composers – Zandonai, Mascagni,

---

dare il peccato della *Rondine*, ma fortunatamente è un momento. C'è l'arioso di Rinuccio sulla gente nova che rinnova Firenze e, pur vivo e schietto nelle parole, minaccia qua e là la solita inutile enfasi canora, ma fortunatamente si ricompone nel disegno del quadro». «L'idea nazionale», *Il successo di Puccini*.

[39] Nuanced accounts of Puccini's wartime activities on which I draw include PHILLIPS-MATZ, *Puccini*, pp. 223-256; and BUDDEN, *Puccini*, pp. 345-351 and *passim*.

[40] «Tu conosci i miei sentimenti e sai anche che, benché io sia un germanofilo, non ho mai voluto mostrarmi pubblicamente né per una né per l'altra parte, deplorando sempre che la guerra sparga i suoi strazi nel mondo, e anche perché desidero rimanermene nel mio guscio e nel mio riserbo, seguendo la neutralità che il nostro paese s'è imposta». The letter, which Dieter Schickling has recently dated 18 December 1914, is excerpted in *Carteggi pucciniani*, ed. by Eugenio Gara, Milan, Ricordi, 1986, p. 433.

Leoncavallo, Franchetti, Boito – contributed songs as well). *Morire?*, the poem by Giuseppe Adami that Puccini chose to set, is no celebration of Italian patriotism, nor does it offer succour to the bereft and wounded. Instead, it reflects ambivalently – and, as adapted by Puccini, perhaps autobiographically – on the competing stakes of military glory and escapist fantasy:

> Morire? E chi lo sa qual è la vita!
> Questa che s'apre luminosa e schietta,
> ai fascini, agli amori, alle speranze,
> o quella che in rinunce s'è assopita?
>
> È la semplicità timida e quieta
> che si tramanda come ammonimento,
> come un segreto di virtù segreta
> perché ognuno raggiunga la sua mèta,
>
> O non piuttosto il vivo balenare
> di sogni nuovi sovra sogni stanchi,
> e la pace travolta e l'inesausta
> fede d'avere per desiderare?

[To die? And who knows what life is! | This one that opens, luminous and pure, | To snares, loves, hopes, | Or that one languished in renunciations? | Is it the bashful and calm simplicity | that is handed down as a warning, | like a secret of secret virtue | so that everyone can reach his goal, | or not rather the lively flash | of new dreams over tired ones, | peace overwhelmed, and the unexhausted | faith necessary to desire?]

Puccini set these verses strophically, to a melody that unfolds slowly over a tonic pedal (see Ex 4.3). The affect is languid and clearly seems to privilege the comfort of «sogni stanchi» over the excitement of «sogni nuovi».

The mood, however, changes in the fourth and final stanza, when the speaker addresses the dead directly:

> Ecco... io non lo so, ma voi che siete
> all'altra sponda sulla riva immensa
> ove fiorisce il fiore della vita,
> son certo lo saprete.

[So... I don't know, but you who are | at the other side on the vast bank | where the flower of life blossoms, | I am sure you will know.]

Puccini could have easily written an additional strophe here. Instead, he does something startlingly new. After the words «io non lo so», the piano comes to rest on a dominant seventh and then drops out entirely, leaving

Ex. 4.3. Puccini, *Morire?*[+1-7]. Opening.

the singer stranded until the conclusion of the song (see Ex. 4.4). The vocal line abandons its previous melodic grace and the singer speaks to the dead in a style close to unmetered recitative. Then, for the final line of Adami's text, the style modulates again. The singer's rhythms slow, and his line rises grandly to a climactic high B. At this point, the piano finally returns to sound a tonic triad, but there is little sense of resolution.[41]

---

[41] Puccini would later recycle this song's music, and some of the key words and phrases of its text, to produce Ruggero's aria «Parigi! è la città dei desideri» for his 'second' version of *La rondine* (1920). The moment in which the speaker of *Morire?* calls out to the dead is paralleled by a similar formal shift in the aria, as Ruggero ceases merely to describe Paris, and instead addresses it directly. Here, too, there is something more than a little mystical about his language: «Ecco: sono qui perché guidate il mio cammino | in questa immensa vastità infinita | ch'è luce della vita» (So: I am here because you guide my path | in this immense infinite vastness | that is the light of life). Has Paris ever been apostrophized in stranger terms?

Ex. 4.4. Puccini, *Morire?*[+42-52]. Conclusion.

What is happening in this final stanza? Has the speaker finally achieved some new assertiveness? Or is he struggling to make his voice heard in the beyond? This latter interpretation would bring Puccini's song within the orbit of *Suor Angelica*, on which he was working concurrently. After all, and as we observed in the previous chapter, that opera also depicted a woman desperate to communicate with the departed. But, unlike *Suor Angelica*, *Morire?* offers no consoling miracle. The piano remains silent as death itself.

Three months before he wrote *Morire?*, Puccini received the libretto for *Gianni Schicchi*. He completed *Suor Angelica* on 14 September 1917, and then turned to his new comedy. His work would soon be clouded by news of the Battle of Caporetto, which raged from 24 October through 19 November of that year. Italian troops, exhausted and demoralized by two years of fruitless battles along the Isonzo river, and unprepared to confront the German army's recent strategic and technological advances, were attacked unawares, and suffered the most humiliating defeat of the entire war: 10,000 dead, 30,000 wounded, an astounding 265,000 taken prisoner. The battle was the downfall of Luigi Cardona, the intransigent supreme commander of the Italian armed forces; it produced a crisis in the government and led to a complete reorganization of the military. The word «Caporetto» is still used as a metonym for devastating failure, and historians point to it as a powerful indictment of the Italian liberal state.

On 15 November 1917, Puccini wrote to Tito Ricordi in despair over *Gianni Schicchi*, blaming Caporetto for his inactivity, and hoping, cautiously, for a brighter future:

You're right, we're waiting; but the calm and faith necessary for work aren't here. And what can be done? Too much sadness is in my heart! Forzano has also thought of another subject, strong and varied; but even he is now on the verge of enlisting. [...] Thanks for the monthlies. And now we have confidence in our army and its new captains! And may God protect us! [42]

The suggestion that Forzano worried *Gianni Schicchi* had become an inappropriate subject during wartime is fascinating, and Puccini's letter also suggests telling differences between librettist and composer. The former (26 years younger than his collaborator) thinks up a new opera, «strong and varied», and toys with joining the army himself; the latter falters and languishes. After the war, Forzano would become a close associate of d'Annunzio,

---

[42] «Hai ragione, aspettiamo; ma la calma e la fede per ora non ci sono per lavorare. E chi lo può fare? Troppo dolore è nel cuore! Forzano ha pensato anche ad altro soggetto, forte e vario; ma anche lui ora è alla vigila di arruolarsi. [...] Grazie dei mensili. Ed ora confidiamo nel nostro esercito e nei suoi nuovi capi! E che Dio ci protegga!». Puccini to Tito Ricordi, 15 November 1917, in *Carteggi pucciniani*, p. 457.

collaborate on three plays with Mussolini, and serve as a minister in the Fascist government.[43] It was he who came up with the idea for *Gianni Schicchi*, and he who persuaded Puccini, amid considerable reservations, of the stage-worthiness of a Tuscan opera. It is tempting to give Forzano credit for much of *Gianni Schicchi*'s belligerence. But it is equally worth asking if Puccini's melancholy passivity had any impact on the final text.

The Arnolfo tower, that symbol of Tuscan virility, makes one more appearance in *Gianni Schicchi*. Schicchi has hatched his plan for rewriting Buoso's will, and dressed himself in the dead man's clothes to prepare for the arrival of the notary. The relatives «*spingono Gianni verso il letto, ma egli li ferma con un gesto quasi solenne*» (*push Gianni toward the bed, but he stops them with an almost solemn gesture*):

> Prima un avvertimento!
> O messeri, giudizio!
> Voi lo sapete il bando?
> «Per chi sostituisce
> se stesso in luogo d'altri
> in testamenti e lasciti,
> per lui e per i complici
> c'è il taglio della mano e poi l'esilio!»
> Ricordàtelo bene! Se fossimo scoperti:
> la vedete Firenze?
> (*accennando la torre di Arnolfo che appare dalla finestra aperta*)
> Addio Firenze, addio, cielo divino,
> ti saluto con questo moncherino,
> e vo randagio come un Ghibellino!...

[First a warning! | O ladies and gentlemen, discretion! | Do you know the risk? | «For him who substitutes | himself in place of others | in wills and bequests, | for himself and for his accomplices | a hand cut off, and then exile!» | Remember it well! If we were discovered: | Do you see Florence? (*nodding toward Arnolfo's tower, which appears through the open window*) | Farewell, Florence, farewell divine sky, | I salute you with this stump, | and I stray off like a Ghibelline!...]

At these words the relatives are «*soggiogati, impauriti*» (subdued, frightened); gazing toward the window, they repeat Schicchi's three-line farewell in chorus.

«Addio Firenze», sung as Schicchi waves his mock-mutilated arm at the horizon, might have been a grotesquely comic song, or a satiric, mocking one. Instead, Puccini makes it into a fragile, haunting set-piece (see Ex. 4.5).

---

43 For more on Forzano, see C.E.J. GRIFFITHS, *The Theatrical Works of Giovacchino Forzano: Drama for Mussolini's Italy*, Lewiston, NY, The Edward Mellen Press, 2000.

Ex. 4.5. PUCCINI, *Gianni Schicchi*, 64-65.

(continues)

Ex. 4.5. *(conclusion)*

Schicchi's melody contains the only Italianate archaisms in the score: grace-ful, improvisatory melismas, and piquant Lydian inflections. One critic re-marked on the aria's «fresh Tuscan flavor», and thought you could almost imagine hearing «one of those salacious and characteristic ritornellos that flourish on the banks of the Arno».[44]

Yet his words do not fully do justice to this music's delicacy. Schicchi's tune resists articulating a clear tonic, and the orchestra provides little in the way of support: it is reduced to a choir of cellos, which double the melody at pitch, and a pair of bassoons that sound a hushed accompaniment. When the other characters repeat Schicchi's melody – itself made up of three nearly identical repetitions of a single phrase – an extended pedal amplifies the sense of stasis. «Addio Firenze» draws on the style of «Che faranno i vecchi miei», Jake Wallace's mournful lament for his lost homeland in *La fanciulla del West*, and anticipates «Ho una casa nell'Honan», the ministers' quite similar lament in *Turandot*. But might early listeners have heard other, more urgent, resonances in this spectacle of a mutilated Tuscan bidding farewell to his city in a distinctively folk-like idiom?[45] Throughout Schic-

---

[44] «La musica acquista un sapore di sempre più schietta comicità. Nel fresco sapore tosca-no dell'"Addio Firenze" par quasi di sentir scandire uno dei salaci e caratteristici ritornelli che fioriscono in riva all'Arno». MATTEO INCAGLIATI, *L'arte di Puccini canta e trionfa tre volte*, «Giorna-le d'Italia», 13 January 1919, p. 3.

[45] Is it a coincidence that Richard Strauss's wartime opera *Die Frau ohne Schatten* (1919), also features mutilated characters? Two of Barak's brothers are identified only as «Der Einäu-gige» and «Der Einarmige». I am grateful to Emanuele Senici for alerting me to the significance of maiming in both Strauss's and Puccini's works. For a related discussion of «Addio Firenze» in the context of the Great War, see ABBATE and PARKER, *A History of Opera*, p. 454.

chi's song, two muted trumpets play a persistent fanfare-like figure, which certainly suggests a call to battle. In many regards, «Addio Firenze» sounds like a negation of «Firenze è come un albero fiorito». Rinuccio's aria describes leaving home as a happy occasion, but Schicchi's song resists and lingers. It imagines Arnolfo's tower not as a goad to future glory, but rather as the symbol of a past that can never be recaptured.

III

Another difference between «Firenze è come un albero fiorito» and «Addio Firenze»: Schicchi knows how to work a crowd. Rinuccio's appeal, as we have seen, fell on deaf ears. In contrast, Schicchi's warning leaves the Donati family «*subdued, frightened*». They repeat his song almost automatically, as if swept up by the force of his performance (see $65^{+2\text{-}13}$). Given the lack of 'authentic' Tuscanisms in the opera as a whole, Schicchi's marked adoption of them in «Addio Firenze» might seem like a self-conscious strategy for manipulating his audience. No similar spectre of inauthenticity hovers over «Che faranno i vecchi miei» or «Ho una casa nell'Honan», both private performances with no concrete aims other than emotional indulgence. Schicchi, however, uses nostalgia for a purpose. His climactic impersonation of Buoso may be the crime that lands him in Hell, but a disturbing ability to adopt different voices and control other characters is in evidence throughout the opera.

The historical Gianni Schicchi, a member of the Cavalcanti family, was famous for his powers of mimicry. The fourteenth-century commentary on which Forzano based his libretto noted that Schicchi «could imitate any man with voice and gesture».[46] For Dante, it was this skill that led to his undoing. In the *Inferno*, we encounter Schicchi near the very bottom of hell, in an area reserved for impersonators, counterfeiters, and alchemists: all people guilty of distorting the true substance of God's love. A man who, in life, had no integral sense of self is now but one member of a pair of «ombre smorte e nude» (pallid, naked shades); he feasts on his companions like an angry pig, just as he formerly consumed the identities of others:

> [...] «Quell'è l'anima antica
> di Mirra scellerata, che divenne
> al padre, fuor del diritto amore, amica.
>   Questa a peccar con esso così venne,
> falsificando sé in altrui forma,
> come l'altro che là sen va, sostenne,
>   per guadagnar la donna de la torma,
> falsificare in sé Buoso Donati,
> testando e dando al testamento norma». (XXX, 37-45)

---

[46] Anonimo Fiorentino, *Commento alla Divina Commedia*, p. 638.

[«That is the ancient soul | of wicked Myrrha, who became enamoured | of her father with more than lawful love. | She contrived to sin with him | by taking on another person's shape, | as did that other, eager to decamp, | to gain the queen mule of the herd, | take on the shape of Buoso Donati, | dictating and giving to the will due form».]

The phrase «falsificare in sé» is repeated twice, a device that further blurs the identities of Myrrha and Schicchi, and allows the words to echo with all the force of Judgement.

Forzano paraphrased the final two lines of this passage toward the conclusion of Schicchi's aria «Si corre dal notaio», placing Dante's condemnation in the mouth of the sinner himself:

> In testa
> la cappellina!
> al viso
> la pezzolina!
> Fra cappellina e pezzolina un naso
> che par quello di Buoso e invece è il mio...
> perché al posto di Buoso ci son io!
> Io lo Schicchi con altra voce e forma!
> «Io falsifico in me Buoso Donati,
> testando e dando al testamento norma!»
> O gente! questa matta bizzarria
> che mi zampilla dalla fantasia
> è tale da sfidar l'eternità!

[On the head | the nightcap! | On the face | the kerchief | Between nightcap and kerchief a nose | that seems to be that of Buoso but instead is mine, | because in the place of Buoso it is I! | I, Schicchi with another voice and shape! | «I falsify in myself Buoso Donati, | Dictating and giving to the will good form!» | O people! This mad caprice | That springs from my fantasy | Is enough to defy eternity!]

This is the most direct quotation of the *Inferno* in *Gianni Schicchi*, and it was clearly designed to stand apart from its immediate context. The alliteration, internal rhymes, and slightly convoluted diction of Dante's line «testando e dando al testamento norma» contrast with the more prosaic original verse by Forzano that surrounds it. Even more striking, in an aria dominated by rhymed quatrains and couplets, is Forzano's sudden attempt to imitate the three-line structure of Dante's *terza rima*. At the start of his invented tercet, the librettist rhymes «norma» with «forma», surely plucking the word from Dante's preceding description of Myrrah. He seems wary of tampering too much with the original and, in the process, produces a verse almost more 'Dantean' than Dante's own.

But even factoring in Schicchi's extraordinary powers of impersonation, this attempt to conjure up the voice of Dante may seem incredible. After all, the *Divina commedia* was written after the action of *Gianni Schicchi* takes place, and the character can't possibly be aware of the poet's post-mortem verdict on his crimes. We have thus arrived at an especially complex instance of what Michal Grover-Friedlander, in an essay on the opera, describes as «a backwards de-animation, as it were, from the perspective of death, an echo from the realm of shades».[47] Schicchi talks about resurrecting the voice of a corpse but, as he does so, he is simultaneously overtaken by another voice, 'echoing' from a future in which he himself is dead. Even more confoundingly, that second voice sounds, to the contemporary audience, like a voice from the distant past. As Schicchi himself warns us, the conceit is «bizarre» enough to «defy eternity».

This might seem considerable interpretive pressure to place on Forzano's poetry. And yet, his text inspired one of Puccini's strangest, most experimental, and violent arias. If Puccini's setting of «Firenze è come un albero fiorito» seemed to deflate Forzano's poetry, his response to «Si corre dal notaio» exaggerates its strange mechanics. And this is fitting. For the aria comes closer than any other moment in *Gianni Schicchi* to stating the opera's central nightmare. Is Gianni Schicchi's attempt to make a dead man speak in any way different from *Gianni Schicchi*'s attempt to revivify the Tuscan past? If Schicchi's sin is acting, and acting too convincingly, what does this say about the premises of realist opera?

Schicchi's aria appears to be composed of three main parts: a fast section in D major («Si corre dal notaio»), a transitional section in C-sharp minor («Ed il notaio viene»), and a slow concluding section in C minor («In testa la cappellina»). Andrew Davis has described the piece as a double aria, although his language betrays the difficulty of such an approach. The first formal movement «is not even close to being a slow movement or even a cantabile, let alone an adagio». Meanwhile, the final *cabaletta* «is 'slower', not faster, and thus opposite of the norm».[48] One could question the relevance of nineteenth-century prototypes for Puccini's «late style», but it might be more accurate to say that the composer is both engaging with and confounding stylistic conventions in a way that will prove characteristic of the aria as a whole. Alternately, and keeping in mind the strange, backwards movement of Forzano's text, one might say that what Puccini has

---

[47] See MICHAL GROVER-FRIEDLANDER, *Operatic Afterlives*, New York, Zone Books, 2011, p. 107.

[48] ANDREW DAVIS, *«Il trittico», «Turandot», and Puccini's Late Style*, Bloomington, Indiana University Press, 2010, p. 158. Original emphasis.

done is write a double aria in reverse. That is to say: the piece begins with a *cabaletta*, and moves crablike through a *tempo di mezzo* and toward a final adagio. This admittedly peculiar notion is supported by Puccini's odd harmonic plan. After all, the aria begins in D major and then slides down the chromatic scale in each successive section. Puccini, like any crowd-pleasing *fin-de-siècle* composer, loves to end passages a half-step higher than they began. But this carefully plotted process of tonal descent has no clear models.

The opening section of the aria gives the listener scant hints of the complexities to come. As the aria begins, Schicchi is busy giving his instructions to the relatives. He behaves rather like a stage director – telling his actors not just what to say, but how to say it:

> Si corre dal notaio:
> (*veloce, affannato*)
> «Messer notaio, presto!
> Via da Buoso Donati!
> C'è un gran peggioramento!
> Vuol fare testamento!
> Portate su con voi le pergamene,
> presto, messere, presto, se no è tardi!...»

[You run to the notary: | (*fast, breathless*) | «Master notary, quick! | Away to Buoso Donati's! | There's been a great decline in his health! | He wants to make his will! | Bring your parchments with you, | Quick, master, quick, or it will be too late!...»]

As critics have long noted, Puccini sets these lines in the style of an eighteenth-century patter song (see 49+$^{1-23}$). Julian Budden speaks of «modernized Paisiello»,[49] and, at the premiere, Matteo Incagliati described «an irresistible page of buffo from the 1700s, revived in modern taste and spirit».[50] The fast tempo, circular runs up and down a D Major scale, and uneven phrase lengths all depict a character in a state of breathless confusion and anxiety.

Although the tempo does not change in the second section, the affect does. The mode shifts from major to minor, and the orchestra's frantic runs and tremolos are stilled by an extended, 26-bar tonic pedal (see 50^{+7-32}). A funeral drum, sigh figures played by a full choir of double reeds, and nervous *pizzicato* strings all set the scene for Schicchi's deception:

> Ed il notaio viene.
> (*pittoresco*)
> Entra: la stanza

---

⁴⁹ BUDDEN, *Puccini*, p. 411.

⁵⁰ «Il canto si svolge con una comicità di rara eleganza – e può dirsi una irresistibile pagina buffa del '700, rinnovata di gusto e di spirito moderno». INCAGLIATI, *L'arte di Puccini*.

> è semioscura,
> dentro il letto intravede
> di Buoso la figura!

[And the notary comes. | He enters: the room | is half dark, | in the bed he glimpses | Buoso's form!]

In contrast to the previous (and following) scenes of mimicry, the libretto is clear that Schicchi's voice here should be «*naturale*». Then again, there is nothing natural about Puccini's setting of the final two lines (see Ex. 4.6). Twice, Schicchi's line rises slowly up a cycle of widely spaced intervals (C-sharp, G-sharp, B). He begins the cycle a third time and falls silent, only to have his melody completed – and then echoed, in a fourth cycle – by muted trumpets. Puccini's style here – upward leaps, melodic repetitions, muted brass – is a calculated imitation of the opening of the Zia Principessa's aria in *Suor Angelica*. It too is in C-sharp minor, and it too describes strange goings-on in a darkened room:

> Di frequente, la sera,
> là, nel nostro oratorio,
> io mi raccolgo...

> Nel silenzio di quei raccoglimenti,
> il mio spirito par che s'allontani
> e s'incontri con quel di vostra madre
> in colloquî eterei e arcani!

Ex. 4.6. PUCCINI, *Gianni Schicchi*, 50$^{+21\text{-}33}$.

(continues)

Ex. 4.6. (conclusion)

[Often, in the evening | There, in our chapel, | I meditate... | In the silence of those meditations, | My spirit seem to move off | and encounters that of your mother | in ethereal and arcane conversations.]

The acoustic connection between these scenes makes sense dramatically, for Schicchi, like the Zia Principessa, is about to summon up the spirits of the dead.

Now comes «In testa la cappellina», the third and longest section of the aria, in which Schicchi's voice is overtaken by that Dantean echo. The tempo slows to less than half its original speed, and Schicchi's slithering, ominous melody unfurls against a hushed, ticking background of *staccato* winds and *pizzicato* strings (see Ex. 4.7). This is the only extended minor mode section in *Gianni Schicchi*, and critics have had some difficulty describing it. For Julian Budden, Schicchi's music has «the slink of the modern ballroom».[51] Mosco Carner, in contrast, hears «a spectral march», and an «automaton-like progression of desiccated chords».[52] Michele Girardi allows room for both perspectives: «The piece is a touch sinister, and, moving in a slow fox-trot, seems like something out of a smoky Berlin cabaret. In reality, it is the grotesque funeral march for a dead man who has been revived».[53]

So, is «In testa la cappellina» a foxtrot, or is it a march? On the one hand, it lacks the tell-tale syncopations of the former genre, whose style Puccini

---

[51] BUDDEN, *Puccini*, p. 411.

[52] CARNER, *Puccini*, p. 432.

[53] GIRARDI, *Puccini*, p. 432.

Ex. 4.7. Puccini, *Gianni Schicchi*, 50^{+40}-51^{+8}.

(continues)

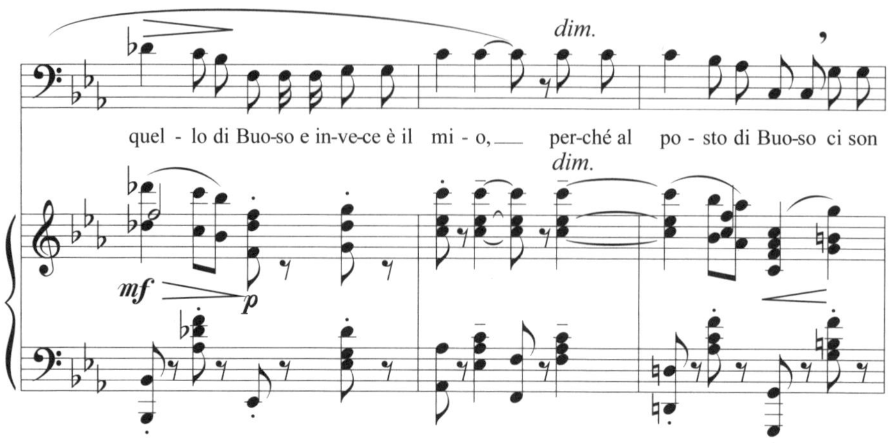

Ex. 4.7. *(conclusion)*

had rendered faithfully in one of *La rondine*'s duets («Perché mai cercate»). On the other hand, the playful, seductive, chromatically inflected melody – constantly stopping, starting, slowing down – is hardly march-like, and the orchestra's extended harmonies do sound quite like jazz. In a sense, choosing between these different options may be less important than noting the very inscrutability of the question: an aria that began with a clear imitation of eighteenth-century style has ended on much stranger, and seemingly more contemporary, turf. What is more, neither a foxtrot nor a jazz-inflected march may seem like an appropriate style for setting the hallowed words of Dante. If «Firenze è come un albero fiorito» flirted with «the sin of *La rondine*», «In testa la cappellina» revels in it.

Both foxtrots and marches are musics for propelling bodies, and it would be grotesque to perform either one alone. Indeed, the real perversity of «In testa la cappellina» resides in its image of a character both leading and following, a strange spectacle that renders the complex double-animation described in Forzano's text, while also capturing its attempt to blur the identities of Schicchi and Buoso.

> […] un naso
> che par quello di Buoso e invece è il mio…
> perché al posto di Buoso ci son io!
> Io lo Schicchi con altra voce e forma!
> «Io falsifico in me Buoso Donati […]

Preparing to put on another man's clothes, to climb into his very bed, Schicchi may begin to seem like Myrrah, the incestuous shade with whom he is paired in the *Inferno*. And yet, unlike that tragic figure, he seems only to be seducing himself.

Schicchi's onanistic dance ends with what the rhetoricians call an ejaculation. «O gente!», he cries out, «questa matta bizzarria | che mi zampilla nella fantasia | è tale da sfidar l'eternità!». The mechanical accompaniment drops away, the «desiccated chords» are replaced by a full complement of bowed strings, the tempo slows excruciatingly (Puccini includes the instructions *«cominciando ad allargare»*, *«ritardando»*, *«sostenendo»*, and *«allargando»* within the space of a mere five bars), and Schicchi's line climaxes on a sustained high G (the highest note he sings in the opera), supported by a ferocious dominant-seventh chord, made harsh through added dissonances (see $51^{+14\text{-}19}$). One critic described a «cadence of extraordinary effect», and his reaction was surely amplified by that of the onstage audience. All the other climactic exhortations we have considered – Rinuccio's «Basta con gli odi gretti e coi ripicchi!» in «Firenze è come un albero fiorito», the speaker's «ma voi che siete | all'altra sponda» in *Morire?* – are greeted by stony silence. Schicchi's, however, provokes an astonishing response.

«Come strozzati dalla commozione i parenti attorniano Gianni Schicchi; gli baciano le mani e le vesti» (As if choked with emotion the relatives surround Gianni Schicchi; they kiss his hands and his garments), the score indicates.[54] This is weird behavior, more appropriate for a saint than a low-level sinner, and Puccini's music makes it even weirder. First, the full ensemble chants «Schicchi!» three times, at the fastest tempo we have heard in this scene, forcibly articulating a hard-earned tonic triad. Then, the voices break apart into phonic chaos. In the course of the next 19 measures, the relatives repeat Schicchi's name some 17 times, in ostinatos based on descending major seconds and (even less attractively) rising octaves. Against this hissing, yelping background – described by one early critic as «a chorus of poisoned laughter» – other characters chant texts that make very little sense.[55] Some of them merely intone catalogues of their own names; Simone, for example, is given the line, «Caro Gherardo, Marco, Zita, Ciesca, Nella, Gerardo, Zita, Betto». Others cry out, «O giorno d'allegrezza! La burla ai frati è bella!» (Oh, day of happiness! The trick on the monks is beautiful!) At the end of the scene, everyone comes together to exclaim, inappropriately, «Com'è bello l'amore fra i parenti!» (How beautiful is love among relatives!). Forzano instructs that *«I parenti si abbracciano, si baciano con grande effusione»* (The relatives embrace and kiss one another with great ef-

---

[54] This stage direction, taken from the score, does not appear in the first published libretto.

[55] DAMON, *The New Work of Puccini*.

fusion) and, once again, Puccini makes the action even more unusual. His newly formed choir sings a melody, if you can call it that, that circles up and down the first three pitches of a whole tone scale. It sounds as if we are listening to a group of school children, or an unprecedentedly inept performance of *The Mikado*.

This scene far exceeds the apparent dramatic situation, straining to its limits the opera's credibility. At first glance, the Donati seem to have been mesmerized, behaving as if the puppets of Schicchi's demonic force. This interpretation, though, does not fully account for what Forzano insists is the overwhelming emotionality of the scene. Indeed, what makes the ensemble strange is its admixture of affect and automation. Perhaps, then, it is better to assume that the relatives have been overwhelmed and rendered incoherent by something miraculous: the return of their dead relative. The course of Schicchi's aria – starting with those eerie echoes of the Zia Principessa's narrative, and ending with his own mesmeric dance – has certainly been pointing in that direction. And given that we are dealing with an opera inspired by a Christian allegory, we might note some telling echoes of biblical scenes of resurrection. Schicchi's strange request to have a kerchief placed on his face – something you would normally only do for a man already dead – recalls John's account of Lazarus: «And he that was dead came forth, bound hand and foot with graveclothes: and his face was bound about with a napkin» (11:44). Meanwhile, Forzano's hyperbolic stage directions bring to mind two verses in Luke's parable of the Prodigal Son. «But when he was yet a great way off, his father saw him, and had compassion, and ran, and fell on his neck, and kissed him». «For this my son was dead, and is alive again; he was lost, and is found. And they began to be merry» (15:20 and 24).

Schicchi's power to summon up dead Buoso may well seem Christlike, but there is nothing pious about the Donati's reaction to his narrative of resurrection. Paying attention not just to their words and actions, but to the sibilant and percussive sound they produce, we may hear an even more telling reference to the world of Dante. The poet famously claimed he needed «rime aspre e chiocce» (harsh and rasping verses) to describe the lowest levels of the Inferno, and the chaotic noise of his underworld is one of its most distinctive features:

> Diverse lingue, orribili favelle,
> parole di dolore, accenti d'ira
> voci alte e fioche, e suon di man con elle [...] (III, 25-27)

[Unfamiliar tongues, horrendous accents, | words of suffering, cries of rage | voices loud and faint, the sound of slapping hands]

Peering down into Gianni Schicchi's trench, Dante hears:

> lamenti saettaron me diversi,
> che di pietà ferrati avean li strali;
> ond'io li orecchi con le man copersi. (XXIX, 43-45)

[strange arrows of lament, their shafts │ with pity at their tips, pierced me, │ so that I pressed my hands against my ears.]

Puccini's awful chorus might well be described as an attempt to render these sounds in music. Such an interpretation helps make sense of many of the strangest aspects of his scene as a whole: Schicchi's backwards double aria, the carefully plotted chromatic descent, the lapse into Dante's own language. By attempting to bring Buoso back to life, both Schicchi and the Donati family seem instead to have joined the miser in Hell.

Right-wing critics were prepared to follow them. Echoing the ensemble's crazed repetitions of Schicchi's name, as well as, tellingly, Dante's onomatopoeic word «chiocce», «L'idea nazionale» proclaimed:

And we arrive at *Gianni Schicchi, Schicchi!* These two syllables, Tuscanly cracking, are truly a fresh call, all ours, all Italian, in the operatic doldrums of the last years. Our people, our Florence, our accents, clear Italic gaiety! Finally![56]

«Clear Italic gaiety» might seem a strange way to described Puccini's chorus. But if the critic for «L'idea nazionale» seems to have missed the implicit moral of *Gianni Schicchi*'s scene of conjuring – beware of charismatic rhetoricians claiming to revive the dead! – that may be because he had other «cries of rage» ringing in his ears.

On the evening of 11 January 1919, just as *Il trittico* was receiving its premiere in Rome, Leonida Bissolati walked onto the stage of La Scala and delivered a speech in which he attempted, once again, to make the case for peace. Mussolini was in the audience that night, as was Marinetti, and the crowd was restless:

For a few minutes Bissolati was allowed to go on, seemingly undisturbed by the confused murmur of the hall. Then at a given moment, as if an invisible baton had given the sign, the infernal symphony began. Squeaks, shrieks, whistles, grumbles, nearly human, and all the thinkable counterfeits of the wild pack's howling made up the bulk of the sound wave; but a human, nay, a patriotic cry became distinguishable now and then and ruled the inarticulate mass with the rhythm of a brutal march. [...]

---

[56] «E siamo a *Gianni Schicchi, Schicchi!* Queste due sillabe, toscanamente schioccanti, sono veramente un richiamo fresco, tutto nostro, tutto italiano, in questa grigia operistica degli ultimi anni. Gente nostra, Firenze nostra, accenti nostri, chiara gaiezza italica! Finalmente!». «L'idea nazionale», *Il successo di Puccini*.

Now suddenly Bissolati recognized Mussolini in the chorus: that unmistakable voice, dishearteningly wooden, peremptorily insistent, like the clacking of castanets.

He turned his head to the friends who were nearest to him and said in a low voice: «*Quell'uomo no!*» – «I will not fight with that man!»[57]

Bissolati's silencing soon entered both left- and right-wing mythology as the first 'official' act of Fascist violence. The account quoted above, with its extraordinary sensitivity to sonorous detail, was written in 1937 by Giuseppe Antonio Borgese: a writer and scholar then living in exile in the United States, where he taught at prominent universities and married a daughter of Thomas Mann.[58] A skilled, if hardly neutral writer, Borgese might seem an untrustworthy historian, but the literary and historical resonances of his language are very much to the point. After all, his influential study of the rise of Fascism began with an extended discussion of Dante, the first Italian who had «distorted the soul of his people, urging it to dislike whatever it had or might have had, and to love a goal which nature and history reproved».[59] If the poet's «infernal symphony» seemed to reemerge on the stages of Italy in January 1919, it was with a grim, you might almost say Dantean, justice. The right-wing press could not have been happier. «And may *Gianni Schicchi* return from Hell!», screamed «L'idea nazionale». «Long live *Gianni Schicchi*!».[60]

---

[57] Giuseppe Antonio Borgese, *Goliath: The March of Fascism*, New York, Viking Press, 1937, p. 143. This passage is also quoted in Thompson, *The White War*, p. 372.

[58] Given the musicality and drama of Borgese's text, it may be worth mentioning that he wrote one opera libretto, for Roger Session's *Montezuma*. The draft of the libretto was completed in 1941, four years after Borgese published his history of fascism.

[59] Borgese, *Goliath*, p. 24.

[60] «E torna dall'Inferno *Gianni Schicchi*! Vive *Gianni Schicchi*!». «L'idea nazionale», *Il successo di Puccini*.

MECHANISM, TRADITION, *TURANDOT*

Not long before he died, Puccini summoned the writer Giuseppe Adami to his home. Ostensibly he hoped to discuss their ongoing revisions to *Turandot*'s libretto, but he also wanted to inform his collaborator of plans for a subsequent opera, one that he would not live long enough to pursue in earnest. In his memoirs, Adami narrates the encounter with palpable excitement:

Immediately, I ran to Viareggio. He spoke. I knew what he would have desired. The Chinese lacquers that cover eighteenth-century Venetian folding screens, the pompous robes that disguise the old Venetian masks as grotesque imperial ministers: these had fascinated the Maestro, guiding his thoughts toward the gilded surfaces of San Marco.

The new work would have had Venice at its base. But not, absolutely not, the nauseating Venice of face powders, beauty spots, and lorgnettes. A Venice full of pathetic, moving, poetic hues: perfumed like a terrace covered with hanging flowers; dark and gloomy like water beating against the smooth marbles of a mysterious canal.

At a certain point he opened a drawer and pulled out a French magazine that throbbed with naked women. He leafed through it slowly, stopping at a page that contained an audaciously suggestive image. And he handed it to me: Venice. A remote canal, bathed in light. A large window with protective grates. Behind it, clinging to the bars for all to see, a wild-haired nude girl, who arched her supple body in a provocative offering to a young boatman resting below, twisting with spasms, his arms stretched out toward the elusive vision.[1]

---

[1] «Corsi subito a Viareggio. Si parlò. Seppi quello che avrebbe desiderato. Le laccature cinesi che coprivano i settecenteschi paraventi veneziani, i paludamenti pomposi che camuffavano da grotteschi ministri imperiali le antiche maschere lagunari, avevano affascinato il Maestro, guidando il suo pensiero verso le dorature di San Marco. La nuova opera doveva aver per sfondo Venezia. Ma non, per carità, la stucchevole cipria coi néi e l'occhialino. Una Venezia piena di riflessi patetici, commoventi, poetici, profumati come i fiori pendenti da un'altana, o cupi e torbidi come lo sciabordare dell'acqua contro i marmi levigati di un rio misterioso. A un certo punto trasse da un cassetto una rivista francese palpitante di nudi femminili. La sfogliò lentamente, fermandosi a una pagina che recava un quadro audacemente suggestivo. E me la

For Adami, this anecdote was a tale of genius at work and great opportunities tragically cut short. It is not difficult, though, to imagine why his story has not found its way into the secondary literature. A specifically Venetian context for *Turandot*, the romantic sheen of an unwritten masterpiece: these are appealing notions. But not when they also remind us of all the aspects of Puccini that have made us most uncomfortable: his exploitative treatment of women, his susceptibility to kitsch.[2]

Adami's narrative does, however, resemble another passage in his book, and one that is considerably better known. It too concerns Puccini's final opera, a meeting between the composer and his poets, a domestic interior, and a peculiar source of inspiration:

We came to Bagni di Lucca to read Puccini the first draft of the libretto. He was waiting for us there with a surprise. The reading took place at the villa of Baron Fassini, who had spent many years at the Italian Embassy in China, and his house was decorated with every sort of *chinoiserie*. And as soon as the manuscript was placed on a little lacquer table, the silence was broken, as if with a magic spell, by the voice of a music box playing the ancient Imperial Hymn, with the solemnity of a sacred and august ceremony. We were astonished, everybody laughed, and Giacomo, who had prepared the trick, was joyful and satisfied. In his hands, the notes of this Hymn would later become the vast chorale that closes the second act.[3]

This anecdote is frequently cited as evidence of Puccini's dedicated realism but read alongside Adami's other story, it suggests an image of a composer inspired less by the real than by the uncanny, of a man fascinated with the strange magic of lithographs and music boxes, those slightly disreputable technologies of reproduction that nonetheless seem able to conjure distant lands. This is a man, after all, who collected racecars and motorboats, and whose decorating tastes combined exotic grace with modern

---

porse: Venezia. Un rio remoto, battuto dalla luna. Una grande finestra armata d'inferriata. E, dietro, in piena luce, aggrappata alle sbarre, una fanciulla scapigliata e ignuda che inarcava il suo corpo flessuoso in procace offerta a un ragazzo rematore che sostava là sotto, torcendosi di spasimo, con le braccia protese verso quella visione inafferrabile». GIUSEPPE ADAMI, *Il romanzo della vita di Giacomo Puccini*, Milan, Rizzoli, 1944, pp. 264-265.

[2] The classic discussion of Puccini in these terms is MOSCO CARNER, *Puccini: A Critical Biography*, New York, Knopf, 1958.

[3] «La prima stesura della trama ci recammo a leggergliela a Bagni di Lucca dove egli ci aspettava con una sorpresa. La lettura avvenne alla villa del barone Fassini, che era stato per molti anni in Cina addetto alla nostra Ambasciata e che aveva arredata la sua casa con ogni sorta di cineserie. Ed ecco che appena fu deposto il manoscritto su un tavolinetto laccato, ruppe il silenzio come per incanto la chiara voce di un cariglione che suonava l'antico Inno Imperiale con la solennità di una cerimonia sacra ed augurale. Stupore nostro, risate dei presenti, gioia soddisfatta di Giacomo che aveva preparato la trovata. Le note di quell'Inno diventarono più tardi in mano sua il vasto corale che chiude il secondo atto». ADAMI, *Il romanzo della vita*, p. 241.

trickery. Describing Puccini's final home, Julian Budden notes «the number of new-fangled gadgets: the aerial for radio reception, the automatic sprinklers that operated from the trees, several of which were hung with Chinese lanterns, the entrance door opened by remote control».[4]

In the context of my own study, Puccini's music box might be said to combine aspects of both the phonograph (as discussed in Chapter Two) and the radio (as discussed in Chapter Three). On the one hand, it offers a promise of objectivity, of seemingly unmediated access to long dead sounds. On the other, it introduces, «as if with a magic spell», geographically remote voices into a domestic space. Simultaneously impersonal and enchanted, the music box seems a technology capable of reconciling the claims of *verismo* opera with the poetics of distance explored in Puccini's later works.

But unlike the fragile, fleeting voices that we observed in Puccini's «radiophonic» operas, the song of the music box is described as vast, ceremonial, and solemn; the music it brings its listeners is cold, inhuman, dead. For many critics, this is how the operatic voice itself had begun to sound by the 1920s. Adorno, for example, suggested that, as technologies of mass dissemination, the phonograph and the radio worked together to empty opera of any vital meaning. «The intellectually advanced public», he wrote in 1954, «is almost no longer capable of responding immediately or spontaneously to a limited store of works, which have long since sunk into the living-room treasure-chests of the petite bourgeoisie, like Raphael's paintings, abused through innumerable reproductions».[5] These phrases cast an ironic light on the world so lovingly evoked in Adami's memoir: the lithograph, the little drawer.

Juxtaposing Adami with Adorno, we arrive at a paradoxical image: Puccini embracing the very technologies that would lead to opera's demise. Perhaps it is no surprise, then, that the composer's name appears frequently in narratives of the death of opera. A trope linking the composer's death, his final, incomplete masterpiece, and the end of the Italian lyric tradition has itself been endlessly reproduced:

As he reached the conclusion of Liù's death scene, Toscanini laid down his baton and said, in effect (he has been quoted variously): «The opera ends here, because at this point the Maestro died. Death was stronger than art». The opera ends here. Toscanini might have been speaking not just of Puccini's last work but of Italian opera in general.[6]

---

[4] Julian Budden, *Puccini: His Life and Works*, Oxford, Oxford University Press, 2002, pp. 419-420.

[5] Theodor Adorno, *Bourgeois Opera*, in *Opera through Other Eyes*, ed. by David J. Levin, Stanford, Stanford University Press, 1993, pp. 25-43: 40-41.

[6] Quoted in William Ashbrook and Harold Powers, *Puccini's «Turandot»: The End of the Great Tradition*, Princeton, Princeton University Press, 1991, p. 3.

This assessment by William Weaver is quoted at the outset of William Ashbrook and Harold Powers' book on the opera, and it is repeated almost verbatim in two of the most important recent studies of Puccini's art. According to Michele Girardi, «Puccini died without leaving heirs. Liù's death scene [...] marked the end of a certain way of composing opera in Italy: this type of opera was dying, attacked on all sides by other types of theater that competed for the same audience».[7] Similarly, for Budden, «With *Turandot* a tradition of Italian opera that had obtained for more than three centuries came to an end. [...] Puccini alone succeeded in pulling the age-old communal tradition of Italian opera into the post-war world, due to that power of self-renewal he shared with Verdi. But alas, there was no-one to follow him».[8]

As Ashbrook and Powers exclaim, «It is not so often that one can put so definite a *finis* to so long-standing a cultural manifestation, saying that with one last Work and the death of its Creator it was all effectively over».[9] But what does it mean for one opera to occupy a position so extraordinary? For Ashbrook and Powers, the answer is clear. With largely unironic capital letters, they describe *Turandot* as «the last Monument in the last Golden Century of one of the world's Great Traditions of musical theater».[10] Puccini, they imply, gathered together all of opera's remaining shards, and recast them in a sort of glowing reliquary. But to treat the death of Italian opera, and the terminal status of *Turandot*, as foregone conclusions is to erase a dimension of self-reflexivity – indeed, of struggle – from Puccini's final work. It discourages us from posing more nuanced questions about the composer's engagement with the past, or with his present moment.

This chapter asks how *Turandot* stages its own relationship with the death of opera, using Puccini's music box as a window onto larger issues concerning mechanism and the Italian canon. As in the previous chapter, I suggest that Puccini's lifelong engagement with questions of sound and realism might serve as a new vantage point from which to consider the politics of the composer's late operas. Although it is becoming increasingly common to assert that there is something 'fascist' about *Turandot*, I am suspicious of over-easy equations between political and operatic spectacle. Instead, I aim to uncover an anxiety about technology and preservation that haunted many of the more eccentric cultural projects in Mussolini's Italy and that was also given voice in Puccini's final work.

---

[7] MICHELE GIRARDI, *Puccini: His International Art*, trans. by Laura Basini, Chicago, University of Chicago Press, 2000, p. 487.

[8] BUDDEN, *Puccini*, pp. 472-473.

[9] ASHBROOK and POWERS, *Puccini's Turandot*, p. 11.

[10] ASHBROOK and POWERS, *Puccini's Turandot*, p. 3.

I

We might as well begin with politics. In her book *Fascist Spectacle*, Simonetta Falasca-Zamponi argues that Italian opera and Italian fascism drink from a common fount. Describing Mussolini's colonial campaign, she writes:

In a country whose popular culture was fully rooted in opera [...] the narrative construction of the Ethiopian conflict contained all elements able to capture people's imagination. The African story, with its moral drama and its repertoire of clichés, including bombastic solemnity, sentimentalism, and noble passions, appealed to what Antonio Gramsci once called the Italians' «melodramatic taste», their operatic conception of life. If, as many affirm, the time of the Ethiopian war witnessed the Italians' utmost support for the regime, some of this support can be explained through reference to the narrative structure of the event.

After all, Mussolini's charisma and oversized gestures led to depictions of him as an «opera star», and the connection Falasca-Zamponi draws between opera and politics, as two different modes of spectacle, seems intuitively just.[11] Writers on opera, however, have tended to disagree. For Michael Steinberg, «Opera, most specifically Italian opera, plays a surprisingly scant role in and for the fascist regime».[12] Similarly, Richard Taruskin cites a memorandum by Mussolini to make the case that opera was a passé form with little value for the new government. The old, despised Italy (Taruskin argues) was represented by emotive tenors like Enrico Caruso. The future lay in the collective discipline of orchestral music: in the «extravagantly vivid nationalism» of Respighi's suites, and in the second-order dictatorship of Toscanini.[13]

Taruskin overlooks much in his account. As was observed in the preceding chapter, Beniamino Gigli's recording of Puccini's *Inno a Roma* suggests how easily the traditional resources of Italian lyricism could be made to serve the aims of the Fascist government; and, in fact, opera was extensively patronized by Mussolini. One thinks of the transformation, in 1928, of the private Teatro Costanzi into the nationalized Teatro Reale dell'Opera, or of the 392 operas staged across Italy as part of the Italian

---

[11] SIMONETTA FALASCA-ZAMPONI, *Fascist Spectacle: The Aesthetics of Power in Mussolini's Italy*, Berkeley, University of California Press, 1997, p. 178.

[12] MICHAEL STEINBERG, *The Politics and Aesthetics of Operatic Modernism*, «Journal of Interdisciplinary History», XXXVI, 2006, pp. 629-648: 635.

[13] RICHARD TARUSKIN, *The Oxford History of Western Music*, IV, Oxford, Oxford University Press, 2005, pp. 748-751: 750. Other important discussions of music and Italian fascism include BEN EARLE, *Luigi Dallapiccola and Musical Modernism in Fascist Italy*, Cambridge, Cambridge University Press, 2013; HARVEY SACHS, *Music in Fascist Italy*, London, Weidenfeld and Nicolson, 1987; and FIAMMA NICOLODI, *Musica e musicisti nel ventennio fascista*, Florence, Discanto, 1984.

Musical Summer of 1938.[14] Money tells another part of the story. The fascist «opera train», described in more detail below, was allotted a fifth of the total budget of the Opera Nazionale Dopolavoro during the depths of the Depression.[15] Between 1933 and 1943, Mascagni was the single largest recipient of the Ministry of Popular Culture's funds.[16] Yet although these statistics are telling, they should not simply send us running back to the generalities of Falasca-Zamponi's study, which tell us little about the complex negotiations enacted in specific works.

Few operas, in this context, would seem more rewarding than *Turandot*. At first glance, it appears utterly remote from the world of power: based on a whimsical eighteenth-century play, steeped in extravagant *chinoiserie*, reliant on the conventions of fairy-tales. Yet it is also quite easy to read *Turandot* as a political allegory, one consistent with fascism's own narrative of the degradation of post-World War I Italy, and of Mussolini's heroic rise.[17] Such an interpretation might begin with the opera's setting: an ancient imperial capital that has, frankly, seen better days; a city dominated by a massive staircase that echoes Rome's Campidoglio, its traditional seat of civic government. Against this backdrop, Puccini's characters appear as familiar interwar types. There is the emperor Altoum, a leader who (like Vittorio Emanuele III and Pius XI) possesses great symbolic, but little practical authority. There are his ministers – bookish, effeminate, and wedded to past ways, as urban liberal-democrats were (and, alas, still are) thought to be. There is the very modern-seeming crowd, as violent as it is irrational and easily swayed. There is Turandot herself, embodying contemporary anxieties about the so-called «donna-crisi», an unnatural lesbian and usurper of male power.[18] And there is, of course, the manly, audacious, and clever prince Calaf, who

---

[14] For one especially useful discussion of popular uses of opera during the fascist regime, see EMANUELA SCARPELLINI, *Organizzazione teatrale e politica del teatro nell'Italia fascista*, Milan, LED, 2004. Many of Scarpellini's findings are cited in FALASCA-ZAMPONI, *Fascist Spectacle*, pp. 178-179. For an exhaustive history of the Costanzi and its mutations, see VITTORIO FRAJESE, *Dal Costanzi all'Opera: Cronache, recensioni e documenti*, Rome, Edizioni Capitolium, 1977.

[15] VICTORIA DE GRAZIA, *The Culture of Consent: Mass Organization of Leisure in Fascist Italy*, Cambridge, Cambridge University Press, 1981, p. 163.

[16] SCARPELLINI, *Organizzazione*, p. 158.

[17] My reading here draws on RICHARD M. BERRONG, *«Turandot» as Political Fable*, «Opera Quarterly», XI, 1995, pp. 65-75. For a more general consideration of the pull between allegory and orientalism in opera, see RALPH P. LOCKE, *Reflections on Orientalism in Opera and Musical Theatre*, «Opera Quarterly», X, 1993, pp. 49-64.

[18] On the figure of the «donna-crisi», see VICTORIA DE GRAZIA, *How Fascism Ruled Women: Italy 1922-1945*, Berkeley, University of California Press, 1992, pp. 212-213. The gender politics of the opera are discussed in PATRICIA JULIANA SMITH, *«Gli enigmi sono tre»: The [D]evolution of Turandot, Lesbian Monster*, in *En Travesti: Women, Gender Subversion, Opera*, ed. by Corinne E. Blackmer and Patricia Juliana Smith, New York, Columbia University Press, 1995, pp. 242-284.

obtains the blessing of the emperor, wins the respect of the masses, brings peace to the land, and successfully restores traditional gender relations.

This interpretation accounts for much in *Turandot*, although it is not unproblematic. For one thing, the character of Liù, the clear focus of the audience's sympathetic identification, has no role in it. For another, the opera's meanings are, as always, contingent on their embodiment in any given performance.[19] If you cast, as one recording did, a passionate Greek soprano in the role of the ice princess and assign Liù to a steely Nazi sympathizer, the allegorical structure becomes hopelessly subverted.[20] And it would seem churlish to despair entirely over the gender politics of the only opera that has ever allowed for a duet between Luciano Pavarotti and Peter Pears.[21]

Nonetheless, *Turandot* is thoroughly embedded in the emerging tropes of fascist discourse. Its elaborate thematic associating Calaf's ascendancy with day and Turandot and her reign with night recalls very similar uses of light and darkness in the propagandistic work of Alessandro Blasetti, fascist Italy's leading filmmaker.[22] A number of recent studies suggest that another of the opera's main polarities – the opposition of virile hero and demonized woman – is 'the' central node of fascist and proto-fascist rhetoric.[23] Even *Turandot*'s fairy-tale atmosphere may have a wider context. There is a suggestive affinity between Puccini's mix of contemporary politics and exotic fantasy and the «realismo magico» advocated (starting in the mid-twenties) by Massimo Bontempelli.[24] One of the most influential dramatists and critics during the fascist regime, Bontempelli encouraged writers to «invent the myths and fairy tales necessary for new times», to give contemporary moral lessons an objective, mystic force.[25] It would

---

[19] On the point, see CAROLYN ABBATE, *Music – Drastic or Gnostic?*, «Critical Inquiry», XXX, 2004, pp. 503-536; and *Wagner, Cinema, and Redemptive Glee*, «Opera Quarterly», XXI, 2006, pp. 597-611.

[20] The studio recording, featuring Maria Callas and Elisabeth Schwarzkopf and conducted by Tulio Serafin, was made in 1957, and is widely available on reissue from EMI Classics.

[21] See Zubin Mehta's 1972 studio recording of the opera (Decca 4582022), with Pears singing the role of Altoum.

[22] For a brief discussion of Blasetti in this context, see JEFFREY SCHNAPP, *Staging Fascism: 18BL and the Theater of Masses for Masses*, Stanford, Stanford University Press, 1996, pp. 57-58. See also *Sole: Soggetto, sceneggiatura, note per la realizzazione*, ed. by Adriano Aprà and Riccardo Redi, Rome, Di Giacomo, 1985.

[23] This is a central thesis of Falasca-Zamponi's study. See also BARBARA SPACKMAN, *Fascist Virilities: Rhetoric, Ideology, and Social Fantasy in Italy*, Minneapolis, University of Minnesota Press, 1996.

[24] Bontempelli's earlier theoretical writings are collected in *L'avventura novecentista*, Florence, Vallecchi, 1974. For a helpful survey of his ideas and influence in this context, see SCHNAPP, *Staging Fascism*, pp. 40-44.

[25] «Dovrà *inventare i miti e le favole necessari ai tempi nuovi*, come li inventò il vecchio medio-

be hard to imagine a better exemplar of this method than Puccini's final opera.

The explicitly fascist wing of the Italian press allowed readers to draw other sorts of connections between the opera and the regime. In the «Rivista illustrata del popolo d'Italia», a monthly publication edited by Mussolini's brother, photographs of *Turandot's mise-en-scène* – faceless crowds gathered in front of massive structures – seem calibrated to resonate with other pictures in the May issue of the journal: throngs of soldiers celebrating the dictator's visit to Tripoli, masses of Italians commemorating the «Natale di Roma». «Il giornale d'Italia», another propagandistic publication, included a section in their review of the *prima* entitled «A Miracle of Reconstruction», which described the opera's sets in language that seems lifted from their awed descriptions of actual fascist building projects:

The walls of the purple city in the first act, with the massive terraces, with the vast arcade adorned with unicorns, monsters, tortoises, with three colossal gates, [...] took us away suddenly from human things. So too the immense curtain of the second act [...] that, in the second scene, revealed the enormous, extremely opulent marble staircase of the Kingdom.[26]

Innocenzo Cappa, writing for the «Rivista illustrata», concluded his review with an outpouring of patriotic sentiment, blending martial rhetoric with claims for artistic immortality in a way that recalls the Duce's own speeches:

Yes, O Italians [...] we have lived together through hours that have been mixed of beauty and sadness, truth and dream, life and death. Giacomo Puccini has won his final battle, up to the point of making everyone, audience and interpreters, suffer, so that it felt as if we had touched the face and struck the heart of that divine pronouncement: Genius is immortal in the works that it creates, and it triumphs over death generation after generation, but it is defeated in individuals. Tragic truth, that would make us weep!... Glory unto Giacomo Puccini.[27]

---

evo romantico: ed esse poterono correre il mondo in mille forme». BONTEMPELLI, *L'avventura*, p. 26.

[26] «Le mura della città violetta al primo atto, con gli spalti massicci, col vasto loggiato adorno di liocorni, mostri, tartarughe, con tre porte colossali, [...] ha tratto subito al di là delle cose umane. Così la immensa tenda del secondo atto [...] che, al secondo quadro, ha discoperto la enorme, doviziosissima scalea di marmo della Reggia». See RAFFAELLO DE RENSIS, *La prima rappresentazione di «Turandot» di Puccini alla Scala*, «Il giornale d'Italia», 27 April 1926, p. 5.

[27] «Sì, o italiani [...] abbiamo vissuto insieme ore che furono commiste di bellezza e di dolore, di verità e di sogno, di vita e di morte. Giacomo Puccini ha vinto la sua ultima battaglia fino ad ottenere di farci soffrire tutti, spettatori ed interpreti, come se ci sentissimo sfiorare il volto e percuotere il cuore da quel divino annuncio: "Il genio è immortale nelle generazioni, ma ne è sconfitto negli individui". Tragica verità, che farebbe piangere! [...] Sia Gloria a Giacomo Puccini». INNOCENZO CAPPA, *«Turandot» alla Scala*, «La rivista illustrata del popolo d'Italia», May 1926, pp. 58-61: 61.

As for the composer's own politics, the evidence is inconclusive. It seems important to note that, in his final years, Puccini did not pursue the aggressively nationalist path that many right-wing critics thought he had set upon with *Gianni Schicchi*. The composer never wrote another *Inno a Roma*, and never produced another opera dedicated to the glories of the Italian past. It is unlikely that his projected Venetian opera – «dark and gloomy», «full of pathetic, moving, poetic hues» – would have presented the city in a light that flattered the dictatorship. And although Puccini did make approving references to Mussolini in a letter to Adami, his one official meeting with Il Duce seems to have left both parties frustrated.[28] Dying in 1924, two years after the March on Rome, but one year shy of Mussolini's final imposition of a dictatorship, may have spared Puccini from making any of the decisions that have marred the reputation of Mascagni and Respighi. Budden's assessment is typically judicious: «Certainly [Puccini] approved of the man who put an end to chaos in Italy, unaware that much of it was the Fascists' own making: and, as with all those who profess indifference to politics, he invariably gravitated towards the right».[29]

The most intriguing biographical link between Puccini and the regime comes in the person of Giovacchino Forzano. A playwright and librettist, director of operas and films, and Fascist cultural administrator, Forzano was heavily involved in Italian operatic life.[30] For Puccini he provided the libretti for *Suor Angelica* and *Gianni Schicchi*; he also crafted another text, never set, and staged *Turandot*'s premiere at La Scala. Historians, however, know Forzano best for two more eccentric projects. As mentioned briefly in the preceding chapter, he co-authored three plays with Mussolini: grand historical tragedies that present the lives of Julius Caesar, Napoleon, and Camillo Cavour as allegories of the dictator's own struggles.[31] Forzano was also the man behind the *carri di tespi*, train cars that transported actors and ambitious but easy-to-assemble sets throughout the Italian provinces, where productions were staged in village squares.[32] (The original *carro tea-*

---

[28] For recent discussions of Puccini's relationship with the dictator, see BUDDEN, *Puccini*, pp. 435-436; and GIRARDI, *Puccini*, pp. 434-435.

[29] BUDDEN, *Puccini*, p. 436.

[30] On Forzano, see C.E.J. GRIFFITHS, *The Theatrical Works of Giovacchino Forzano: Drama for Mussolini's Italy*, Lewiston, NY, The Edward Mellen Press, 2000; and *Il piccolo Marat: storia e rivoluzione nel melodramma verista*, ed. by Pietro and Nandi Ostali, Milan, Sonzogno, 1990.

[31] These plays are reprinted, along with an extensive introduction and facsimiles of relevant Mussolini letters, in GIOVACCHINO FORZANO, *Mussolini autore drammatico*, Florence, Barbera, 1954. For Forzano's memoir of a life spent among musical and political luminaries (he also met Lenin), see *Come li ho conosciuti*, Turin, ERI, 1957.

[32] Among numerous discussions of these cars, see especially SCARPELLINI, *Organizzazione*, pp. 114-20; DE GRAZIA, *Culture of Consent*, pp. 162-164; and SCHNAPP, *Staging Fascism*, pp. 17-22.

trale, which presented spoken plays, debuted in 1929. A much more popular *carro lirico*, devoted to the performance of Italian opera, was launched the following year). The thespian cars were massive affairs, involving an 890-square meter theatre, as many as 300 stage hands for lyric productions, and enough seating for two-thirds of the population of the towns they visited. Designed, according to one official publication, to inspire a «sense of the miraculous», the cars cleverly served the aims of fascist policy.[33] On the one hand, they aimed to interpolate provincial and lower-class audiences into a centrally planned vision of Italian culture. On the other hand, they advertised the technological mastery that was one of the central accomplishments of Mussolini's regime.

Pointing to Forzano's involvement in *Turandot*, Michael Steinberg and Suzanne Stewart-Steinberg conclude that «*Turandot* delivers opera to spectacle». «The delivery of opera to spectacle», they write, «is also its delivery to fascism, to its aesthetic of power through spectacle».[34] But by focusing on primarily biographical connections, Steinberg and Stewart-Steinberg might overstate something of *Turandot*'s place within the fascist theater of power. Looking through the repertory of the *carro lirico* (which traveled up through 1939) we find a predictable selection of nineteenth-century Italian classics; *La bohème* was programmed more frequently than any other work.[35] Yet despite its apparent propagandistic value, its apropos combination of the political and the miraculous, *Turandot* never made the list. This omission cannot solely be attributed to its scenic and vocal demands, or to a bias for sentimental operas. Two comparably challenging warhorses, *Aïda* and *La Gioconda*, were the second and third most programmed works. Of course, it is easy to imagine other reasons for *Turandot*'s omission. Perhaps its dissonances were deemed too harsh for provincial ears. Or perhaps it was too recent to be accorded the status of a masterwork.

Neither of these hypotheses, however, explain the opera's exclusion from what was perhaps Mussolini's most grandiose cultural project. In 1942, the regime planned to stage a huge Universal Exhibition, to show the world that, as an inscription written in giant font on each face of one of the exhibition buildings (collectively known as «EUR») puts it, Italians are «A PEOPLE OF POETS OF ARTISTS OF HEROES OF SAINTS OF THINKERS OF SCIENTISTS OF EXPLORERS OF

---

[33] Quoted in DE GRAZIA, *Culture of Consent*, p. 162.

[34] See MICHAEL P. STEINBERG and SUZANNE STEWART STEINBERG, *Fascism and the Operatic Unconscious*, in *Opera and Society in Italy and France from Monteverdi to Bourdieu*, ed. by Victoria Johnson, Jane F. Fulcher, and Thomas Ertman, Cambridge, Cambridge University Press, 2007, pp. 267-288: 276. This essay is somewhat at odds with Steinberg's own approach, discussed above.

[35] A list of all operas performed is included in SCARPELLINI, *Organizzazione*, p. 360.

SETTLERS». Although the war prevented the realization of this vision, the government did construct a network of boulevards, gardens, piazzas, and immense white halls in Rome's southern periphery: together, they form Italy's most chillingly visible reminder of its fascist past. The center of this whole complex was to have been a great theater, and plans were underway to celebrate its opening with a number of suitably ambitious dramatic cycles.[36] One of these was to have been a sequence of ten plays, which together illustrated the development of Italian drama from medieval mysteries through Pirandello. Along similar lines, if more impressively, twenty-four operas were scheduled: a cycle of twelve works designed again to trace the history of the form, and a cycle of twelve works by living authors to demonstrate its ongoing vitality. The program for the first eleven evenings in the former cycle reads as follows: opera through Monteverdi; opera in the eighteenth-century; Spontini's *La vestale*; Rossini's *Il barbiere di Siviglia* and *Guillaume Tell*; Bellini's *Norma*; Donizetti's *Poliuto*; Verdi's *La traviata* and *Falstaff*; Puccini's *La bohème*; a double bill of Mascagni's *Cavalleria rusticana* and *L'amico Fritz*. But in twelfth place, a place *Turandot* would seem destined to occupy, we find instead Pizzetti's Old Testament drama *Debora e Jaele*.

What, then, was the problem with *Turandot*? On the one hand, there are numerous aspects of the work – its blatant eroticism, its unsympathetic heroine, its lack of a proper ending – that might have made it seem a less than perfect bookend. On the other hand, I suspect that festival programmers (not unlike Pizzetti himself) must have been more comfortable with the Puccini of the 1890s – the bourgeois, liberal poet of «piccole cose» – than with the more confusing composer he had become in the 1910s and 20s. If Pizzetti's operas represented a clear, and comforting path forward, Puccini's later works seem more ambivalent about the relationship between tradition and innovation. Indeed, *Turandot*'s omission from the Exposition, and from the program of the *carro lirico*, might serve as an invitation to investigate ways in which the opera undermines the confidence of these large-scale projects. In what follows, I suggest that aspects of *Turandot* might be said to call the premises of the Universal Exposition and the *carro lirico* into question. To begin, it may be helpful to consider one final experiment in fascist spectacle.

II

Among the countless initiatives launched under Mussolini's rule, surely none was stranger than *18BL*, a three-act play staged for 20,000 spectators

---

[36] On these celebrations, see *ibid.*, pp. 299-313.

in 1934, on the banks of the Arno outside of Florence. The production employed, according to Jeffrey Schnapp:

2,000 to 3,000 amateur actors, an air squadron, an infantry brigade, a cavalry brigade, 50 trucks, 8 tractor plows, 4 field and machine-gun batteries, 10 field radio stations, and 6 photoelectric units in a stylized Soviet-style representation of the fascist revolution's past, present, and future. However titanic its scale, its ambitions were even greater: to launch a theater of the future, for the future, a modern theater 'for' and 'of' the masses that would once and for all end the crisis of bourgeois theater.[37]

The protagonist of this pageant was, infamously, an actual truck, shown participating in various key moments in the history of the fascist state.

General connections between the use of mass spectacle in *18BL* and *Turandot* have already been explored by Steinberg and Stewart-Steinberg, but in this context my interest lies with one specific scene, a corrupt celebration that takes place sometime in the dark days between the end of World War I and the March on Rome:[38]

An immense banquet table bearing the word PARLIAMENT appears atop the central hillock bathed in red light. Seated at the table is a group of geriatric politicians representing the liberal, socialist, and populist parties, as well as the Freemasons [...] A few minutes later, applause rings out. A socialist politician has stood up to begin his speech. Instead of a voice, however, the sound of a barrel organ issues from his mouth [...] playing the Dance of the Seven Veils from Richard Strauss's opera *Salomé* [...] The barrel organ churns away for several minutes, after which it begins to wind down as a newsboy cries out headlines announcing the foundation of fascist groups.[39]

For Schnapp, the combination of socialist rhetoric, Strauss opera, and mechanized music in this scene forges «a symbolic link between the menace of decadent sensuality and Marxian materialism [...] with its false promises of technico-mechanical utopia».[40] It is not the only instance of an association between empty, repetitive sound and 'outmoded' political speech in fascist art. In Blasetti's 1929 film *Sole*, the voices of characters who doubt fascist progress are at times replaced by the sound of chirping frogs. It is not difficult to imagine Leonida Bissolati's silencing at La Scala, discussed at the conclusion to the preceding chapter, as the 'real life' model for the scenes in both *Sole* and *18BL*.

---

37 SCHNAPP, *Staging Fascism*, pp. 7-8.

38 See STEINBERG and STEWART-STEINBERG, *Fascism and the Operatic Unconscious*, pp. 271-272.

39 SCHNAPP, *Staging Fascism*, pp. 71-72.

40 *Ibid.*, p. 91.

It may seem counterintuitive to stage a critique of «technico-mechanical utopia» in a work so obviously enamored with machinery and science. According to Schnapp, however, one of the main aims of *18BL* was to counter Soviet dreams of a fully mechanized, but (from the fascist perspective) soulless, society with another fantasy: that of technology placed in the service of «vague terms such as soul, spirit, beauty, heroism, individualism, and Latinity».[41] These latter values are easily associated with nineteenth-century opera, and it is possible to perceive an affinity here between *18BL* and the *carro lirico*, which attempted, quite literally, to fuse modern technology with the traditional powers of Italian art. But there is also an important difference here. The *carro lirico* presents the union of opera and technology as essentially transparent: new media are used to present old repertory, without any worry that the meanings of the canon might themselves be changed in the process. *18BL*, in contrast, seems much more anxious: worried enough about the relationship between mechanization and spirit to represent both its negative and positive potentials, embodied in the barrel organ and the hero truck. And it is here that *Turandot* enters the scene. It dwells on *18BL*'s technological «bad object», exploring the deathly aspects of technology and the mechanical aspects of the musical museum, teasing out the implications of marrying an operatic classic with a wind-up box.

As mentioned at the outset of this chapter, one of Puccini's earliest musical inspirations for *Turandot* was the mechanical music box owned by his friend the Baron Fassini. Three melodies from the box would find their way into the opera's score.[42] Scholars have long assumed that Puccini was looking for authentic Chinese folk material (he also consulted ethnomusicological texts), but I wonder if he was also drawn to the music box as an object in itself.[43] In *Il tabarro*, Puccini had written an extended passage of dissonant, *Pétrouchka*-like music to characterize the sound of a Parisian barrel-organ and, as discussed in the Introduction, as far back as *Madama Butterfly* he had attempted to recreate the actual sound of a Chinese music box. What is more, there are many other modernist works that use *chinoiserie* as a screen for the mechanical: think of wind-up characters like the Chinese teacup in Maurice Ravel's *L'Enfant et les sortilèges* and the Chinese conjurer in Erik Satie's *Parade*,

---

[41] *Ibid.*, p. 84.

[42] On Puccini's manipulation of these themes, see ASHBROOK and POWERS, *Puccini's «Turandot»*, pp. 94-95; and W. ANTHONY SHEPPARD, *Puccini and the Music Boxes*, «Journal of the Royal Musical Association», CXL, 2015, pp. 41-92. Sheppard's discussion of *Turandot* responds to an earlier, article version of my chapter.

[43] For a discussion of the philosophical and musical problems raised by music boxes, one deeply influential on my own account, see CAROLYN ABBATE, *Outside the Tomb*, in *In Search of Opera*, Princeton, Princeton University Press, 2001, pp. 185-246.

as well as the imperial Chinese courtiers in Igor Stravinsky's *Le Rossignol,* who are entranced by the sound of a nightingale machine. One critic at *Turandot's* premiere was on the right track when he suggested that «of real China there exists only that little bit that, used in Puccini's usual fashion, serves to add bizarre or strident tones, exotic or mechanical rhythms».[44]

The longest melody Puccini quotes from the music box is assigned, in the first act, to Ping, Pang, and Pong: the «old Venetian masks» disguised as «grotesque imperial ministers», who, in the allegorical reading of the plot, function as representatives of the outmoded liberal-democratic order. The ministers sing the melody on their first appearance in the opera and, like their political counterparts in *18BL* and *Sole,* they are busy instilling doubt: attempting, in this case, to dissuade Calaf from his heroic quest (see Ex. 5.1). Like the politicians in *18BL,* they go on far too long. The essentially

Ex. 5.1. PUCCINI, *Turandot,* I, 28[+1-10].

(continues)

---

44 «Di colorismo ambientale cinese ce n'è abbastanza per staccare *Turandot* dalle partiture anteriori dedicate alla espressione folkloristica di altri paesi. Ma chi osservi sotto le apparenze della pura materia, vedrà che di Cina vera e propria esiste solo quel poco che, usato puccinianamente, serve a raggiungere i toni bizzarri o stridenti, i ritmi esotici o meccanici, di cui ha bisogno il grottesco quando voglia essere tale». G. CESARE, quoted in «Musica d'Oggi», May 1926, p. 143.

Ex. 5.1. *(conclusion)*

pentatonic tune unfolds over the course of thirty bars and then, after a brief interruption by the Prince, repeats almost verbatim. The ministers are starting the melody for a third time when Turandot's servants call out «Silenzio, olà!», and abruptly cut them off.

The association of the ministers with mechanical music continues through the second act. The first scene of that act – in which Ping, Pang, and Pong lament the state of the empire and reflect, nostalgically, on lost time – was universally condemned by early critics. As they noted, accurately, Puccini had never before written music with such leisure and so little dramatic point. One way of making sense of the scene is to note how it anticipates the banquet in *18BL*. Both are lengthy meditations on past ways, interrupted by a heroic action: in the play, the founding of fascist leagues; in the opera, Calaf's trial and victory. Both are the only interior, domestic scenes in very public dramas.

As for the music box, it plays at the very heart of the scene, as the ministers' thoughts turn to a vanished idyll (see Ex. 5.2):

> Ho una casa nell'Honan
> con il suo laghetto blu
> tutto cinto di bambù...[45]

[I have a house in Honan | with a little blue lake | all girded with bamboo...]

Ex. 5.2. PUCCINI, *Turandot*, II, 9-10[+1].

(continues)

---

[45] All citations of the libretto refer to the edition edited by Eduardo Rescigno (Milan, Ricordi, 1988), which is based on the first published version of the text.

Ex. 5.2.

(continues)

Ex. 5.2. *(conclusion)*

The telltale sign here is the celesta, which chimes rocking eighth-note figures throughout the passage. But the music is excessively repetitive on almost every formal level. The basic generative cell is a directionless little motive that returns, again and again, to the fifth scale degree; the main melody itself is nothing more than a threefold repetition of this fragment. The structure of the passage as a whole is based on three repetitions, with only slight variation, of the initial melody. It is possible to hear other mechanical effects as well. After the first strophe comes to an end, there is a moment of silence and then a harp glissando. It sounds like the music box is winding up.[46]

There is another dimension to this scene, although one that will require us to wade briefly into the murky waters of operatic form. Ashbrook and Powers have argued that the whole of *Turandot* can be analyzed as a succession of double-arias, oscillating endlessly between moments of action and stasis, with passages of free declamation placed between more formalized *cantabiles* and *cabalettas*. For them it is this structural principle, inherited from Donizetti and early Verdi, that marks the opera as a monument to the Great Tradition.[47] This interpretation rings false to my ears, and Ashbrook and Powers offer no explanation as to why Puccini would suddenly embrace a formal logic in which he had exhibited little interest throughout his career,

---

[46] Although this passage in many ways resembles *Gianni Schicchi*'s «Addio Firenze», as described in the preceding chapter, the mechanical effects created by the celesta and the harp, as well as the lack of quasi-improvisatory ornamentation in the vocal line, produce an altogether colder piece.

[47] *Puccini's «Turandot»*, 12-38. For a more recent approach to *Turandot* in these terms, see ANDREW DAVIS, *«Il trittico», «Turandot», and Puccini's Late Style*, Bloomington, Indiana University Press, 2010, pp. 168-221.

and which had arguably taken its last gasps long before *Manon Lescaut*. But their reading does work, surprisingly well, for Act 2, Scene 1: a single four-part double-aria. In this interpretation, «Ho una casa nell'Honan» should be labeled the *cantabile*, and this seems right, given its repose, formal independence, and lyric affect. If this is the case, however, then the music allows for an uncomfortable association between nostalgia and mechanicity, on the one hand, and the Italian operatic tradition (as embodied in the most lyric moment of its most hallowed form), on the other. A formal gesture to the musical past is itself cast as an act of empty repetition.

A similar case might be made for «Non v'è in Cina», the scene's concluding section. As with «Ho una casa nell'Honan», this movement has a number of features in common with a traditional *cabaletta*: an accelerated tempo, long passages of unison singing. But if the *cabaletta* was traditionally a showcase for virtuoso display, here it is distorted through a number of intentionally ugly (froglike?) gestures: *falsetto* singing, hummed passages, wide leaps, a climactic bent pitch. The ministers' impotence is further underscored, I think, by an implicitly ironic relationship between this scene and the most obvious model for a male trio in the Italian repertoire, the heroic oath-taking in Rossini's *Guillaume Tell*.

III

Another passage that baffled early critics was «In questa reggia», Turandot's entrance aria in Act 2, Scene 2. This is the only music Turandot sings before presenting her three riddles in a sparse, dissonant duet with Calaf. As such, the aria bears a double burden: introducing the protagonist – who, quite unusually, has not sung during the first half of the opera – and explaining the psychology of a character whose motivations have up to this point been far from clear. Judging by the opening-night reviews, «In questa reggia» failed on both counts. For the «Rivista musicale italiana», an aria that should have revealed «the essence of Turandot's soul», instead «begins and unfolds, for a long stretch, like a cantilena or a lullaby».[48] The «Nuova antologia» found the vocal line similarly slight: «raw declamation lacking in ecstatic splendor».[49] In his play-by-play description of the work, the critic for «L'Ambrosiana» rushed over the aria to get to the enigma scene:

---

48 «Il lungo brano con il quale essa si presenta nell'azione, colla scena centrale del secondo atto, dove appunto dovrebbe concentrarsi, per così dire, l'essenza dell'anima di Turandot, comincia e si svolge per buon tratto con un andamento da cantilena, di ninna-nanna». MICHELE LESSONA, «*Turandot*» *di Giacomo Puccini*, «Rivista musicale italiana», XXXIII/2, 1926, pp. 239-247: 244.

49 «È aspra declamazione senza estatico splendore come nella invettiva ai barbari dopo il racconto del regno vinto ("In questa reggia or son mill'anni"... e poi "O principi che a lunghe carovane")». SAVERIO PROCIDA, «*Turandot*» *nel teatro di Puccini*, «Nuova antologia», 16 May 1926, pp. 180-188: 185.

For the first time we hear Turandot, evoking with mystery her vengeful fate, then proclaiming the three enigmas: solemn in the first, angry in the second, hissing like a wounded snake in the third.[50]

A very similar movement appears in the review published by «La stampa»: first a dismissal of «In questa reggia», then a celebration of the relative clarity of the following scene:

There is little interest in the first words of Turandot, in the middle of the second act. There is little interest in her narration of the reasons why she decided to refuse all contact with foreigners. But when the contest begins, and the torturous theme of the enigmas explodes in the orchestra, and the voice of the Princess vibrates with hate, and the orchestra provides a trembling comment on the dramatic action, we are at the best page in the opera and an important point in Puccini's art.[51]

For contemporary listeners, the modernistic enigma scene would seem to be the more 'challenging' of the two passages. But early critics took an exactly opposite approach.

Describing «In questa reggia» as blank or withholding, as somehow void of clear meaning, writers were perhaps responding to an affect that I again would call mechanical. (Indeed, it is tempting to say that Italian critics knew how to recognize, and condemn, machine *topoi*, but lacked a concrete vocabulary to pin their dislike to the music). The aria might be divided into two parts: the first, largely in F-sharp minor, involving Turandot's narration of the torture and murder of her ancestor Lo-u-ling; the second, in G-flat major, constructed around repetitions of the phrase «Mai nessun m'avrà». It is in the first section, in this account, that I hear another sort of music machine (see Ex. 5.3). The section is constructed around three ticking ostinato figures: first an eighth-note tonic-dominant pattern in F-sharp minor, played by the strings; then a 'white key' ostinato played by both strings and winds; then a reprise of the original ostinato, now with winds added, decorated with sixteenth-note figurations, and featuring the telltale

---

[50] «Udiamo per la prima volta Turandot evocare con mistero il proprio destino di vendicatrice e proclamare poi i tre enigmi; solenne nel primo, irosa nel secondo, sibilante come serpe ferita nel terzo». G.C. Paribeni, *«Turandot» di Giacomo Puccini*, «L'ambrosiana», 26 April 1926, p. 3.

[51] «Poco interessano le prime parole di Turandot, a metà del secondo atto. Poco interessa la narrazione ch'ella fa delle ragioni per le quali ha deciso di rifiutare ogni contatto con stranieri. Ma quando s'inizia la gara e prorompe in orchestra il tortuoso tema degli enigmi e nel canto della Principessa vibra l'odio e nell'orchestra è un fremente commento dell'attimo drammatico, siamo alla pagina migliore dell'opera e a un punto importante dell'arte di Puccini». A. della Corte, quoted in «Musica d'oggi», May 1926, p. 149.

Ex. 5.3. PUCCINI, *Turandot*, II, 44$^{+3\text{-}12}$.

chiming of glockenspiel, celesta, and harp. Turandot's line is not repetitive in the manner of «Ho una casa nell'Honan», but it lacks the spontaneity and naturalness that characterizes so many of Puccini's other arias. Mosco Carner describes the first section of «In questa reggia» as «chant-like and visionary» and notes that it «may be said to be, on the whole, more striking in its powerful dramatic characterization than in melodic invention».[52] Indeed, it would be hard to think of a less self-consciously inventive melody than the line that is sung over the first and third ostinati; entirely diatonic, it returns obsessively to C-sharp, obstinately refusing to develop. Similarly, the melody supported by the second ostinato is constructed out of a slight two-bar scalar figure, repeated again and again in rising sequence.

All this repetition does, however, support the meaning of the text: Turandot's commitment to act out – for all time, and at enormous cost – the murder of her ancestor. When the Princess looks for a metaphor to describe her tale of trauma and repetition, she comes close to imagining herself as an actual music box, a device for preserving and replaying sound:

> In questa Reggia, or son mill'anni e mille,
> un grido disperato risuonò.
> E quel grido, del fior della mia stirpe,
> qui nell'anima mia si rifugiò!

[In this kingdom, thousands and thousands of years ago, | a desperate cry resounded. | And that cry, of the flower of my ancestors, | here, in my soul, took refuge!]

And, as with the trio in the previous scene, psychological and musical repetition are linked to the return to an obsolete operatic style. As Ashbrook and Powers point out, «In questa reggia» is a textbook *aria di sortita*, a stodgy dramatic convention utterly at odds with the more naturalistic ways in which Puccini's characters normally enter the stage.[53] The classic *recitativo* opening of the aria – the voice begins over a sustained triad, declaims freely, and ends with a scalar ascent to the tonic – further emphasizes its conventionality. Turandot, like the ministers, is imprisoned in both the historical and the operatic past. But here the point is perhaps even clearer: the continuation of the Great Tradition is figured as both a senseless music machine, and as aberrant, hysterical compulsion.

---

[52] CARNER, *Puccini*, p. 458.

[53] ASHBROOK and POWERS relate «In questa reggia» to this convention, *Puccini's «Turandot»*, p. 14.

IV

The interplay of tradition and mechanicity that I have been exploring has been analyzed somewhat differently by Alexandra Wilson.[54] For her, these polarities are embodied in the opera's two female protagonists: warm, sentimental Liù represents the past strengths of Italian opera, while «mechanical Turandot» looks to a much colder future.[55] In crafting Turandot, Wilson argues, Puccini drew on tropes from Italian Futurism and other forms of modernism, noting that, «A new type of metallic and mechanistic heroine became a key part of the modernist renunciation of sentimental excess, a particularly effective vehicle through which to sever links to the past». Wilson suggests that this renunciation «is exemplified particularly clearly in the works of [the Futurist painter and writer] "Filia" (Luigi Colombo)», citing the hyperbolic titles of several of his texts from the 1920s to seal her case.[56]

Yet Wilson simplifies the history of Futurism's engagement with technology and the past. The art historian Christine Poggi, in contrast, sees a contrast between Filia's prewar poems – where «machines, weapons, and electricity appear as metaphors for the power to create anew» – and his work from the twenties and thirties, in which «the machine becomes an object, not of violent revolution, but of cultic (and erotic) veneration»:[57]

Although Filia's ideas of a «mechanical idol» were consistent with Futurism's «heroic», nonutilitarian enthusiasm for the machine, they may still seem astonishing in the context of its long-standing anticlericalism. They also reveal the extent to which postwar Futurism had abdicated its revolutionary demand to destroy the museums and the aura that attended traditional works of art. Whereas before the war Futurism had defined itself as an oppositional social force, the movement later strove to identify with the regime and to reassert the ritual function of art [...] If the dogmas of the Catholic Church, its authority, and its humanitarian ethics had been rejected, the quest for experience of otherworldly mysteries had not.[58]

In other words, Filia's postwar corpus – the work contemporaneous with *Turandot*, and that which Wilson cites – uses technology not as a means to renounce «sentimental excess», but rather as a way to build links, however tentative, with emotion, magic, and history.

---

[54] See ALEXANDRA WILSON, *A Suitable Ending?*, in *The Puccini Problem: Opera, Nationalism, and Modernity*, Cambridge, Cambridge University Press, 2007, pp. 185-220.

[55] *Ibid.*, p. 196.

[56] *Ibid.*, pp. 209-210.

[57] CHRISTINE POGGI, *Inventing Futurism: The Art and Politics of Artificial Optimism*, Princeton, Princeton University Press, 2009, p. 249.

[58] *Ibid.*, pp. 253-254.

The key term here, of course, is 'aura', defined by Walter Benjamin as «the unique apparition of a distance, however near it may be».[59] The common feature shared by religious objects and museum art, to cite a now familiar argument, aura was threatened by technologies of mass reproduction, a process that both fascism and the American culture industry sought speciously to counteract. *18BL* clearly partakes of this world. But, as Poggi suggests, the quest for aura also had a more fragile, private side: less mass rallies than Filia's odd devotional paintings «populated by vibrant red spheres and floating atmospheric crucifixes».[60]

This eccentric longing for auratic mystery also plays a role in *Turandot*, one that complicates and vies with the largely pessimistic stance toward technology I have tried to explicate thus far. Filia's dream of technology as a bridge to otherworldly mysteries occupies the same imaginative world as the music box in Adami's memoir, summoning the voices of ancient China, «as if with a magic spell». It similarly recalls Puccini's magazine, with its image of a man with «arms outstretched toward [an] elusive vision», which could hail the mysteries of Venice into being. How might these fantasies be related to the opera's music?

Let us return once more to Baron Fassini's enchanted box. Another melody Puccini took from it is a traditional song known as «Mo Li Hua», a rocking pentatonic tune that Puccini treats thematically throughout the opera. The melody makes its first, and lengthiest, appearance in Act I, where it is sung by the children's chorus: a self-contained little set-piece, an oasis of four-square tunefulness between the expressionism of the choral prayer to the moon, and the dissonance of the Prince of Persia's funeral march (see Ex. 5.4). As with the ministers' music box theme, the passage semaphores its mechanical origins. A two-bar ostinato sounds endlessly underneath the melody, and the texture is punctured by metallic chords played (in a combination we have already encountered in «In questa reggia») by glockenspiel, celesta, and harp.

The D-flats and A-flats in the ostinato bass give the pentatonic tune a Mixolydian tinge, and Girardi describes a medieval «aura [that] serves to distance the listener, who instinctively notices archaism but cannot identify it».[61] The mysterious effect is intensified by other details as well. Simply put, «Mo Li Hua» is the single most bizarrely orchestrated passage in Puccini's *œuvre*. The children's chorus sings offstage, and their melody is doubled

---

[59] *The Work of Art in the Age of its Technological Reproducibility: Third Version*, in *Walter Benjamin: Selected Writings*, IV, ed. by Howard Eiland and Michael W. Jennings, Cambridge, Belknap, 2003, pp. 251-283: 255.

[60] Poggi, *Inventing Futurism*, p. 260.

[61] Girardi, *Puccini*, p. 452.

at pitch by two offstage alto saxophones. Meanwhile, the ostinato accompaniment is hummed, onstage, by the entire chorus proper. What we see is a choir standing inert, with its mouths closed. What we hear is music that is neither offstage nor on, its source unclear because it partakes of both worlds simultaneously. This passage literally sutures distance, connecting the space before and beyond the flats. It summons both the actual sound of a music box and something of its mystic charm.[62]

Ex. 5.4. PUCCINI, *Turandot*, I, 19[+1-12].

(continues)

[62] Although the metallic chiming is the passage's most obviously mechanical timbral feature, it is possible that the saxophones were chosen to evoke the distinctive sound of a reed-organ music box. See SHEPPARD, *Puccini and the Music Boxes*, p. 89.

Ex. 5.4. *(conclusion)*

The «Mo Li Hua» theme has, since the opera's premiere, been linked to the character of Turandot. Although it can be risky to attach concrete meanings to Puccini's leitmotivs, this particular association between character and theme seems too persistent to brook much doubt. The melody sounds every time Turandot appears on stage, and is played when Calaf cries out her name in the first act. Admittedly, it is unusual to introduce a theme like this in a choral passage, and «Mo Li Hua» lacks the sort of affective iconicity that marks many of Puccini's other leitmotivs. But, seen in this context, the association has a certain logic. Turandot, after all, is herself a sort of «mechanical idol»: physically remote, a guardian of enigmas, an object of cultic and erotic veneration. Indeed, one might say that the opera's whole contradictory relationship to technology is embodied in Turandot: she is both *18BL*'s heartless Salomé and its beloved truck, her extremes of mechanism and enchantment represented, alternately, by «In questa reggia» and «Mo Li Hua». The contrast between mechanicity and tradition is not simply an opposition between Turandot and Liù, in other words, but rather a tension that unfolds in the theater of the princess's own voice.

V

No critic that I have encountered articulated this doubleness, although Raffaello de Rensis, writing for the fascist «Giornale d'Italia», came close. Immediately after praising the set's impressive «scalea di marmo» (marble staircase), he complained about what he called «la marmorea Turandot» (marmoreal Turandot).[63] The use of the same word for both set and character is telling, and it encapsulates the ways in which *Turandot* both embraces and (in so doing) undermines its monumental status. This was not just a problem with Puccini's opera. In his study *The Body of Il Duce*, Sergio Luzzatto suggests that Mussolini too occupied an uncomfortable place between 'good' and 'bad' monumentality:

Mussolini, celebrating the fourth anniversary of the March on Rome, told the crowd gathered under his balcony that his watchword was «a verb, to endure» – to endure day after day, month after month, year after year [...] Rhetoric aside, Mussolini's watchword points to a greater mission than politics, one that Il Duce genuinely perceived as ageless, a will to power defying time and reaching for eternity. Eternity here is not to be confused with immortality; to say something is dead does not mean it cannot last. Like other twentieth-century totalitarian regimes, Fascism tried to cloak the body of its charismatic leader with the durability of a monument, to turn Il Duce into a lasting entity not much different from the embalmed corpses of Soviet memory.[64]

This dead eternity led to strange fantasies. Luzzatto reports that «One elaborate story [from the late thirties] had Mussolini "embalmed with his right arm raised in the Roman salute", so that he could be wheeled onto the balcony of the Palazzo Venezia, concealing his inability to walk».[65] It is tempting to associate this image of Mussolini on his balcony with that of Turandot atop her staircase, and to hear another music-box chiming somewhere in the background.

Two years after *Turandot*'s posthumous premiere, Bontempelli compared Italian opera to «certain old men who have lived robust lives, and who, when they reach seventy, live for another twenty years, full of strong memories and lucid visions, to the amazement of their children and neph-

---

[63] See DE RENSIS, *La prima rappresentazione*.

[64] SERGIO LUZZATTO, *The Body of Il Duce: Mussolini's Corpse and the Fortunes of Italy*, trans. by Frederika Randall, New York, Metropolitan Books, 2005, p. 23.

[65] *Ibid.*, p. 31.

ews».[66] «For glorious lives full of action», he mused, «I like to imagine complicated and hardy deaths».[67] The event that inspired Bontempelli's remarks was the posthumous performance of another incomplete opera – Boito's *Nerone*, which inaugurated the new Teatro Reale dell'Opera a decade after the composer's own death. If my study began with Boito, on the cusp of articulating a new acoustics, it seems just to also end with him, wheeled out for one more performance, a ghost-like presence in a new world in which he would never fully fit.

The situation of opera has changed remarkably little in the nearly ninety years since Bontempelli wrote these words, and technology has remained central both to fantasies of renewal and to narratives of what went wrong. As for *Turandot*, its incomplete last act has recently been seized on as an opportunity for revivifying the operatic canon itself. Reflecting on Luciano Berio's experimental and open-ended 'completion' of Puccini's text, Roger Parker is prompted to reverse the «last Italian opera» tropes with which this chapter began:

Puccini's last opera, interrupted as it was by the composer's death, is often thought the end of a great tradition, as the last Italian repertory piece in a line that goes back more than three hundred years. But Luciano Berio's ending might just be a beginning, the start of a great tradition, of a proliferation of new ways in which the music that lies at the center of operatic works might be reconfigured.[68]

It is hard not to applaud such optimism. It may still be worth remembering, however, that when Puccini himself tried to devise an ending for his opera, imagining a way to transform Turandot from vengeful despot into loving wife, the best magic he could muster was a mechanical repetition of a hallowed classic. In a sketch for the final section of the Act 3 duet he would not live to complete, Puccini penned a short melody followed by an indication that seems both absurdly optimistic and hopelessly self-defeating. «*Poi Tristano*», he wrote. «Next, *Tristan*».

---

[66] «Certi vecchi, la cui vita fu robusta, dopo i settant'anni vivono per altri venti ancora di una vita fisiologica piena di forti memorie e lucide visioni, che fanno la maraviglia dei figli e dei nipoti». BONTEMPELLI, *L'avventura novecentista*, pp. 236-237.

[67] «Amo immaginare alle vite ricche d'azione e gloriose, morti complicate e resistenti». BONTEMPELLI, *L'avventura*, p. 236.

[68] ROGER PARKER, *Remaking the Song: Operatic Visions and Revisions from Handel to Berio*, Berkeley, University of California Press, 2006, p. 120.

EPILOGUE

But, a sceptical reader asks, is there any evidence of what Puccini himself thought of sound and sound recording, or of larger questions concerning realism and technology? Puccini's letters are resolutely practical in tone, and he penned no manifestos on the state of opera in modernity. For one (ambivalent, and inevitably partial) response to these questions, we might however turn to a long-forgotten portrait of Puccini published in the «New York Times». It is worth reading closely, as it engages with many of this study's central themes.

In 1923, one year before the composer's death, the retired United States Army colonel F. L. Minnigerode visited Puccini at his new home in the Tuscan city of Viareggio. (This is the same house, with its array of technological wonders, to which Giuseppe Adami was summoned at the start of the last chapter). A veteran of the Great War, and now the representative of an ascending imperial power, Minnigerode seems to have hoped that he would find a charmingly old world scene in this «sandy strip between the Versillia [sic] mountains, whose jagged peaks are still streaked with shining snow, and the Mediterranean, where the bathers are splashing under a cloudless sky».[1] The reality was rather different:

The most distinctly American thing in this little town is the Puccini bungalow – «My California Bungalow» – he calls it. And yet there is a tone of the Orient about it, for on the porches and from the great plane trees here and there hang Japanese lanterns and over the main gate there is a sort of pagoda effect, while in one corner is a round, grass-roofed little house that might have been brought from a village in old Nippon.

Such cosmopolitanism, however unexpected, might seem appropriate for a composer nearing the end of an international career. But it is also possible to detect a strain of melancholy. Puccini, after all, had never visited «old Nippon» or California. Instead of surrounding himself with the souvenirs

---

[1] See F.L. MINNIGERODE, *Puccini, His New Opera, and His Singing Birds: The Composer of «Madame Butterfly» Talks about Chinese «Turandot»*, «New York Times», 29 July 1923.

of lived experience, he seems to have chosen to dwell amidst the exotic sets of his own previous operas: *Madama Butterfly* and *La fanciulla del West*.

As Minnigerode soon discovered, an air of the museum also hung over the composer's studio. He noted a framed letter of Wagner's from 1861 (the year of the *Tannhäuser* fiasco) and a group of «stuffed song birds» on the mantel. Minnigerode was more impressed with another artifact: a letter from Thomas Edison, which proclaimed «Men die and Governments change, but the melodies of *La Bohème* will live forever». The missive was dated September 1920, a month of extraordinary unrest in Italy, with factories occupied from Turin through Palermo. Had news of the chaos reached the laboratories in New Jersey, Edison might have intended his words to be consoling. Nonetheless, the idea of melodies that «will live forever» sounds strange when coming from the inventor of the phonograph, a man who had attempted to ensure the immortality of the human voice by fixing it in wax.

The conversation turns to *Turandot*. Puccini rushes into another room and returns excitedly with a «much-handled and tattered paper-covered yellow book». «Inside the mutilated covers the pages were alive with Chinese characters and bars of Chinese music», observed Minnigerode, in language that resonates with his previous quotation of Edison's letter. His strange claim that the volume's melodies were «alive», despite manifest dislocations of time and space, seems to imagine the mutilated songbook as a second-order phonograph, preserving the sounds of distant lands. (As such, it shares an affinity with those other surrogate sound recording devices – bells and music boxes – that we have had occasion to discuss). Yet Puccini is not unironic about his own claims to authenticity. He notes, laughing, that while he may have never visited Peking, «I have been through New York's Chinatown».

A California bungalow and a Japanese hut close to the beach in Tuscany, a studio alive with the voice of Edison and the songs of ancient China: Puccini's villa may begin to resemble a modern-day version of Klingsor's palace, the terrain of an aging magician who surrounds himself with dangerous chimeras in which he only half believes. It seems fitting, then, that Minnigerode would attempt to break the magic spell: first, by informing the composer that he has actually travelled through Peking; then, by casting doubt on the very survival of his art. «What effect will the present rapidly increasing system of broadcasting and the increasing perfection of the phonograph have on grand opera?» asked Minnegerode, sounding quite a bit like Walter Benjamin. «Will not many people sit at home and listen to the opera instead of taking the trouble to dress and go out at night?»:

«Never!» was the emphatic reply. «Nothing can replace the living presence of the singer nor make the story a reality without the carefully prepared setting. The wireless and the phonograph may sing, but they can never act, can never be more than a piece of mechanism for the reproduction of sound. You may sit at home and read a play or you may visit the cinema and see the movement, but that is a very poor substitute for the living, vital, speaking characters».

Puccini's vehemence is striking, yet this is a curious defense of live performance. What, exactly, does it mean to claim that «The wireless and the phonograph may sing, but they can never act»? Puccini seems here to imagine opera as a collection of discrete components (voice, gesture, scenery, language), any one of which may indeed be faithfully reproduced. What makes a sound recording, a printed script, or a silent film a «poor substitute» for the live event is not its deadness, nor its lack of 'aura', but the fact that each medium only captures one of opera's many systems. One wonders what Puccini would have made of synchronized sound cinema, as it developed later in the 1920s. Would it have provided the unified 'reality' that he seems to have prized above all else?

Before he abandoned the composer to work on his new opera, Minnigerode had one final question. «I had been told by a number of people in a number of places», he wrote:

that whether you sat in the top gallery of the Scala Theatre in Milan or at the opera house in Paris or shone resplendently in the «diamond horseshoe» at the Metropolitan in New York, or, for that matter, sat by your radio or phonograph in your own room, listening to the voice of Caruso or Farrar in *La Bohème, Tosca, Madame Butterfly*, or any other Puccini composition, you were not only hearing the voices of the great and the songs of Puccini, but were being carried back to nature and were, in truth, hearing the songs of many birds from many lands.

They say that the notes of the Japanese nightingale and the English skylark and the Baltimore oriole had been taken by Puccini and made into *La Bohème*. The great composer maintained at his villa near Torre del Lago a great aviary, so the story went, and he sat for hours and listened to the carolling of his birds.

Puccini denied this suggestion (how could he not?) and Minnigerode ended his interview on a triumphant note: «Thus is a legend exploded by the very person around whom it was woven». Yet the extended anecdote casts a shadow over his essay as a whole. What relation is there between those stuffed song birds on the mantle and the living ones outside? What would it mean, even as a thought experiment, to describe *La bohème* as a phonograph-like repository of natural sound? Or to imagine the overwhelmingly present voices Caruso and Farrar as containing, within themselves, something distant and inhuman, «the songs of many birds from many lands»?

Tropes linking composers and songbirds have, of course, a long and complex history. (Indeed, the origins of Western notation are founded on one such myth). Mozart famously befriended a starling and taught it a melody from one of his piano concertos – an allegory of the Enlightenment's sympathetic conquest of nature if there ever was one. Olivier Messiaen, already a star conservatory student when Minnigerode conducted his interview, would pursue an exactly opposite path, making his own voice conform to the sounds of the natural world in a style that drew heavily on his experiments with *musique concrète*. In the present study, I have tried to capture an image of Puccini as a composer poised ambivalently between these different poles: his operas are neither the naive assertions of human subjectivity they have often seemed, nor are they entirely comfortable with the new and disenchanted values they often struggle to embrace. As Minnigerode seems to have intuited, nature and artifice, life and death, existed in an uneasy balance on Puccini's last estate. Let us leave him there, in that narrow strip between the «shining snow» of the Versilia mountains and the warm, blue Italian sea.

SELECT BIBLIOGRAPHY

Newspapers and journals

«L'ambrosiana»
«Avanti!»
«Corriere della sera»
«Il cosmorama pittorico»
«The Dial»
«The Evening World»
«Fanfulla della domenica»
«Gazzetta musicale di Milano»
«Il giornale d'Italia»
«Life»
«L'idea nazionale»
«Il mondo artistico»
«Musica»
«Musica d'oggi»
«La nazione»
«New York Times»
«New York Tribune»
«Nuova antologia: rivista di scienze, lettere ed arti»
«La Revue d'art dramatique»
«La rivista illustrata del popolo d'Italia»
«Rivista teatrale italiana»
«The Sun»
«Il teatro illustrato»
«La tribuna»
«La voce»

Primary and secondary sources

ABBATE, CAROLYN, *Elektra's Voice: Music and Language in Strauss's Opera*, in *Richard Strauss: «Elektra»*, ed. by Derrick Puffett, Cambridge, Cambridge University Press, 1989, pp. 107-127.

— *Music: Drastic or Gnostic?*, «Critical Inquiry», XXX, 2004, pp. 503-536.

— *In Search of Opera*, Princeton, Princeton University Press, 2001.

— *Unsung Voices: Opera and Musical Narrative in the Nineteenth Century*, Princeton, Princeton University Press, 1991.

— *Wagner, Cinema, and Redemptive Glee*, «Opera Quarterly», XXI, 2006, pp. 597-611.

ABBATE, CAROLYN – PARKER, ROGER, *A History of Opera*, New York, Norton, 2012.

ADAMI, GIUSEPPE, *Il romanzo della vita di Giacomo Puccini*, Milan, Rizzoli, 1944.

ADAMSON, WALTER L., *Avant-Garde Florence: From Modernism to Fascism*, Cambridge, MA, Harvard University Press, 1993.

ADORNO, THEODOR W., *Bourgeois Opera*, in *Opera through Other Eyes*, ed. by David J. Levin, Stanford, Stanford University Press, 1993, pp. 25-43.

— *The Radio Voice*, in *Current of Music*, ed. by Robert Hullot-Kentor, Cambridge, Polity Press, 2009, pp. 345-391.

— *Schreker*, in *Quasi una fantasia: Essays on Modern Music*, trans. by Rodney Livingstone, London, Verso, 1992, pp. 130-144.

— *In Search of Wagner*, trans. by Rodney Livingstone, London, Verso, 2005².

ALBRIGHT, DANIEL, *Verdi*, in *Berlioz, Verdi, Wagner, Britten*, ed. by Daniel Albright, London, Bloomsbury, 2014 («Great Shakespeareans», XI), pp. 77-134.

ALIGHIERI, DANTE, *The Inferno*, trans. by Robert and Jean Hollander, New York, Anchor Books, 2002.

— *Purgatorio*, trans. by Robert and Jean Hollander, New York, Anchor Books, 2004.

APOLITO, PAOLO, *The Internet and the Madonna*, Chicago, University of Chicago Press, 2005.

ASHBROOK, WILLIAM – POWERS, HAROLD, *Puccini's «Turandot»: The End of the Great Tradition*, Princeton, Princeton University Press, 1991.

AUDEN, W. H., *Cav & Pag*, in *The Dyer's Hand and Other Essays*, New York, Vintage Books, 1968, pp. 475-482.

BARAGWANATH, NICHOLAS, *The Italian Traditions and Puccini: Compositional Theory and Practice in Nineteenth-Century Opera*, Bloomington, Indiana University Press, 2011.

BARNABY, PAUL, *The Haunted Monastery: Capuana's «Profumo» and the Ghosts of the «Nuova Italia»*, «Romance Studies», XIX, 2001, pp. 109-121.

BASINI, LAURA, *Cults of Sacred Memory: Parma and the Verdi Centennial Celebration of 1913*, «Cambridge Opera Journal», XIII, 2001, pp. 141-161.

— *Reviving the Past: Italian Music History and Verdi*, PhD diss., University of California Berkeley, 2003.

BEN GHIAT, RUTH, *Fascist Modernities: Italy, 1922-1945*, Berkeley, University of California Press, 2001.

BENJAMIN, WALTER, *The Work of Art in the Age of its Technological Reproducibility: Third Version*, in *Walter Benjamin: Selected Writings*, IV, ed. by Howard Eiland and Michael W. Jennings, Cambridge, Belknap, 2003, pp. 251-283.

BERGERON, KATHERINE, *How to Avoid Believing (while Reading Iago's «Credo»)*, in *Reading Opera*, ed. by Arthur Groos and Roger Parker, Princeton, Princeton University Press, 1988, pp. 184-199.

— *Verdi's Egyptian Spectacle: On the Colonial Subject of «Aida»*, «Cambridge Opera Journal», XIV, 2002, pp. 149-159.

BERNARDONI, VIRGILIO, *Le 'tinte' del vero nel melodramma dell'ottocento*, «Il saggiatore musicale», V, 1998, pp. 43-68.

BERRONG, RICHARD M., *«Turandot» as Political Fable*, «Opera Quarterly», XI, 1995, pp. 65-75.

BLASETTI, ALESSANDRO, *«Sole»: Soggetto, sceneggiatura, note per la realizzazione*, ed. by Adriano Aprà and Riccardo Redi, Rome, Di Giacomo, 1985.

BLACKBOURN, DAVID, *Marpingen: Apparitions of the Virgin Mary in a Nineteenth-Century German Village*, New York, Vintage, 1993.

BOITO, ARRIGO, BOITO, *Il primo Mefistofele*, ed. by Emanuele d'Angelo, Venice, Marsilio, 2012.

— *Tutti gli scritti*, ed. by Piero Nardi, Verona, Mondadori, 1942.

BOITO, CAMILLO, *Il maestro di setticlavio*, in *Storielle vane*, ed. by Chiara Cretella, Bologna, Edizioni Pendragon, 2007, pp. 237-284.

BONTEMPELLI, MASSIMO, *L'avventura novecentista*, Florence, Vallecchi, 1974.

BORGESE, GIUSEPPE ANTONIO, *Goliath: The March of Fascism*, New York, Viking Press, 1937.

BRAIDA, ANTONELLA, *Dante's «Inferno» in the 1900s: From Drama to Film*, in *Dante on View: The Reception of Dante in the Visual and Performing Arts*, ed. by Antonella Braida and Luisa Calè, Aldershot, Ashgate, 2007, pp. 39-52.

BUDDEN, JULIAN, *The Operas of Verdi*, 3 vols., Oxford, Oxford University Press, 1981².

— *Puccini: His Life and Works*, Oxford, Oxford University Press, 2002.

— *Wagnerian Tendencies in Italian Opera*, in *Music and Theatre: Essays in Honour of Winton Dean*, ed. by Nigel Fortune, Cambridge, Cambridge University Press, 1987, pp. 299-332.

BUSCH, HANS, *Verdi's «Falstaff» in Letters and Contemporary Reviews*, Bloomington, Indiana University Press, 1997.

BURTON, DEBORAH, *Recondite Harmony: Essays on Puccini's Operas*, Hillsdale, NY, Pendragon Press, 2012.

BUSONI, FERRUCCIO, *A Fairy-like Invention*, in *The Essence of Music and Other Papers*, trans. by Rosamond Ley, London, Rockliff, 1957, pp. 190-193.

The Cambridge Companion to Modern Italian Culture, ed. by Zygmunt G. Baranski and Rebecca J. West, Cambridge, Cambridge University Press, 2001.

CAMPANA, ALESSANDRA, *Opera and Modern Spectatorship in Late Nineteenth-Century Italy*, Cambridge, Cambridge University Press, 2015.

CAMPBELL, TIMOTHY, *Wireless Writing in the Age of Marconi*, Minneapolis, University of Minnesota Press, 2006.

CARNER, MOSCO, *Giacomo Puccini: «Tosca»*, Cambridge, Cambridge University Press, 1985.

— *Puccini: A Critical Biography*, New York, Knopf, 1958.

Carteggio Verdi-Ricordi 1880-1881, ed. by Pierluigi Petrobelli, Marisa Di Gregori Casati, and Carlo Matteo Mossa, Parma, Istituto di Studi Verdiani, 1988.

Carteggi Pucciniani, ed. by Eugenio Gara, Milan, Ricordi, 1986.

CHESSA, LUCIANO, *Luigi Russolo, Futurist: Noise, Visual Arts, and the Occult*, Berkeley, University of California Press, 2012.

CHRISTIAN, WILLIAM, *Visionaries: The Spanish Republic and the Reign of Christ*, Berkeley, University of California Press, 1996.

CHOATE, MARK I., *Emigrant Nation: The Making of Italy Abroad*, Cambridge, MA, Harvard University Press, 2008.

CODE, DAVID. *Hearing Debussy Reading Mallarmé: Music après Wagner in the «Prélude à l'après-midi d'une Faune»*, «Journal of the American Musicological Society», LII, 2001, pp. 493-554.

COHN, RICK, *Uncanny Resemblances: Tonal Signification in the Freudian Age*, «Journal of the American Musicological Society», LVII, 2004, pp. 285-324.

Commento alla Divina Commedia d'Anonimo Fiorentino del secolo XIV, ed. by Pietro Fanfani, Bologna, Romagnoli, 1866.

Corbin, Alain, *Village Bells: Sound and Meaning in the Nineteenth-Century French Countryside*, trans. by Martin Thom, New York, Columbia University Press, 1998.

Croce, Benedetto, *Arrigo Boito*, in *La letteratura della nuova Italia: saggi critici*, I, Bari, Laterza e figli, 1967, pp. 255-273.

Cruz, Gabriella, *Aida's Flutes*, «Cambridge Opera Journal», XIV, 2002, pp. 177-200.

Dahlhaus, Carl, *Realism in Nineteenth-Century Music*, trans. by Mary Whittall, Cambridge, Cambridge University Press, 1985.

d'Angelo, Emanuele, *Arrigo Boito drammaturgo per musica: Idee, visioni, forma e battaglie*, Venice, Marsilio, 2010.

Davis, Andrew, *«Il trittico», «Turandot», and Puccini's Late Style*, Bloomington, Indiana University Press, 2010.

de Grazia, Victoria, *The Culture of Consent: Mass Organization of Leisure in Fascist Italy*, Cambridge, Cambridge University Press, 1981.

— *How Fascism Ruled Women: Italy, 1922-1945*, Berkeley, University of California Press, 1992.

del Fiorentino, Dante, *Immortal Bohemian: An Intimate Memoir of Giacomo Puccini*, New York, Prentice Hall, 1952.

Della Coletta, Cristina, *World's Fairs Italian Style: The Great Exhibitions in Turin and Their Narratives, 1860-1915*, Toronto, University of Toronto Press, 2006.

di Blasi, Corrado, *Luigi Capuana: originale e segreto*, Catania, Giannotta, 1968.

Döhring, Sieghart, *Musikalischer Realismus in Puccinis «Tosca»*, «Analecta Musicologica», XXII, 1984, pp. 249-295.

Dolan, Emily I., *The Orchestral Revolution: Haydn and the Technologies of Timbre*, Cambridge, Cambridge University Press, 2013.

Donatello among the Blackshirts: History and Modernity in the Visual Culture of Fascist Italy, ed. by Claudio Lazzaro and Roger J. Crum, Ithaca, Cornell University Press, 2005.

Earle, Ben, *Luigi Dallapiccola and Musical Modernism in Fascist Italy*, Cambridge, Cambridge University Press, 2013.

Falasca-Zamponi, Simonetta, *Fascist Spectacle: The Aesthetics of Power in Mussolini's Italy*, Berkeley, University of California Press, 1997.

Forzano, Giovacchino, *Come li ho conosciuti*, Turin, Edizioni Radio Italiana, 1957.

Forzano, Giovacchino – Benito Mussolini, *Mussolini autore drammatico*, Florence, Barbera, 1954.

Frajese, Vittorio, *Dal Costanzi all'Opera: Cronache, recensioni e documenti*, 4 vols., Rome, Edizioni Capitolium, 1977.

Gere, Cathy, *Gnossos and the Prophets of Modernism*, Chicago, University of Chicago Press, 2009.

Gerhard, Anselm, *Ultimi baci nei «giardini del Decameron». Allusioni intertestuali nei libretti di Boito per Verdi*, in *L'opera prima dell'opera. Fonti, libretti, intertestualità*, ed. by Alessandro Grilli, Pisa, Plus, 2006, pp. 141-150.

Giger, Andreas, *Verismo: Origin, Corruption, and Redemption of an Operatic Term*, «Journal of the American Musicological Society», LX, 2007, pp. 271-316.

Girardi, Michele, *Puccini: His International Art*, trans. by Laura Basini, Chicago, University of Chicago Press, 2000.

GRAMSCI, ANTONIO, *Selections from the Cultural Writings*, ed. by David Forgacs and Geoffrey Nowell-Smith, Cambridge, MA, Harvard University Press, 1991.

GREENWALD, HELEN, *Verdi's Patriarch and Puccini's Matriarch: «Through the Looking Glass and What Puccini Found There»*, «19th-Century Music», XVII, 1994, pp. 220-236.

GRIFFITHS, C. E. J., *The Theatrical Works of Giovacchino Forzano: Drama for Mussolini's Italy*, Lewiston, NY, The Edward Mellen Press, 2000.

GROOS, ARTHUR – PARKER, ROGER, *Giacomo Puccini: «La bohème»*, Cambridge, Cambridge University Press, 1986.

GROVER-FRIEDLANDER, MICHAL, *Operatic Afterlives*, New York, Zone Books, 2011.

— *Vocal Apparitions: The Attraction of Cinema to Opera*, Princeton, Princeton University Press, 2005.

GUARNIERI CORAZZOL, ADRIANA, *Musica e letteratura in Italia tra Ottocento e Novecento*, Milan, Sansoni, 2001.

— *Opera and Verismo: Regressive Points of View and the Artifice of Alienation*, trans. by Roger Parker, «Cambridge Opera Journal», V, 1993, pp. 39-53.

GUMBRECHT, HANS-ULRICH, *In 1926: Living at the Edge of Time*, Cambridge, MA, Harvard University Press, 1997.

HAVLEY, NICK, *Dante and Early Italian Cinema: The 1911 Milano-Films «Inferno» and Italian Nationalism*, in *Dante in the Long Nineteenth Century: Nationality, Identity, and Appropriation*, ed. by Aida Audeh and Nick Havely, Oxford, Oxford University Press, 2012, pp. 353-371.

HEPOKOSKI, JAMES, *Giuseppe Verdi: «Falstaff»*, Cambridge, Cambridge University Press, 1983.

— *Structure, Implication, and the End of «Suor Angelica»*, «Studi pucciniani», 3, 2004, pp. 241-264.

HILLER, JONATHAN ROBERT, *Bodies that Tell: Physiognomy, Criminology, Race, and Gender in Late Nineteenth- and Early Twentieth-Century Italian Literature and Opera*, Ph.D. Diss., University of California, Los Angeles, 2009.

Italian Cultural Studies: An Introduction, ed. by David Forgacs and Robert Lumley, Oxford, Oxford University Press, 1996.

Italian Sound, ed. by Deanna Shemek and Arielle Saiber, *California Italian Studies*, IV, 2013.

JAMES, HENRY, *Italian Hours*, ed. by John Auchard, New York, Penguin Books, 1995.

KATZ, MARK, *Capturing Sound: How Technology Has Changed Music*, Berkeley, University of California Press, 2010.

KAUFMAN, SUZANNE K., *Consuming Visions: Mass Culture and the Lourdes Shrine*, Ithaca, Cornell University Press, 2004.

KENNER, HUGH, *The Pound Era*, Berkeley, University of California Press, 1971.

KERMAN, JOSEPH, *Opera as Drama*, Berkeley, University of California Press, 1988[2].

KITTLER, FRIEDRICH A., *Gramophone, Film, Typewriter*, trans. by Geoffrey Winthrop-Young and Michael Wutz, Stanford, Stanford University Press, 1999.

— *World-Breath: On Wagner's Media Technology*, in *Opera through Other Eyes*, ed. by David J. Levin, Stanford, Stanford University Press, 1993, pp. 215-235.

KÖRNER, AXEL, *Politics of Culture in Liberal Italy: From Unification to Fascism*, New York, Routledge, 2009.

LASANSKY, D. MEDINA, *The Renaissance Perfected: Architecture, Spectacle, and Tourism in Fascist Italy*, University Park, The Pennsylvania State University Press, 2004.

LEE, SHERRY D., *A Minstrel in a World without Minstrels: Adorno and the Case of Schreker*, «Journal of the American Musicological Society», LVIII, 2005, pp. 639-696.

LEUKEL, JÜRGEN. *Sulla rappresentazione dell'extramusicale nelle opere di Puccini*, in *Esotismo e colore locale nell'opera di Puccini. Atti del primo Convegno internazionale sull'opera di Giacomo Puccini (Torre del Lago, 1983)*, ed. by Jürgen Maehder, Pisa, Giardini, 1985, pp. 241-245.

LEVRA, UMBERTO, *Fare gli italiani: memoria e celebrazione del Risorgimento*, Turin, Comitato di Torino dell'Istituto per la storia del Risorgimento, 1992.

LOCKE, RALPH P., *Reflections on Orientalism in Opera and Musical Theatre*, «Opera Quarterly», X, 1993, pp. 49-64.

LOCKHART, ELLEN, *Photo-Opera: «La fanciulla del West» and the Staging Souvenir*, «Cambridge Opera Journal», XXIII, 2011, pp. 145-166.

LOMBROSO, CESARE, *After Death – What?: Spiritistic Phenomena and their Interpretation*, trans. by William Sloane Kennedy, Boston, Small, Maynard, and Company, 1909.

LUCKHURST, ROGER, *The Invention of Telepathy, 1870-1901*, Oxford, Oxford University Press, 2001.

LUZZATTO, SERGIO, *The Body of Il Duce: Mussolini's Corpse and the Fortunes of Italy*, trans. by Frederika Randall, New York, Metropolitan Books, 2005.

MACDONALD, MALCOM, *Varèse: Astronomer in Sound*, London, Kahn and Averill, 2003.

MAEHDER, JÜRGEN, *«La giusta prospettiva dell'orchestra»: Grundlagen der Orchesterbehandlung bei Komponisten der «giovane scuola»*, «Studi pucciniani», 3, 2004, pp. 105-149.

MALLACH, ALAN, *The Autumn of Italian Opera: From Verismo to Modernism*, Boston, Northeastern University Press, 2007.

MANCINELLI, LUIGI, *Epistolario*, ed. by Antonio Mariani, Lucca, Akademos, 2000.

Mefistofele di Arrigo Boito, ed. by William Ashbrook and Gerardo Guccini, Milan, Ricordi, 1998.

MOE, NELSON, *The View from Vesuvius: Italian Culture and the Southern Question*, Berkeley, University of California Press, 2002.

NARDI, PIERO, *Vita di Arrigo Boito*, Verona, Mondadori, 1941.

NICOLAISEN, JAY, *Italian Opera in Transition, 1871-1893*, Ann Arbor, UMI Research Press, 1980.

NICOLODI, FIAMMA, *Musica e musicisti nel ventennio fascista*, Florence, Discanto, 1984.

OSBORNE, CHARLES, *The Complete Operas of Puccini: A Critical Guide*, London, Gollancz, 1981.

OSTHOFF, WOLFGANG, *Il sonetto nel «Falstaff» di Verdi*, in *Melodramma italiano dell'Ottocento: studi e ricerche per Massimo Mila*, ed. by Giorgio Pestelli, Turin, Einaudi, 1977, pp. 157-183.

PANICHELLI, PIETRO, *Il 'pretino' di Giacomo Puccini*, Pisa, Nistri-Lischi, 1962[4].

PAPPACENA, FLAVIA, *Excelsior: Documenti e saggi/Documents and Essays*, Rome, Di Giacomo, 1998.

PARKER, ROGER, *Leonora's Last Act: Essays in Verdian Discourse*, Princeton, Princeton University Press, 1997.

— *Remaking the Song: Operatic Visions and Revisions from Handel to Berio*, Berkeley, University of California Press, 2006.

PHILLIPS-MATZ, MARY JANE, *Puccini: A Biography*, Boston, Northeastern University Press, 2002.

Il piccolo Marat: storia e rivoluzione nel melodramma verista, ed. by Piero and Nandi Ostali, Milan, Sonzogno, 1990.

PICKER, JOHN M., *Victorian Soundscapes*, Oxford, Oxford University Press, 2003.

PIZZETTI, ILDEBRANDO, *Musicisti contemporanei: Saggi critici*, Milan, Treves, 1914.

POGGI, CHRISTINE, *Inventing Futurism: The Art and Politics of Artificial Optimism*, Princeton, Princeton University Press, 2009.

Puccini: Manon Lescaut, ed. by Roger Parker, «Opera Quarterly», 24, 2008.

REHDING, ALEXANDER, *On the Record*, «Cambridge Opera Journal», XVIII, 2006, pp. 59-82.

ROSS, PETER, *Die multidimensionale Szenenstruktur in der italienischen Oper am Ende des 19. Jahrhunderts*, «Studi pucciniani», 3, 2004, pp. 151-175.

SACHS, HARVEY, *Music in Fascist Italy*, London, Weidenfeld and Nicolson, 1987.

SANSONE, MATTEO, *Giordano's «Mala vita»: A 'Verismo' Opera too True to Be Good*, «Music and Letters», LXXV, 1994, pp. 381-400.

— *Verga and Mascagni: The Critics' Response to «Cavalleria rusticana»*, «Music and Letters», LXXI, 1990, pp. 198-214.

SCARDOVI, STEFANO, *L'opera dei bassifondi: Il melodramma 'plebeo' nel verismo musicale italiano*, Lucca, Libreria Musicale Italiana, 1994.

SCARPELLINI, EMANUELA, *Organizzazione teatrale e politica del teatro nell'Italia fascista*, Milan, LED, 2004.

SCHAFER, R. MURRAY, *The Soundscape: Our Sonic Environment and the Tuning of the World*, Rochester, VT, Destiny Books, 1993.

SCHNAPP, JEFFREY, *Staging Fascism: 18BL and the Theater of Masses for Masses*, Stanford, Stanford University Press, 1996.

SCHWARTZ, ARMAN, *Manon in the Desert, Wagner on the Beach*, «Opera Quarterly», XXIV, 2008, pp. 51-61.

SCHWARTZ, VANESSA R., *Spectacular Realities: Early Mass Culture in Fin-de-Siècle Paris*, Berkeley, University of California Press, 1999.

SCONCE, JEFFREY, *Haunted Media: Electronic Presence from Telegraphy to Television*, Durham, Duke University Press, 2000.

SENICI, EMANUELE, *Landscape and Gender in Italian Opera: The Alpine Virgin from Bellini to Puccini*, Cambridge, Cambridge University Press, 2005.

— *Verdi's «Falstaff» at Italy's Fin-de-Siècle*, «Musical Quarterly», LXXXV, 2001, pp. 274-310.

Seven Puccini Librettos, trans. by William Weaver, New York, Norton, 1981.

SHEINBAUM, JOHN J., *Adorno's Mahler and the Timbral Outsider*, «Journal of the Royal Musical Association», CXXXI, 2006, pp. 38-82.

SHEPPARD, W. ANTHONY, *Puccini and the Music Boxes*, «Journal of the Royal Musical Association», CXL, 2015, pp. 41-92.

SOLINAS, ROSA, «Arrigo Boito: The Legacy of Scapigliatura», PhD diss., Oxford University, 1999.

SMART, MARY ANN, *Mimomania: Music and Gesture in Nineteenth-Century Opera*, Berkeley, University of California Press, 2004.

SMITH, MATTHEW WILSON, *The Total Work of Art: From Bayreuth to Cyberspace*, New York, Routledge, 2007.

SMITH, PATRICIA JULIANA, «*Gli enigmi sono tre*»: *The [D]evolution of Turandot, Lesbian Monster*, in *En Travesti: Women, Gender Subversion, Opera*, ed. by Corinne E. Blackmer and Patricia Juliana Smith, New York, Columbia University Press, 1995, pp. 242-284.

Spackman, Barbara, *Fascist Virilities: Rhetoric, Ideology, and Social Fantasy in Italy*, Minneapolis, University of Minnesota Press, 1996.

Steege, Benjamin, *Helmholtz and the Modern Listener*, Cambridge, Cambridge University Press, 2012.

Steimatsky, Noa, *Italian Locations: Reinhabiting the Past in Postwar Cinema*, Minneapolis, University of Minnesota Press, 2008.

Steinberg, Michael, *The Politics and Aesthetics of Operatic Modernism*, «Journal of Interdisciplinary History», XXXVI, 2006, pp. 629-648.

Steinberg, Michael – Stewart-Steinberg, Suzanne, *Fascism and the Operatic Unconscious*, in *Opera and Society in Italy and France from Monteverdi to Bourdieu*, ed. by Victoria Johnson, Jane F. Fulcher, and Thomas Ertman, Cambridge, Cambridge University Press, 2007, pp. 267-288.

Stewart-Steinberg, Suzanne, *The Pinocchio Effect: On Making Italians: 1860-1920*, Chicago, University of Chicago Press, 2007.

Sterne, Jonathan, *The Audible Past: Cultural Origins of Sound Reproduction*, Durham, University of North Carolina Press, 2003.

Stokowski, Leopold, *New Vistas in Radio*, «The Atlantic Monthly», CLV, 1935, pp. 1-16.

Suisman, David, *Selling Sounds: The Commercial Revolution in American Music*, Cambridge, MA, Harvard University Press, 2009.

Taruskin, Richard, *The Oxford History of Western Music*, IV, Oxford, Oxford University Press, 2005.

— *Text and Act: Essays on Musical Performance*, Oxford, Oxford University Press, 1995.

Thomas, Alex, *The Darkened Room: Women, Power, and Spiritualism in Late Victorian England*, Chicago, University of Chicago Press, 2004.

— *The Place of Enchantment: British Occultism and the Culture of the Modern*, Chicago, University of Chicago Press, 2004.

Thompson, Mark. *The White War: Life and Death on the Italian Front, 1915-1919*, London, Faber and Faber, 2008.

Tomlinson, Gary, *Learning to Curse at Sixty-Seven*, «Cambridge Opera Journal», XIV, 2002, pp. 229-241.

— *Metaphysical Song: An Essay on Opera*, Princeton, Princeton University Press, 1999.

Torrefranca, Fausto, *Giacomo Puccini e l'opera internazionale*, Turin, Bocca, 1912.

Vandiver Nicassio, Susan, *Tosca's Rome: The Play and the Opera in Historical Perspective*, Chicago, University of Chicago Press, 1999.

Venturini, Domenico, *Dante Alighieri e Benito Mussolini*, Rome, Casa Editrice Nuova Italia, 1927.

Verga, Giovanni, *The She-Wolf and Other Stories*, trans. by Giovanni Cecchetti, Berkeley, University of California Press, 1962.

Viglino, Sergio, *La fortuna italiana della «Carmen» di Bizet (1879-1900)*, Turin, De Sono, 2003.

Voss, Egon, *Il verismo nell'opera*, in *Cavalleria rusticana, 1890-1990: cento anni di un capolavoro*, ed. by Piero Ostali and Nandi Ostali, Milan, Sonzogno, 1990, pp. 47-55.

Wilson, Alexandra, *Golden Age Thinking: Updated Stagings of «Gianni Schicchi» and the Popular Historical Imagination*, «Cambridge Opera Journal», XXV, 2013, pp. 185-201.

— *The Puccini Problem: Opera, Nationalism, and Modernity*, Cambridge, Cambridge University Press, 2007.

Zimdars-Swartz, Sandra, *Encountering Mary: From La Salette to Medjugorje.* Princeton, Princeton University Press, 1991.

Zoppelli, Luca. *«Stage Music» in Early Nineteenth-Century Opera*, trans. by Arthur Groos, «Cambridge Opera Journal», II, 1990, pp. 29-39.

TABLE OF CONTENTS

FINITO DI STAMPARE
PER CONTO DI LEO S. OLSCHKI EDITORE
PRESSO ABC TIPOGRAFIA • SESTO FIORENTINO (FI)
NEL MESE DI MAGGIO 2016

CENTRO STUDI GIACOMO PUCCINI

Collana diretta da Arthur Groos e Virgilio Bernardoni

Atti di Convegno

1. *Madama Butterfly: l'orientalismo di fine secolo, l'approccio pucciniano, la ricezione.* Atti del convegno internazionale di studi, Lucca-Torre del Lago, 28-30 maggio 2004, a cura di A. Groos e V. Bernardoni. 2008, viii-414 pp. con 15 figg. n.t. e numerosi es. mus.

Testi e Documenti

Madama Butterfly. Fonti e documenti della genesi, a cura di A. Groos, V. Bernardoni, G. Biagi Ravenni e D. Schickling, 2005, 518 pp. (esclusività di vendita).

———

1. V. Bernardoni, *Verso Bohème. Gli abbozzi del libretto negli archivi di Giuseppe Giacosa e Luigi Illica.* 2008, x-276 pp. con 1 fig. n.t.

2. *Tosca di V. Sardou, G. Giacosa e L. Illica. Musica di G. Puccini. I. Facsimile della copia di lavoro del libretto.* 2009, 140 pp. II. Copia di lavoro del libretto. Edizione e commento a cura di Gabriella Biagi Ravenni. 2009, xli-140 pp. con 1 ill. n.t.

Premio Rotary Giacomo Puccini Ricerca

1. R. Pecci, *Puccini e Catalani. Il principe reale, il pertichino e l'«eredità del Wagner».* 2013, x-252 pp. con 8 figg. n.t., 84 es. mus. e 2 tavv. f.t. a colori.

2. Arman Schwartz, *Puccini's Soundscapes: Realism and Modernity in Italian Opera.* 2016, x-180 pp. con 20 es. mus.

Studi Pucciniani

Rassegna sulla musica e sul teatro musicale
nell'epoca di Giacomo Puccini

A cura di Virgilio Bernardoni, Michele Girardi e Arthur Groos

(I volumi 1-3 sono in esclusività di vendita)

Vol. 1. 1998, 232 pp. con 9 figg. n.t., 21 es. mus. e 8 tavv. f.t. a colori.
Vol. 2. 2000, 242 pp. con 16 es. mus.
Vol. 3. 2004, 288 pp. con 6 figg. n.t., 47 es. mus.
Vol. 4. 2010, 202 pp. con 24 figg. n.t., 33 es. mus. e 1 tav. f.t. a colori.